iOS Development Using MonoTouch Cookbook

109 simple but incredibly effective recipes for developing and deploying applications for iOS using C# and .NET

Dimitris Tavlikos

[PACKT] PUBLISHING

BIRMINGHAM - MUMBAI

iOS Development Using MonoTouch Cookbook

Copyright © 2011 Packt Publishing

All rights reserved. No part of this book may be reproduced, stored in a retrieval system, or transmitted in any form or by any means, without the prior written permission of the publisher, except in the case of brief quotations embedded in critical articles or reviews.

Every effort has been made in the preparation of this book to ensure the accuracy of the information presented. However, the information contained in this book is sold without warranty, either express or implied. Neither the author, nor Packt Publishing, and its dealers and distributors will be held liable for any damages caused or alleged to be caused directly or indirectly by this book.

Packt Publishing has endeavored to provide trademark information about all of the companies and products mentioned in this book by the appropriate use of capitals. However, Packt Publishing cannot guarantee the accuracy of this information.

First published: December 2011

Production Reference: 1071211

Published by Packt Publishing Ltd.
Livery Place
35 Livery Street
Birmingham B3 2PB, UK.

ISBN 978-1-84969-146-8

www.packtpub.com

Cover Image by Rakesh Shejwal (shejwal.rakesh@gmail.com)

Credits

Author
Dimitris Tavlikos

Reviewers
Jayant Varma
Andreas Zimnas
Chris Flethcer

Acquisition Editor
Usha Iyer

Development Editor
Meeta Rajani

Technical Editor
Lubna Shaikh

Project Coordinator
Shubhanjan Chatterjee

Proofreader
Jonathan Todd

Indexer
Hemangini Bari
Tejal Daruwale

Graphics
Valentina D'silva

Production Coordinator
Shantanu Zagade

Cover Work
Shantanu Zagade

About the Author

Dimitris Tavlikos discovered that computer programming was a passion during his school days. He knew this was what he wanted to do ever since he participated in a course for a few hours a week and learned how to write simple console programs on monochrome monitors.

While working as a programmer for a major IT company in Greece, he stumbled upon the quite promising and new language at the time, named C#. When MonoTouch was released, providing .NET developers with the ability to create software for the iOS platform, he was overwhelmed by the potential it offered.

With almost 10 years of professional programming experience with .NET and Mono, he now works as a freelance C# and MonoTouch software developer and offers his expertise to various projects for companies around the world.

In his spare time, he enjoys blogging about his "adventures" in coding (`http://software.tavlikos.com`) and tries to fill his camera's memory cards.

About the Reviewers

Jayant Varma, is the founder of OZ Apps, an Australian consultancy specializing in mobile development, training, and consulting. He had been involved with mobile devices in 2000, when Microsoft first released the Compaq iPaq (PocketPC).

He started his career in IT as a developer and then managed the IT departments for the BMW and Nissan dealerships in a couple of countries. His enterprising work demonstrated the gap and the niche that existed for mobile devices.

He is working on a Lua Cookbook for CoronaSDK developers and intends to write a book for beginners on game development principals.

Andreas Zimnas, was born in Kaufbeuren, Germany in 1982. Later, he moved with his parents to Edessa, Greece where he finished high school. In 2007, he graduated from the Technological Institute of Thessaloniki, obtaining his degree in software development, after a four-year attendance. While a student, his paper *Instructional Design E-Learning Systems* was presented in the 3rd International Scientific Conference eRA in September 2008 and in the World Congress on Science, WCSET 2009, Dubai, United Arab Emirates, in January 2009. He is now attending the Master's program in Applied Informatics at the University of Macedonia in Thessaloniki. Mr. Zimnas is currently employed as a software developer for a private company in Thessaloniki, Greece, developing applications for the .NET platform. He is also developing applications for the iOS platform, having currently published six applications.

Chris Fletcher, as a long-time Apple fan with extensive programming experience, has developed and beta tested many applications spanning various programming languages. Recently starting his own company, Empoc, LLC, Chris now develops applications mostly for the Mac App Store and iOS devices. Chris also spends time on his blog, chris-fletcher.com, writing tutorials and reviews. Most importantly, though, Chris values his time with his family.

www.PacktPub.com

Support files, eBooks, discount offers and more

You might want to visit `www.PacktPub.com` for support files and downloads related to your book.

Did you know that Packt offers eBook versions of every book published, with PDF and ePub files available? You can upgrade to the eBook version at `www.PacktPub.com` and as a print book customer, you are entitled to a discount on the eBook copy. Get in touch with us at `service@packtpub.com` for more details.

At `www.PacktPub.com`, you can also read a collection of free technical articles, sign up for a range of free newsletters and receive exclusive discounts and offers on Packt books and eBooks.

PACKTLiB

`http://PacktLib.PacktPub.com`

Do you need instant solutions to your IT questions? PacktLib is Packt's online digital book library. Here, you can access, read and search across Packt's entire library of books.

Why Subscribe?

- Fully searchable across every book published by Packt
- Copy and paste, print and bookmark content
- On demand and accessible via web browser

Free Access for Packt account holders

If you have an account with Packt at `www.PacktPub.com`, you can use this to access PacktLib today and view nine entirely free books. Simply use your login credentials for immediate access.

Table of Contents

Preface	**1**
Chapter 1: Development Tools	**7**
Introduction	7
Installing pre-requisites	8
Creating an iPhone project with MonoDevelop	13
Interface builder	24
Creating the UI	26
Accessing the UI with outlets	29
Adding actions	35
Compiling	37
Debugging our application	40
Chapter 2: User Interface: Views	**43**
Introduction	43
Adding and customizing views	44
Receiving user input with buttons	48
Using labels to display text	53
Displaying images	58
Displaying and editing text	62
Using the keyboard	65
Displaying progress	68
Displaying content larger than the screen	72
Navigating through content divided into pages	74
Displaying a toolbar	78
Creating a custom view	80
Chapter 3: User Interface: View Controllers	**85**
Introduction	85
Loading a view with a view controller	86

Navigating through different view controllers	88
Providing controllers in tabs	91
Creating a table controller	94
Modal view controllers	96
Creating a custom view controller	99
Using view controllers efficiently	101
Combining different view controllers	103
iPad view controllers	105
Creating a user interface for different devices	109

Chapter 4: Data Management — 113

Introduction	113
Creating files	114
Creating an SQLite database	115
Inserting and updating data	118
Querying an SQLite database	119
Using an already existing SQLite database	121
Storing data with serialization	123
Storing data with XML	126
Managing XML data with LINQ to XML	127

Chapter 5: Displaying Data — 131

Introduction	131
Providing lists	132
Displaying data in a table	135
Customizing rows	138
Editing a table: deleting rows	142
Editing a table: inserting rows	145
Table indexing	147
Searching through the data	149
Creating a simple web browser	152
Displaying local content	153
Displaying formatted text	155
Displaying documents	157

Chapter 6: Web Services — 161

Introduction	161
Consuming web services	161
Invoking web services	164
Consuming WCF services	167
Reading JSON data	169

Chapter 7: Multimedia Resources — 173
- Introduction — 173
- Selecting images and videos — 174
- Capturing media with the camera — 177
- Playing video — 180
- Playing music and sounds — 182
- Recording with the microphone — 185
- Managing multiple album items directly — 187

Chapter 8: Integrating iOS Features — 191
- Introduction — 191
- Starting phone calls — 192
- Sending text messages and e-mails — 194
- Using text messaging in our application — 197
- Using e-mail messaging in our application — 200
- Managing the address book — 203
- Displaying contacts — 205
- Managing the calendar — 208

Chapter 9: Interacting with Device Hardware — 211
- Introduction — 211
- Detecting device orientation — 212
- Adjusting UI orientation — 215
- Proximity sensor — 217
- Retrieving battery information — 219
- Handling motion events — 221
- Handling touch events — 223
- Recognizing gestures — 225
- Custom gestures — 228
- Using the accelerometer — 230
- Using the gyroscope — 233

Chapter 10: Location Services and Maps — 237
- Introduction — 237
- Determining location — 238
- Determining heading — 242
- Using region monitoring — 245
- Using significant-change location service — 247
- Location services in the background — 249
- Displaying maps — 252
- Geocoding — 255

Table of Contents

Adding map annotations	258
Adding map overlays	262

Chapter 11: Graphics and Animation — 267

Introduction	267
Animating Views	268
Transforming views	270
Animation with images	274
Animating layers	276
Drawing lines and curves	279
Drawing shapes	282
Drawing text	284
A simple drawing application	286
Creating an image context	290

Chapter 12: Multitasking — 295

Introduction	295
Detecting application states	296
Receiving notifications for application states	298
Running code in the background	300
Playing audio in the background	303
Network connectivity maintenance	305

Chapter 13: Localization — 309

Introduction	309
Creating an application for different languages	309
Localizable resources	312
Regional formatting	315

Chapter 14: Deploying — 319

Introduction	319
Creating profiles	319
Creating an ad-hoc distribution bundle	324
Preparing an application for the App Store	328
Submitting to the App Store	332

Chapter 15: iOS 5 Features — 337

Introduction	337
Reproducing the page curl effect	338
Styling views	342
Twitter integration	344
Working with the split keyboard	346

Index — 351

Preface

Technology is advancing quite rapidly. Portable devices, such as media players, smartphones, and tablets, have brought huge advancements and changes in the way people communicate, share, and consume digital content. Developers need to be up-to-date with the available platforms these devices work on, if they want to be "part of the game".

iOS, Apple's operating system for its own portable devices, is undoubtedly one of the leading portable platforms today. If it weren't for MonoTouch, .NET developers would have to spend time to learn a new programming language to expand their creativity to the iOS ecosystem.

This book, through a series of multiple recipes and with an almost equal number of complete projects, will help you become part of this ecosystem, with the help of MonoTouch and C#. When you finish reading it, you will be a capable iOS developer, ready to unleash your creativity to one of the most popular portable platforms today.

What this book covers

Chapter 1, Development Tools, will walk you through all the available IDEs and SDKs that you will need for using MonoTouch for iOS development. You will create your first MonoTouch project and learn how to debug on the simulator.

Chapter 2, User Interface: Views, introduces the concept of views and how they are part of a complete iOS application. Exploring a large number of various view components, you will create different applications that will help you understand how each component works.

Chapter 3, User Interface: View Controllers, discusses the Model-View-Controller (MVC) pattern and how to use it to create applications suitable for enhanced user experience. Through this chapter, you will also learn about the most useful controllers, which will be part of many of your projects in the future, and how to create iPad-specific and universal applications.

Chapter 4, Data Management, will walk you through a series of techniques that will allow you to incorporate data management in your applications. You will learn how to use SQLite databases, XML, LINQ-to-XML, and Serialization, formerly only available to .NET desktop and web projects.

Preface

Chapter 5, Displaying Data, expands on the available components to display data effectively on the smaller-than-desktop screens of iOS devices. You will get accustomed to using the `UITableView` for displaying lists of data, as well as the `UIWebView` for HTML (and more) content.

Chapter 6, Web Services, discusses creating applications that communicate online to exchange data. With the help of MonoTouch, you will not only learn how to use common .NET and WCF web services in iOS applications, but also how to read and parse JSON objects.

Chapter 7, Multimedia Resources, will teach you to create applications that capture, reproduce, and manage multimedia content through the device's hardware. You will not only learn to use the camera to capture images and video, but also how to play back and record audio.

Chapter 8, Integrating iOS Features, will walk you through the ways to incorporate the platform's native applications and components. You will learn how to provide e-mail, text messaging, and address book features in your application and how to use the native calendar to create events.

Chapter 9, Interacting with Device Hardware, discusses creating applications that are fully aware of their surrounding environment, through the device's sensors. You will learn to adjust the user interface according to device orientations and how to respond to accelerometer and gyroscope events.

Chapter 10, Location Services and Maps, is a detailed guide for using the built-in location services to create applications that provide location information to the user. You will not only learn how to use the GPS hardware, but also how to display maps and layout information.

Chapter 11, Graphics and Animation, introduces 2D graphics and animation. You will learn to animate components and create simple graphics. By the end of this chapter, you will create a small finger-drawing application.

Chapter 12, Multitasking, will walk you through the details for implementing multitasking in iOS applications, which helps enhance user experience by executing code behind the scenes.

Chapter 13, Localization, discusses providing localized content in applications. You will learn how to prepare your application to target users worldwide.

Chapter 14, Deploying, will not only walk you through the required steps to deploy your finished application to devices, but also to prepare and distribute it to the App Store.

Chapter 15, iOS 5 Features, discusses some of the many new features that were introduced with the latest iOS version, such as page-curl content navigation, split keyboard for the iPad, and styling multiple views easily.

What you need for this book

The minimum requirement for this book is a Mac computer running Mac OS X Snow Leopard (10.6.*) or Lion (10.7.*). Almost all projects you will create with the help of this book work on the iOS Simulator. However, some projects will require a device to work correctly. You will find all the appropriate details in *Chapter 1*, Development Tools.

Who this book is for

This book is essential for C# and .NET developers with no previous experience in iOS development and Objective-C developers that want to make a transition to the benefits of MonoTouch and the C# language for creating complete, compelling iPhone, iPod, and iPad applications and deploying them to the App Store.

Conventions

In this book, you will find a number of styles of text that distinguish between different kinds of information. Here are some examples of these styles and an explanation of their meaning.

Code words in text are shown as follows: "Apple provides another base class, the `UIViewController`, which is responsible for managing views."

A block of code is set as follows:

```
public override void ViewDidLoad (){
  base.ViewDidLoad();
  this.myLabel.Text = "View loaded!";
}
```

When we wish to draw your attention to a particular part of a code block, the relevant lines or items are set in bold:

```
public override void ViewDidLoad (){
  base.ViewDidLoad ();
  UIButton.Appearance.BackgroundColor = UIColor.Gray;
  UIButton.Appearance.SetTitleColor(UIColor.White,
    UIControlState.Normal);
    this.buttonPresent.TouchUpInside += delegate(object sender,
      EventArgs e) {
      this.PresentModalViewController(new ModalController(), true);
    } ;
}
```

New terms and important words are shown in bold. Words that you see on the screen, in menus or dialog boxes for example, appear in the text like this: " Any file that is marked as **Content** is being copied as-is in the application bundle".

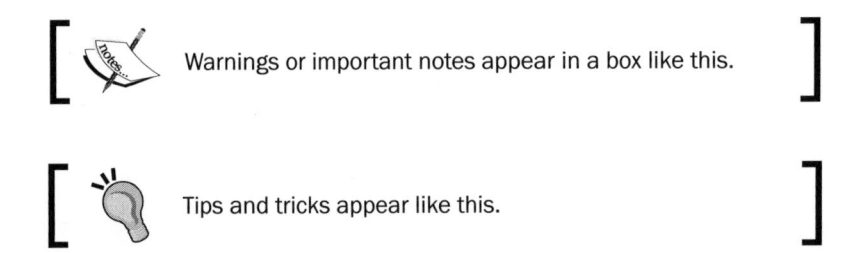

> Warnings or important notes appear in a box like this.

> Tips and tricks appear like this.

Reader feedback

Feedback from our readers is always welcome. Let us know what you think about this book — what you liked or may have disliked. Reader feedback is important for us to develop titles that you really get the most out of.

To send us general feedback, simply send an e-mail to feedback@packtpub.com, and mention the book title via the subject of your message.

If there is a book that you need and would like to see us publish, please send us a note in the **SUGGEST A TITLE** form on www.packtpub.com or e-mail suggest@packtpub.com.

If there is a topic that you have expertise in and you are interested in either writing or contributing to a book, see our author guide on www.packtpub.com/authors.

Customer support

Now that you are the proud owner of a Packt Publishing book, we have a number of things to help you to get the most from your purchase.

Downloading the example code

You can download the example code files for all Packt books you have purchased from your account at http://www.PacktPub.com. If you purchased this book elsewhere, you can visit http://www.PacktPub.com/support and register to have the files e-mailed directly to you.

Errata

Although we have taken every care to ensure the accuracy of our content, mistakes do happen. If you find a mistake in one of our books — maybe a mistake in the text or the code — we would be grateful if you would report this to us. By doing so, you can save other readers from frustration and help us improve subsequent versions of this book. If you find any errata, please report them by visiting http://www.packtpub.com/support, selecting your book, clicking on the **errata submission form** link, and entering the details of your errata. Once your errata are verified, your submission will be accepted, and the errata will be uploaded on our website, or added to any list of existing errata, under the Errata section of that title. Any existing errata can be viewed by selecting your title from http://www.packtpub.com/support.

Piracy

Piracy of copyright material on the Internet is an ongoing problem across all media. At Packt Publishing, we take the protection of our copyright and licenses very seriously. If you come across any illegal copies of our works, in any form, on the Internet, please provide us with the location address or website name immediately so that we can pursue a remedy.

Please contact us at copyright@packtpub.com with a link to the suspected pirated material.

We appreciate your help in protecting our authors and our ability to bring you valuable content.

Questions

You can contact us at questions@packtpub.com if you are having a problem with any aspect of the book, and we will do our best to address it.

1
Development Tools

In this chapter, we will cover:

- Installing pre-requisites
- Creating an iPhone project with MonoDevelop
- Interface builder
- Creating the UI
- Accessing the UI with outlets
- Adding actions
- Compiling
- Debugging our application

Introduction

One of the most important things professionals care about is the tools that are required to perform their work. Just as carpenters need a chisel to scrape wood, or photographers need a camera to capture light, we as developers need certain tools that we cannot work without.

In this chapter, we will provide information on what **Integrated Development Environments** (**IDEs**) and **Software Development Kits** (**SDKs**) are needed to develop applications for iOS, Apple's operating system for the company's mobile devices. We will describe what every tool's role is in the development cycle and step through each one's important features that are essential to develop our first application.

The tools needed to develop applications for iOS are the following:

- **An Intel-based Mac computer running Snow Leopard (10.6.*) or Lion (10.7.*) operating system**: The essential programs we need cannot be installed on other computer platforms.

Development Tools

- **iOS SDK version 3.2 or higher**: To be able to download iOS SDK, a developer must be registered as an Apple developer. iOS SDK, among other things, includes two essential components.
    - **Xcode**: Apple's IDE for developing native applications for iOS and Mac with the Objective-C programming language.
    - **iOS Simulator**: An essential program to debug iOS apps on the computer, without the need of a device. Note that there are many iOS features that do not work on the simulator; hence, a device is needed if an app uses these features.

    Both the registration and SDK download are free of charge from Apple's Developer portal (http://developer.apple.com). If we want to run and debug our applications on the device or distribute them on the App Store, we need to enroll with the iOS developer program, which requires a subscription fee.

- **Mono for Mac**: Mono is an open source implementation of Microsoft's .NET framework. It provides a multi-platform set of tools, libraries, and compilers to develop .NET applications on all mainstream computer operating systems (Linux, Mac, and Windows). We need the latest Mac installer, available from Mono's website.

- **MonoTouch**: MonoTouch is an SDK, based on Mono. It provides .NET developers with the ability to develop applications for iOS, using C# as a programming language. A free evaluation version is available on the MonoTouch website (http://ios.xamarin.com), which has all the features of the commercial versions to debug and run applications on iOS Simulator, without an expiration limit. For deploying applications on a device, or distributing on Apple's App Store, purchasing a commercial license is required.

- **MonoDevelop**: MonoDevelop is an open source IDE for .NET development. It provides developers with lots of features, such as code completion, database browsing, debuggers, and so on. The Mac version provides iOS project templates and MonoTouch integration.

This chapter will also describe how to create our first iPhone project with MonoDevelop, construct its UI with Interface Builder, and how to access the application's user interface from within our code, with the concepts of **Outlets** and **Actions**.

Last but not least, we will learn how to compile our application, the available compilation options we have, and how to debug on the simulator.

Installing pre-requisites

Information on how to download and install the necessary tools to develop with MonoTouch.

Chapter 1

Getting ready

We need to download all the necessary components on our computer. The first thing to do is register as an Apple Developer on `http://developer.apple.com`. The registration is free and easy and provides access to all necessary development resources. After the registration is confirmed through e-mail, we can log in and download the iOS SDK from the address `https://developer.apple.com/devcenter/ios/index.action#downloads`. At the time of writing, Xcode's latest version is 4.2, and iOS SDK's latest version is 5.0.

At times, when Apple introduces beta versions of its components, they are made available through its portal. Although everyone registered can download and use these components, our already installed version of MonoTouch might not work correctly with the beta version of iOS SDK or Xcode. So, this must be taken into account when downloading and installing new beta versions from Apple Developer portal.

How to do it...

To prepare our computer for iOS development, we need to download and install the necessary components in the following order:

1. **Xcode and iOS SDK on OS X Snow Leopard**: After downloading the image file, mount it, and in the window that will pop up, double-click on the Xcode and iOS SDK icon to start the installation. For the installation to proceed, it is necessary to read and accept the two licensing agreements that will be shown. After that, all you need to do is select the destination of the installation and click on **Continue**.

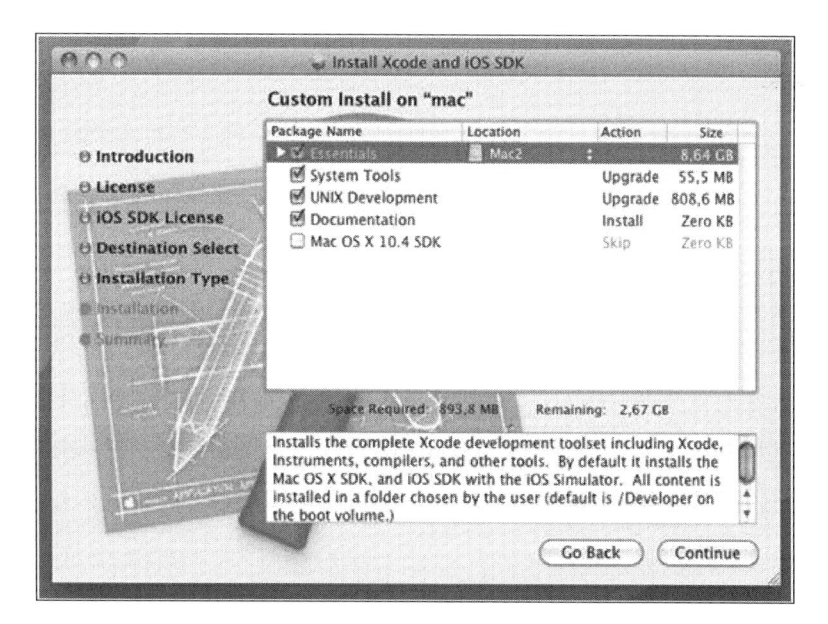

Development Tools

2. **Xcode and iOS SDK on OS X Lion**: To install Xcode and the SDK, a login to the Mac App Store is required. The downloaded files are basically an installer for Xcode and the SDK. When the download completes, run the Install Xcode application, and follow the installation instructions.

3. **Download and install Mono for Mac**: The Mac version of Mono can be downloaded through the Mono Project's website: `http://www.mono-project.com`.

4. **Download and install MonoTouch**: The latest evaluation version can be downloaded from `http://ios.xamarin.com/DownloadTrial` by providing an e-mail address.

5. **Download and install MonoDevelop 2.8+**: Although creating iOS applications with MonoTouch does not require MonoDevelop, installing it will make developing much easier. It can be downloaded from `http://monodevelop.com/Download`.

How it works...

Now that we have everything ready, let's see what each component is needed for.

As stated in the introduction of this chapter, the iOS SDK contains three important components. The first component, **Xcode**, is Apple's IDE for developing applications for both iOS and Mac platforms. It is targeted on the Objective-C programming language, which is the main language to program in, with the iOS SDK. Since MonoTouch is an SDK for the C# language, one might wonder what we need Xcode for. Apart from providing various tools for debugging iOS applications, Xcode provides us with three important components that we need. The first one is a device information window, called **Organizer**, shown in the following screenshot, which is necessary to install the various certificates and provisioning profiles that are required for deploying our application on a device or distributing through the App Store. From within the Organizer, we can view debugging information of our applications, crash logs, and even take screenshots from the device! Of course, these are only a few of the many features Xcode provides, but they are outside of the scope of this book to discuss.

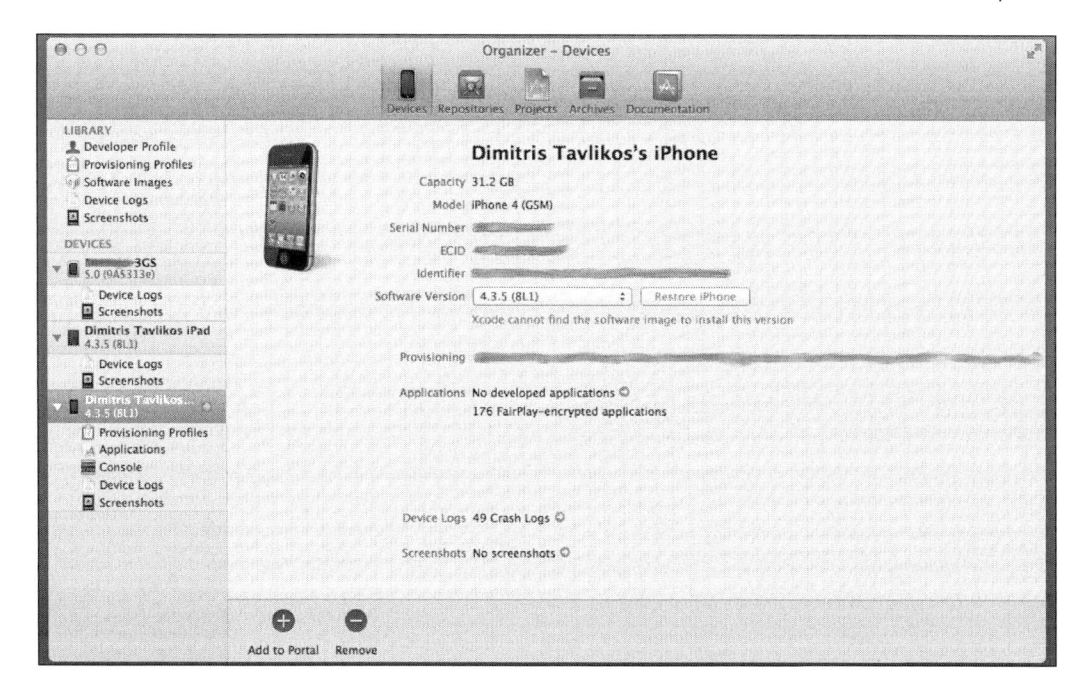

The second component is **Interface Builder**. This is the user interface designer, which was formerly a standalone application. Starting with Xcode 4.0, it is integrated into the IDE. Interface Builder provides all the necessary functionality to construct an application user interface. It is also quite different to what .NET developers have been accustomed to.

The third component is **iOS Simulator**. It is exactly what its name suggests: a device simulator, which we can use to run our applications on, without the need for an actual device. The important thing of iOS Simulator is that it has the option of simulating older iOS versions (if they are installed on the computer); both iPhone and iPad interfaces and device orientations. But, the simulator lacks some device features that are dependent on hardware, such as the compass or accelerometer. Applications using these features must be tested and debugged on an actual device.

Mono is an open source implementation of the .NET framework. It has been around for quite some time now and provides .NET developers the ability to program applications with .NET languages, while targeting all mainstream operating systems: Linux, Mac, and Windows. Both MonoTouch and MonoDevelop depend heavily on Mono, making it a necessary asset.

MonoDevelop is an open source IDE for developing applications with Mono (and the .NET framework on Windows). It provides code completion, database browser, GTK# designer, debuggers, and, in our case, the necessary components to develop iOS applications easily and effectively. It integrates with MonoTouch perfectly, classifying both as a complete iOS development environment.

Development Tools

MonoTouch is the SDK that allows .NET developers to develop applications for the iOS, using the C# programming language. There is a common misconception, mostly among new developers: since MonoTouch provides the ability to program with C#, one can install and use it on a Windows computer. This is totally wrong, since MonoTouch is wrapped around iOS SDK's libraries, which can only be installed on a Mac computer. Another misconception is that applications developed with MonoTouch being ".NET capable" require a virtual machine of some kind to be installed on the device to run, and they will run slower due to this virtual machine. This is also wrong, since MonoTouch's advanced compiler takes care of it by compiling our C# ".NET powered" code to native machine code. Also, a virtual machine being installed on a device is against Apple's guidelines.

There's more...

Applications developed with MonoTouch have the same chances of making it to the App Store as all other applications developed with the native Objective-C programming language! Meaning, if an application does not conform to Apple's strict policy about application acceptance, it will fail, whether it is written in either Objective-C or C#. The MonoTouch team has done a great job in creating an SDK that leaves the developer to only worry about the design and best practice of the code and nothing else. In April 2010, Apple made a modification on its application submission policy, which actually banned all applications from being submitted to the App Store that weren't created with the company's development tools. MonoTouch was one of them. Apart from the concern that emerged among developers who had already invested in MonoTouch, applications created with it were normally accepted on the App Store. In September 2010, Apple modified its policy and relaxed the matter, bringing relief to C# developers.

Useful links

The following is a list of the links that contain the tools and information for installing them:

- **Apple iOS developer portal**: http://developer.apple.com/devcenter/ios/index.action
- **Mono**: http://www.mono-project.com
- **MonoDevelop**: http://www.monodevelop.com
- **MonoTouch**: http://ios.xamarin.com
- **MonoTouch installation guide**: http://ios.xamarin.com/Documentation/Installation
- **Info about Apple developer tools**: http://developer.apple.com/technologies/tools/xcode.html

Updates

MonoDevelop has a feature for checking for available updates. Whenever the program starts, it checks for updates of MonoDevelop itself, MonoTouch, and the Mono framework. It can be turned off, but it is not recommended, since it helps staying up-to-date with the latest versions. It can be found under **MonoDevelop | Check for Updates**.

See also

In this chapter:

- *Compiling*
- *Debugging our application*

Chapter 14, Deploying:

- *Debugging on other devices*
- *Preparing our application for the App Store*

Creating an iPhone project with MonoDevelop

In this task, we will discuss creating our first iPhone project with the MonoDevelop IDE.

Getting ready...

Now that we have all the pre-requisites installed, we will discuss how to create our first iPhone project with MonoDevelop.

Start MonoDevelop. It can be found in the `Applications` folder. MonoDevelop's default project location is the folder `/Users/{yourusername}/Projects`. If it does not exist on the hard disk, it will be created when we create our first project. If we want to change the folder, go to **MonoDevelop | Preferences** from the menu bar.

Development Tools

Select **Load/Save** in the pane on the left, enter the preferred location for the projects in the field **Default Solution** location, and click on **OK**.

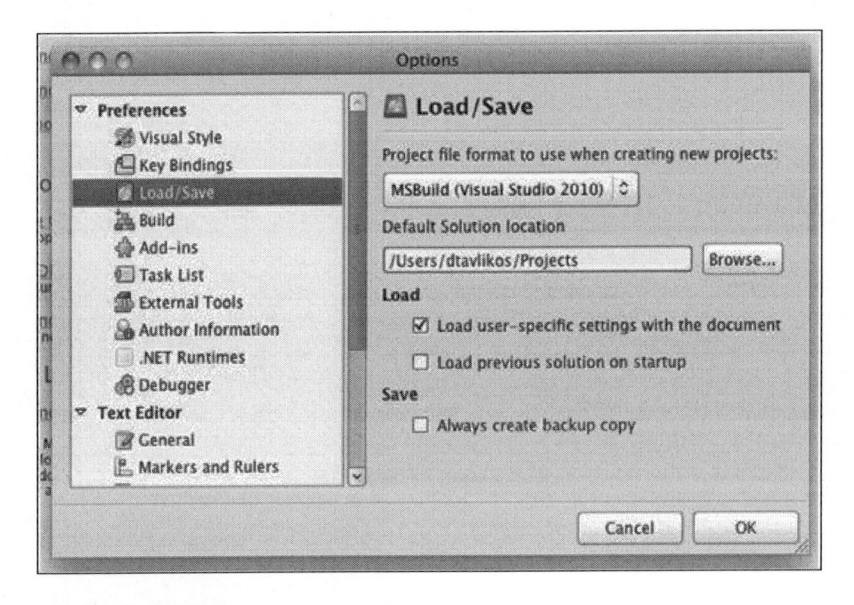

How to do it...

1. The first thing that is loaded when starting MonoDevelop is its **Start** page. Select **File | New | Solution...** from the menu bar. A window will be shown that provides us with the available project options.

2. In this window, on the pane on the left, select **C# | MonoTouch | iPhone**. The iPhone project templates will be presented on the middle pane.

3. Select **iPhone Single View Application**. Finally, enter `MyFirstiPhoneProject` for **Solution name** and click on **Forward**. The following screenshot displays the **New Solution** window:

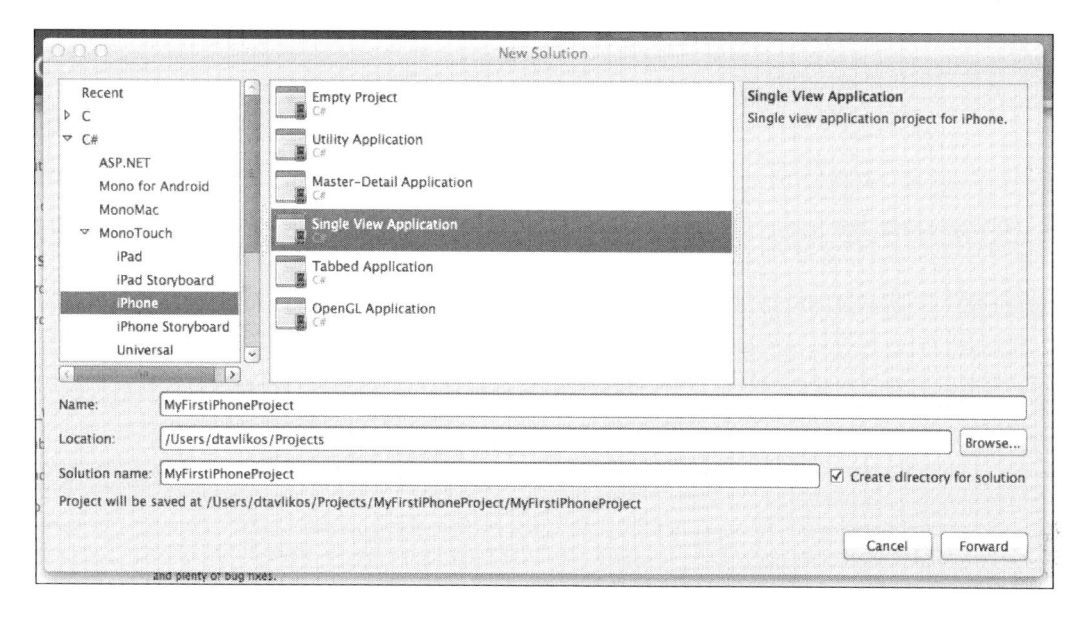

That was it! You have just created your first iPhone project! You can build and run it. The **iOS Simulator** will start, with just a blank light-gray screen nevertheless.

> If the MonoTouch section on the left pane is not shown for some reason, it means that something went wrong with the installation of MonoTouch and/or MonoDevelop. Refer to the previous recipe for proper installation.
>
> If the project templates in the middle are different than what is shown in this screenshot, it must be because you have a different version of MonoTouch and/or MonoDevelop than what was used for this book.

How it works...

Let's see what goes on behind the scenes.

When MonoDevelop creates a new iPhone, or better, iOS project, it creates a series of files. The solution structure is the same as if a .NET/Mono project was created, but with some extra files. The solution files can be viewed in the **Solution** pad on the left side of the MonoDevelop window. If the **Solution** pad is not visible, it can be activated by checking on **View | Pads | Solution** from the menu bar.

Development Tools

These files are the essential files that form an iPhone project:

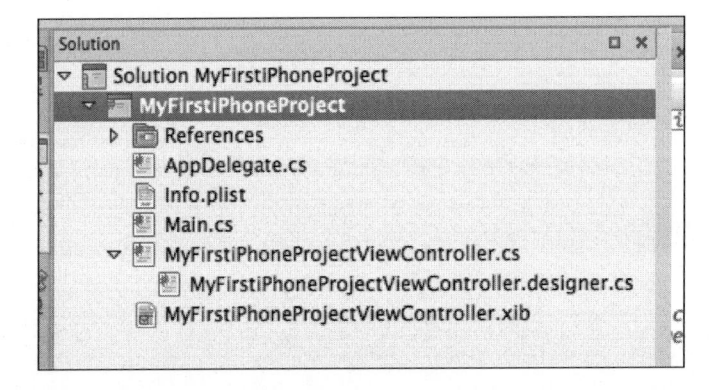

MyFirstiPhoneProjectViewController.xib

This file is the file that contains the view of the application. XIB files are basically XML files with a specific structure that is readable from Interface Builder. They contain various information about the user interface, such as the type of controls it contains, their properties, Outlets, and so on.

> If `MyFirstiPhoneProjectViewController.xib`, or any other file with the `.xib` suffix is double-clicked, then MonoDevelop starts Xcode with the contents of the XIB file open in Interface Builder.

When we create a new interface with Interface Builder and save it, it is saved in the XIB format.

MyFirstiPhoneProjectViewController.cs

This is the file that implements the view's functionality. These are the contents of the file when it is created:

```
namespace MyFirstiPhoneProject{
public partial class MyFirstiPhoneProjectViewController :
  UIViewController{
  public MyFirstiPhoneProjectViewController (string nibName, NSBundle
    bundle) : base (nibName, bundle){}
  public override void DidReceiveMemoryWarning (){
    // Releases the view if it doesn't have a superview.
    base.DidReceiveMemoryWarning ();
    // Release any cached data, images, and so on that aren't in use.
  }
```

```
    public override void ViewDidLoad (){
      base.ViewDidLoad ();
      //any additional setup after loading the view, typically from a
        nib.
    }
    public override void ViewDidUnload (){
      base.ViewDidUnload ();
      // Release any retained subviews of the main view.
      // e.g. myOutlet = null;
    }
    public override bool ShouldAutorotateToInterfaceOrientation
      (UIInterfaceOrientation toInterfaceOrientation){
      // Return true for supported orientations
      return (toInterfaceOrientation !=
        UIInterfaceOrientation.PortraitUpsideDown);
      }
    }
  }
```

The code in this file contains the class that corresponds to the view that will be loaded, along with some default method overrides. These methods are the ones that we will be using more frequently when we create view controllers. A brief description of each method is listed as follows:

- `ViewDidLoad`: This method is called when the view of the controller is loaded. This is the method we use to initialize any additional components.
- `ViewDidUnload`: This method is called when the view is unloaded from memory.
- `DidReceiveMemoryWarning`: This method is called when the application receives a memory warning. This method is responsible for unloading the view.
- `ShouldAutorotateToInterfaceOrientation`: We implement this method when we want our application to support multiple orientations.

MyFirstiPhoneProjectViewController.designer.cs

This is the file that holds our main window's class information in C# code. MonoDevelop creates one `.designer.cs` file for every `XIB` that is added in a project. The file is auto-generated every time we save a change in our `XIB` through Interface Builder. This is being taken care of by MonoDevelop, so that the changes we make in our interface are reflected right away in our code. We must not make changes to this file directly, since when the corresponding XIB is saved with Interface Builder, they will be lost. Also, if nothing is saved through Interface Builder, if changes are made to it manually, it will most likely result in a compilation error.

Development Tools

These are the contents of the file when a new project is created:

```
namespace MyFirstiPhoneProject{
  [Register ("MyFirstiPhoneProjectViewController")]
  partial class MyFirstiPhoneProjectViewController{}
}
```

Just like any other .NET project, a namespace is created with the name of the solution:

```
namespace MyFirstiPhoneProject
```

This file contains the other partial declaration of our `MyFirstiPhoneProjectViewController` class. It is decorated with the `RegisterAttribute`.

The `RegisterAttribute` is used to expose classes to the underlying Objective-C runtime. The string parameter declares by what name our class will be exposed to the runtime. It can be whatever name we want it to be, but it is a good practice to always set it to our C# class' name. The attribute is used heavily in the internals of MonoTouch, since it is what binds all native `NSObject` classes with their C# counterparts.

> `NSObject` is a root class or base class. It is the equivalent of `System.Object` in the .NET world. The only difference between the two is that all .NET objects inherit from `System.Object`, but most, not all, Objective-C objects inherit from `NSObject` in Objective-C. The C# counterparts of all native objects that inherit from `NSObject` also inherit from its MonoTouch `NSObject` counterpart.

AppDelegate.cs

This file contains the class `AppDelegate`. The contents of the file are listed below:

```
using System;
using System.Collections.Generic;
using System.Linq;
using MonoTouch.Foundation;
using MonoTouch.UIKit;
namespace MyFirstiPhoneProject{
  // The UIApplicationDelegate for the application. This class is
    responsible for launching the
  // User Interface of the application, as well as listening (and
    optionally responding) to application events from iOS.
```

```
    [Register ("AppDelegate")]
    public partial class AppDelegate : UIApplicationDelegate{
      // class-level declarations
      UIWindow window;
      MyFirstiPhoneProjectViewController viewController;
      // This method is invoked when the application has loaded and is
        ready to run. In this
      // method, you should instantiate the window, load the UI into it,
        and then make the window visible.
      // You have 17 seconds to return from this method, or iOS will
        terminate your application.
      public override bool FinishedLaunching (UIApplication app,
        NSDictionary options){
        window = new UIWindow (UIScreen.MainScreen.Bounds);
        viewController = new MyFirstiPhoneProjectViewController
          ("MyFirstiPhoneProjectViewController", null);
        window.RootViewController = viewController;
        window.MakeKeyAndVisible ();
        return true;
      }
    }
}
```

The first part is familiar to .NET developers and consists of the appropriate `using` directives that import the required namespaces to use.

```
using System;
using System.Collections.Generic;
using System.Linq;
using MonoTouch.Foundation;
using MonoTouch.UIKit;
```

The first three `using` directives allow us to use the specific and familiar namespaces from the .NET/Mono world with MonoTouch!

> Although the functionality the three namespaces (`System`, `System.Collections.Generic`, `System.Linq`) provide is almost identical to their well-known .NET/Mono counterparts, they are included in assemblies specifically created for use with MonoTouch and shipped with it, of course. An assembly compiled with .NET or Mono cannot be directly used in a MonoTouch project.

Development Tools

The `MonoTouch.Foundation` namespace is a wrapper around the native Objective-C foundation framework, which contains classes that provide basic functionality. These objects' names share the same "NS" prefix that is found in the native foundation framework. Some examples are `NSObject`, `NSString`, `NSValue`, and so on. Apart from `NS`-prefixed objects, the `MonoTouch.Foundation` namespace contains all of the attributes that are used for binding to native objects, such as the `RegisterAttribute` that we saw earlier. The `MonoTouch.UIKit` namespace is a wrapper around the native Objective-C `UIKit` framework. As its name suggests, the namespace contains classes, delegates, and events that provide us with interface functionality. Except for two classes, `DraggingEventArgs` and `ZoomingEventArgs`, all the objects' names share the same "UI" prefix. It should be clear at this point that these two namespaces are essential for all MonoTouch applications, and their objects will be used quite frequently.

The class inherits from the `UIApplicationDelegate` class, qualifying it as our application's `UIApplication` **Delegate** object.

> The concept of a Delegate object in the Objective-C world is somewhat different than a delegate in C#. It will be explained in detail in *Chapter 2, User Interface: Views*.

The `AppDelegate` class contains two fields and one method:

```
UIWindow window;
MyFirstiPhoneProjectViewController viewController;
public override bool FinishedLaunching (UIApplication app,
NSDictionary options) {
```

The `UIWindow` object defines the main window of our application, while the `MyFirstiPhoneProjectViewController` is the variable, which will hold the application's view controller.

> An iOS application typically has only one window, of type `UIWindow`. The concept of a `UIWindow` is somewhat different from a .NET `System.Windows.Form`. The `UIWindow` is the first control that is displayed when an application starts, and every subsequent views are hierarchically added below it.

The `FinishedLaunching` method, as its name suggests, is called when the application has completed its initialization process. This is the method where we must present the user interface to the user. The implementation of this method must be lightweight, since if it does not return in time from the moment it is called, iOS will terminate the application. This is for providing faster user interface loading times to the user by preventing developers from performing complex and long-running tasks upon initialization, such as connecting to a web service to receive data. The application parameter is the application's `UIApplication` object, which is also accessible through the static property `UIApplication.SharedApplication`. The options parameter may or may not contain information about the way the application was launched. We do not need it for now.

The default implementation of the `FinishedLaunching` method for this type of project is the following:

```
window = new UIWindow (UIScreen.MainScreen.Bounds);
```

The `UIWindow` object is initialized with the size of the screen.

```
viewController = new MyFirstiPhoneProjectViewController
  ("MyFirstiPhoneProjectViewController", null);
window.RootViewController = viewController;
```

The view controller is initialized and set as the window's root view controller.

```
window.MakeKeyAndVisible ();
return true;
```

The window is displayed on the screen with the `window.MakeKeyAndVisible()` call and the method returns. This method must be called inside the `FinishedLaunching` method, otherwise the application's user interface will not be presented as it should to the user. Last but not least, the `return true` line returns the method by marking its execution completion.

Main.cs

Inside the `Main.cs` file is where the runtime life-cycle of the program starts:

```
namespace MyFirstiPhoneProject{
  public class Application{
    // This is the main entry point of the application.
    static void Main (string[] args){
      // if you want to use a different Application Delegate class
        from "AppDelegate",
      // you can specify it here.
      UIApplication.Main (args, null, "AppDelegate");
    }
  }
}
```

Much like the following call in a .NET `System.Windows.Forms` application, the `UIApplication.Main` method starts the message loop, or run loop that is responsible for dispatching notifications to the application through the `AppDelegate` class, with event handlers that we can override.

```
// In a .NET application
Application.Run(new Form1());
```

Development Tools

Event handlers such as `FinishedLaunching`, `ReceiveMemoryWarning`, or `DidEnterBackground` are only some of these notifications. Apart from the notification dispatching mechanism, the `UIApplication` object holds a list of all `UIWindow` objects that exist; typically one. An iOS application must have one `UIApplication` object, or a class that inherits from it, and this object must have a corresponding `UIApplicationDelegate` object. This is the `AppDelegate` class implementation we saw earlier.

Info.plist

This file is basically the application's settings file. It has a simple structure of properties with values that define various settings for an iOS application, such as the orientations it supports, its icon, supported iOS versions, what devices it can be installed on, and so on. If we double-click on this file in MonoDevelop, it will open in the embedded editor, specifically designed for `.plist` files. This is what our file in a new project looks like:

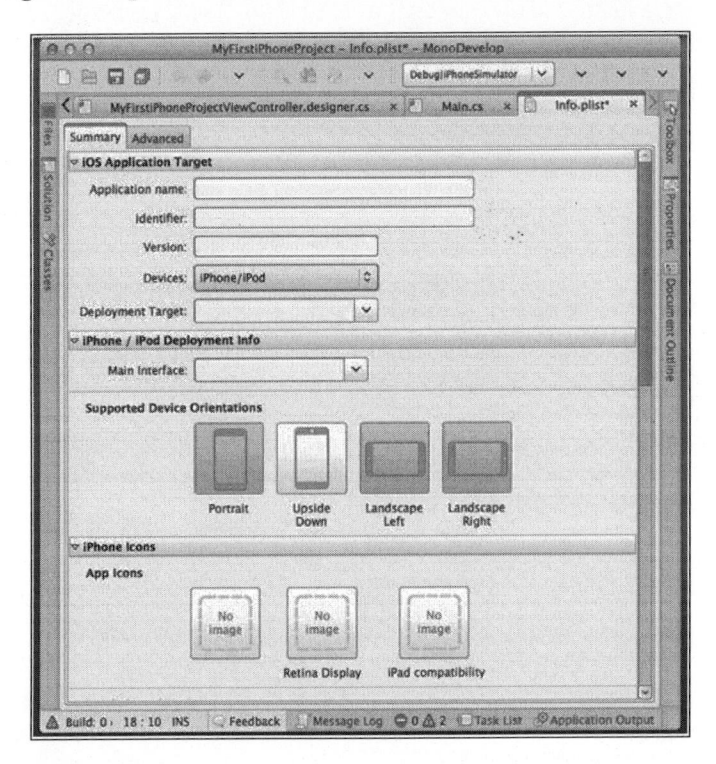

The `Info.plist` is an XML file. Although we can edit the file manually in a text editor, for example, it is not recommended. The embedded editor is the best way of editing.

There's more...

MonoDevelop provides many different project templates for developing iOS applications. Here is a list that describes what each project template is for:

- **Empty project**: It is an empty project without any views.
- **Utility application**: It is a utility application is a special type of iOS application that provides one screen for functionality, and in many cases another one for configuration.
- **Master-detail application**: This type of project creates a template that supports navigating through multiple screens. It contains two view controllers.
- **Single view application**: This template type is the one we used in this recipe.
- **Tabbed application**: It is a template that adds a tab bar controller that manages two view controllers in a tab-like interface.
- **OpenGL application**: It is a template for creating OpenGL-powered applications or games.

These templates are available for the iPhone, the iPad, and Universal (both iPhone and iPad) projects. They are also available in Interface Builder's **Storyboarding** application design.

> Unless otherwise stated, all project templates referring to the iPhone are suitable for the iPod Touch as well.

List of MonoTouch assemblies

MonoTouch supported assemblies can be found in the following link: http://ios.xamarin.com/Documentation/Assemblies.

See also

In this chapter:

- *Creating the UI*
- *Accessing the UI with outlets*

In this book:

Chapter 2, User Interface: Views:

- *Adding and customizing views*

Development Tools

Interface builder

Introduction to Apple's user interface designer.

How to do it...

If you have installed the iOS SDK, then you already have Xcode with Interface Builder installed on your computer.

1. Go to MonoDevelop and open the project `MyFirstiPhoneProject` that we created earlier.
2. In the **Solution** pad on the left, double-click on **MyFirstiPhoneProjectViewController.xib**. MonoDevelop starts Xcode with the file loaded in Interface Builder!
3. On the right side of the toolbar, on the top of the Xcode window, select the appropriate editor and viewing options, as shown below:

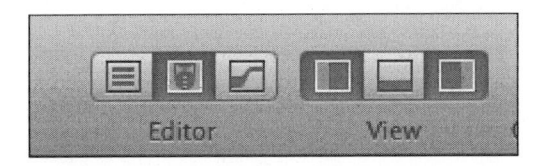

The following screenshot demonstrates what Interface Builder looks like with a XIB file open:

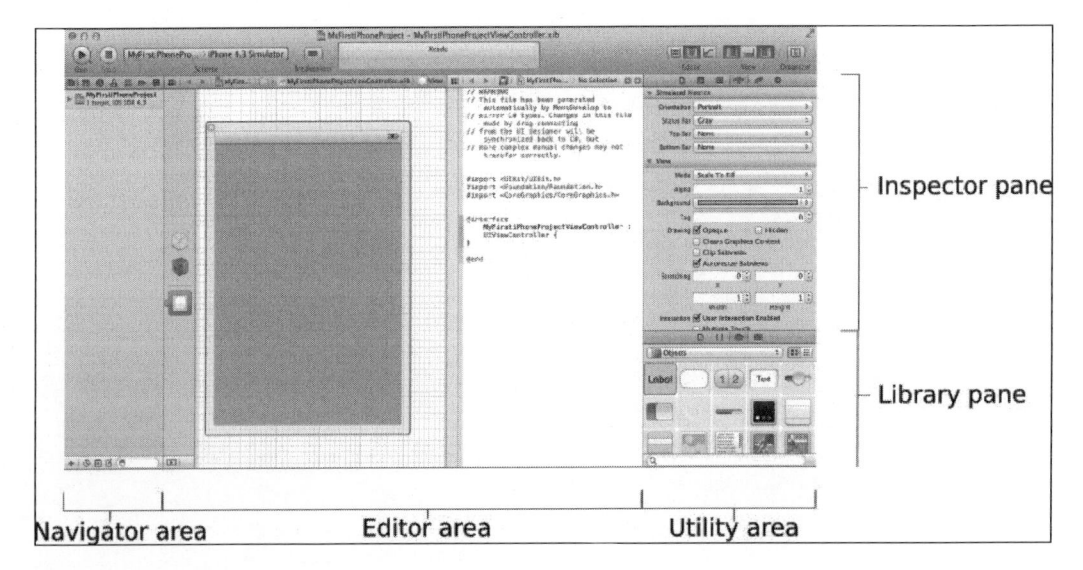

How it works...

Now that we have loaded Interface Builder with the view controller of our application, let's familiarize ourselves with it.

The user interface designer is directly connected to an Xcode project. When we add an object, Xcode automatically generates code to reflect the change we made. MonoDevelop takes care of this for us, as when we double-click on a XIB file, it automatically creates a temporary Xcode project so that we can make the changes we want in the user interface. Therefore, we have nothing more to do than just design the user interface for our application:

Interface Builder is divided into three areas. A brief description of each area is described below.

1. **Navigator area**: In this area, we can see the files included in the Xcode project.
2. **Editor area**: This area is where we design the user interface.
3. **Utility area**: This area contains the **Inspector** and **Library** panes. The **Inspector** is where we configure each object, while the **Library** pane is where we find the objects.

The Editor area is divided into two sections. The one on the left is the **Designer**, while the one on the right is the **Assistant** editor. Inside the assistant editor, we see the underlying Objective-C source code file that corresponds to the selected item in the designer. Although we do not need to edit the Objective-C source, we will need the assistant editor later.

There's more...

We saw what a `XIB` file looks like in Interface Builder. But, there is more as far as these files are concerned. We mentioned earlier that `XIB` files are XML files with appropriate information readable by Interface Builder. The thing is that when a project is compiled, the compiler also compiles the `XIB` file, converting it to its binary equivalent: the `NIB` file. Both `XIB` and `NIB` files contain the exact same information. The only difference between them is that `XIB` files are in a human-readable form, while the `NIB` files are not. For example, when we compile the project we created, the `MyFirstiPhoneProjectViewController.xib` file will become `MyFirstiPhoneProjectViewController.nib` in the output folder. Apart from the binary conversion, the compiler also performs a compression on `NIB` files. So, NIB files will be significantly smaller in size than `XIB` files.

That's not all about `XIB` files. The way a developer manages the `XIB` files in a project is very important in an application's performance and stability. It is better to have many, smaller in size `XIB` files, instead of one or two large ones. This can be accomplished by dividing the user interface in many `XIB` files. It may seem a bit difficult, but as we'll see later in this book, it is actually very easy. We need many, smaller `XIB` files instead of few and large ones because of the way iOS manages its memory. When an application starts, iOS loads the `NIB` files as a whole in memory, and thereafter, all the objects in it are instantiated. So, it is a waste of memory to keep objects in `NIB` files that are not always going to be used. Also, remember that you are developing for a mobile device whose available resources are not a match against desktop computers', no matter what its capabilities are.

Development Tools

More info

You may have noticed that in the **Attributes** tab in the **Inspector** pane, there is a section called **Simulated Metrics**. Options under this section help us see directly in the designer what our interface looks like with the device's status bar, a toolbar, or a navigation bar. Although these options are saved in the XIB files, they have nothing to do with the actual application at runtime. For example, if we set the **Status Bar** option to **None**, it does not mean that our application will start without a status bar.

> **Status Bar** is the bar that is shown on the top portion of the device's screen, which displays certain information to the user, such as the current time, battery status, carrier name on the iPhone, and so on.

See also

In this chapter:

- *Creating the UI*
- *Accessing the UI with outlets*
- *Adding actions*

In this book:

Chapter 2, User Interface:Views:

- *Adding and customizing views*

Chapter 3: User Interface:View Controllers:

- *View controllers and views*

Creating the UI

In this recipe, we will learn how to add and manage controls in the user interface.

Getting ready

Let's add a few controls in an interface. Start by creating a new iPhone Single View Application project in MonoDevelop. Name the project `ButtonInput`. When it opens, double-click on `ButtonInputViewController.xib` in the **Solution** pad to open it with Interface Builder.

How to do it...

Now that we have a new project and Interface Builder has opened the `ButtonInputViewController.xib` file, we'll add some controls to it.

Add a label

1. Go to the **Library** pane and select **Objects** from the drop-down list, if it is not already selected. Select the **Label** object.
2. Drag-and-drop the **Label** onto the gray space of the view in the designer, somewhere in the top half.
3. Select and resize the **Label** from both the left and right side, so that it snaps to the dashed line that will show up when you reach close to the edges of the view.
4. Again, with the **Label** selected, go to the **Inspector** pane, select the **Attributes** tab, and in the **Layout** section, click on the middle alignment button. Congratulations, you have just added a **Label** in your application's main view!

Add a button

We will perform similar steps to add a button in our interface.

1. Again, in the **Library** pane, in the **Objects** section, select the **Button** object. It is next to the **Label** object.
2. Drag-and-drop it onto the bottom half of the view. Align its center with the center of the **Label** we added earlier. A dashed line will show up, and the **Button** will snap to it when the centers of the two controls are almost aligned.
3. Resize the **Button** to the same width of the **Label**. Since the **Label** has a transparent background and you cannot see how wide it is exactly, you will know when the **Button** is the same width when three dashed lines will show up while you are resizing it.
4. Now, let's add some text to the **Button**. Select it and go to the **Inspector** pane. In the **Attributes** tab, in the **Title** field, enter `Tap here please!`.

Development Tools

5. After adding the button, save the document through **File | Save** in the menu bar. The main view should now look like the following screenshot (shown resized here):

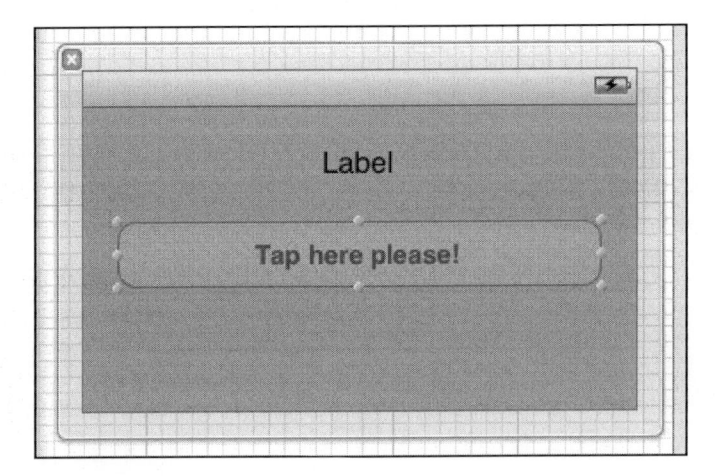

How it works...

As you can see, although some concepts of Interface Builder seem difficult, it is quite easy to use. It also provides a lot of feedback. When we drag objects, a green-circled cross appears on the cursor to declare that we can drop the object there. Also, when we resize a control, we see its dimensions next to it.

You can also resize and position the controls by modifying the values in the **Size** tab of the **Inspector** pane. Another useful feature in the **Size** tab is **Autosizing**. **Autosizing** provides layout options for the controls and can be very useful when we want our application to support different device orientations. You can select a control you want, and then click on the lines that are outside or inside of the square on the left in the **Autosizing** section. The image next to it animates to give you an impression of how the control will behave when the layout changes.

There's more...

Now, let's try running the application on the iOS Simulator. Back at MonoDevelop, select the project configuration at **Debug | iPhoneSimulator** if it is not already selected. No need to do anything else in the code for now; just click on the **Run** button. It is the third button on the right of the configuration combo box, with the double gear icon. When the compilation finishes, iOS Simulator will start automatically and will run the application we just created! You can even "tap" on the **Button** by clicking on it with the mouse and see it responding. Of course, our application does not have any other functionality right now.

Setting titles on buttons

Setting the title of a **Button** or a **Label** can easily be done just by double-clicking on it and typing the preferable title. Do it, and watch how Interface Builder behaves to show you what action is to be performed.

See also

In this chapter:

- *Compiling*
- *Debugging our application*

In this book:

Chapter 2, User Interface: Views:

- *Receiving user input with buttons*
- *Using labels to display text*

Accessing the UI with outlets

In this recipe, we will discuss the concept of **Outlets** and their usage with MonoTouch.

Getting ready

In the previous task, we learned how to add controls to form a basic interface for our application. In this task, we will discuss how to access and use these controls in our code. Launch MonoDevelop, and open the project `ButtonInput` that we created earlier. Open the project's `ButtonInputViewController.xib` in Interface Builder by double-clicking on it in the **Solution** pad.

Development Tools

How to do it...

1. With the **Assistant Editor** open, *Ctrl*-drag from the label to the Objective-C source file, as displayed in the following screenshot:

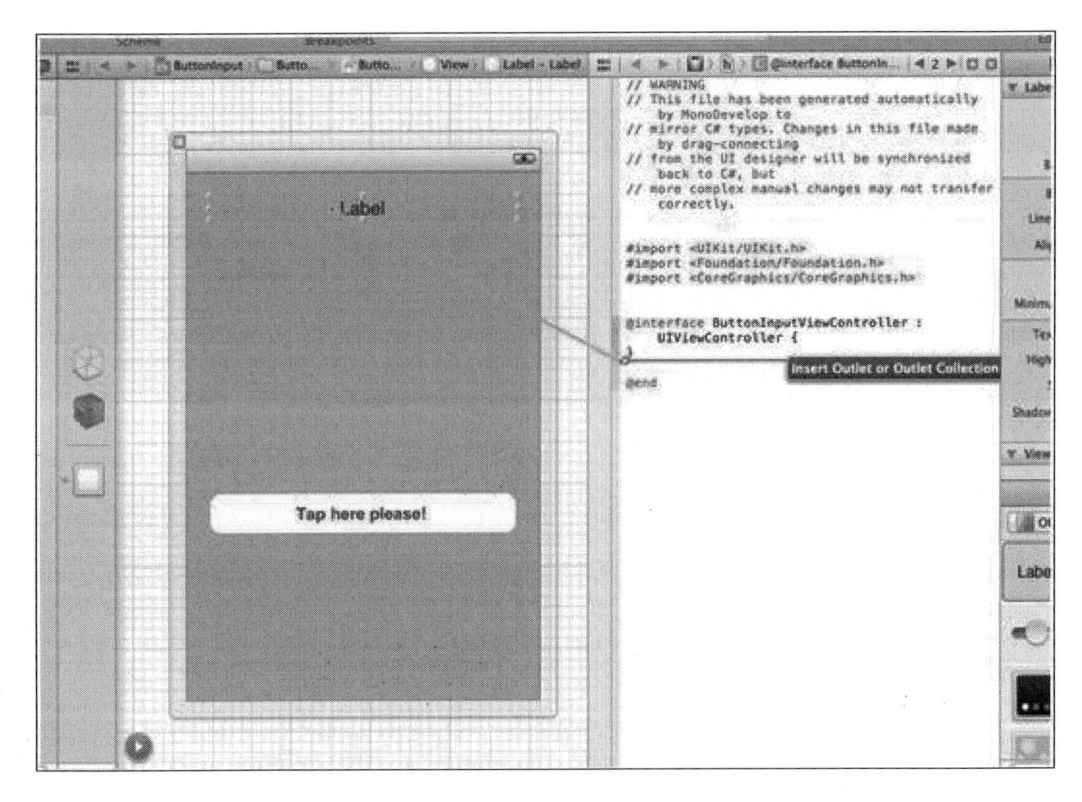

When you release the cursor, a context window will appear, similar to the one in the following screenshot:

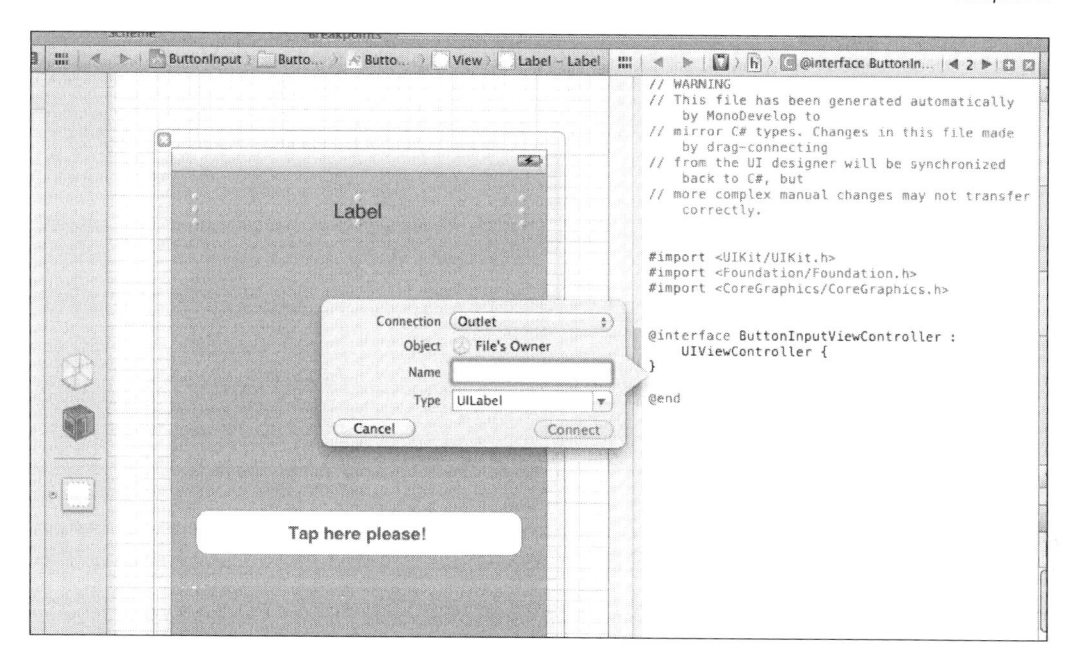

2. In the **Name** field of the context window, enter `labelStatus`, and click on **Connect**.

3. Do the same for the button, and name it `buttonTap`. Save the Interface Builder document by selecting **File | Save** in the menu bar, or by pressing *Option - S* on the keyboard.

4. Back in MonoDevelop, enter the following code in the `ViewDidLoad` method of the `ButtonInputViewController` class:

   ```
   // Create and hook a handler to our button's TouchUpInside event
   // through its outlet
   this.buttonTap.TouchUpInside += delegate(
     object sender, EventArgs e) {
     this.labelStatus.Text = "Button tapped!";
   };
   ```

   This code snippet adds a handler to the button's `TouchUpInside` event. This event is similar to the `Clicked` event of a **Button** control in `System.Windows.Forms`. It also displays the usage of an anonymous method, which just shows how MonoTouch provides C# features to .NET developers. That's it! Our application is now ready with functional controls.

5. Compile and run it on the simulator. See the label changing its text when you tap on the button.

Development Tools

How it works...

The outlet mechanism is basically a way of connecting Interface Builder objects with the code. They are necessary, since it is the only way we can access user interface objects that we create with Interface Builder. This is how Interface Builder works, and it is not just a MonoTouch workaround. An outlet of an object provides a variable of this object, so that we will be able to use it in a project. MonoTouch makes a developer's life much easier, because when we create outlets in Interface Builder and connect them, MonoDevelop works in the background by auto-generating code regarding those outlets. This is what the `ButtonInputViewController.designer.cs` has added to provide us access to the controls we created:

```
[Outlet]
MonoTouch.UIKit.UILabel labelStatus { get; set; }
[Outlet]
MonoTouch.UIKit.UIButton buttonTap { get; set; }
```

These are the properties that provide us access to the controls. They are decorated with the `OutletAttribute`. You can see that the names of the properties are the exact same names we entered for our outlets. This is very important, since we only have to provide names once for the outlets and do not have to worry about repeating the same naming conventions in different parts of our code. Notice also that the types of the variables of the controls are exactly the same as the types of controls we dragged-and-dropped in our user interface. This information is stored in the `XIB` file, and MonoDevelop reads this information accordingly.

There's more...

To remove outlets, you first have to disconnect them. For example, to remove the `buttonTap` outlet, *Ctrl* - click on the button. In the panel that will appear, click on the small (**x**) next to the outlet. This will disconnect the outlet.

Chapter 1

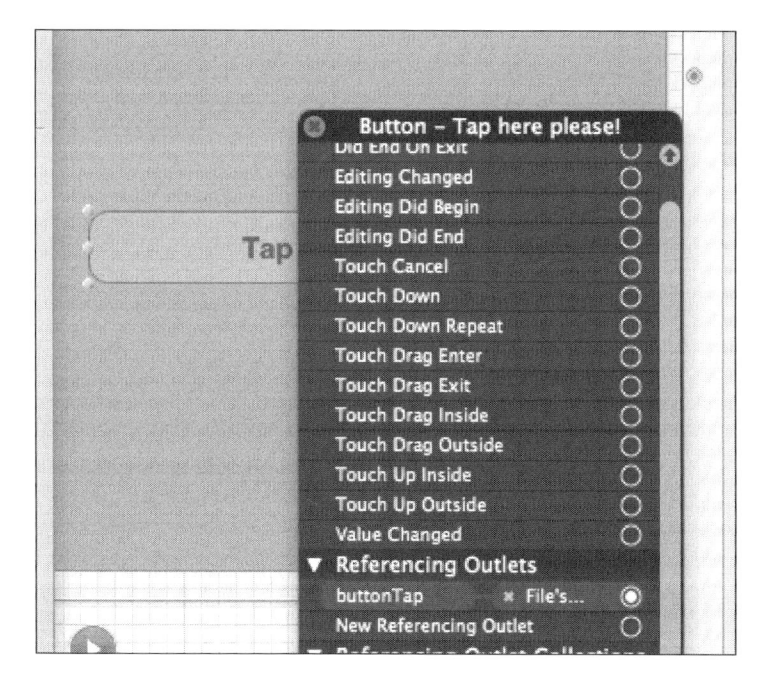

After that, delete the following code from the Objective-C source file:

```
@property (retain, nonatomic) IBOutlet UIButton *buttonTap;
```

When you save the document, the outlet will be removed from the MonoDevelop project.

Adding outlets through code

Another way of adding outlets is to create a property in your C# class and decorate it with the `OutletAttribute`:

```
[Outlet]
UIButton ButtonTap { get;    set; }
```

Development Tools

When you open the `XIB` file in Interface Builder, the outlet will have been added to the user interface. However, you would still have to connect it to the corresponding control. The easiest way to do this is to *Ctrl* - click on the control the outlet corresponds to and click-drag from **New Referencing Outlet** to the **File's Owner** object on the left of the designer area:

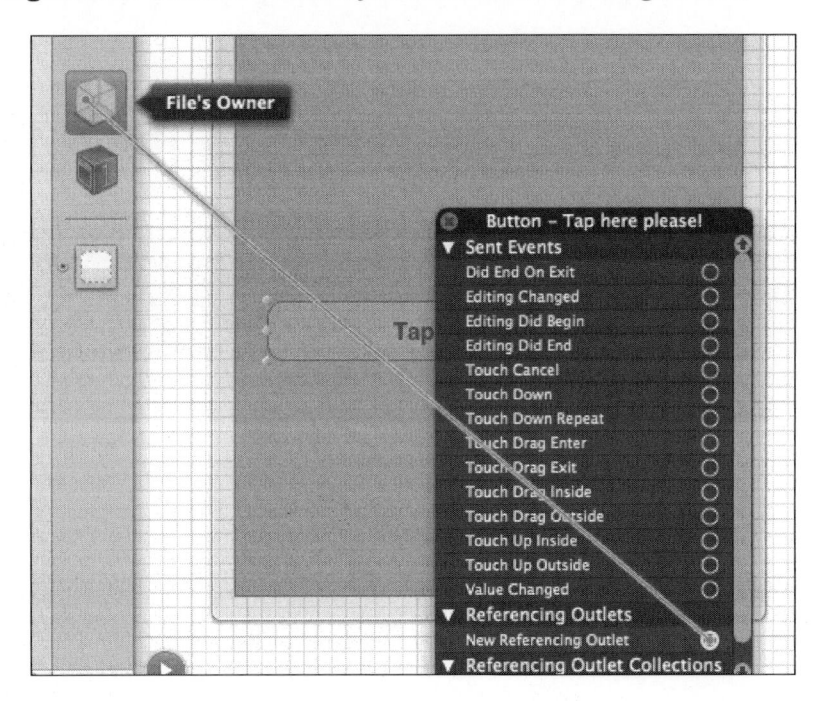

When you release the cursor, select the **ButtonTap** outlet from the small context menu that will appear.

> Note that it is MonoDevelop that monitors for changes made in Interface Builder and not the other way around. When making changes in the MonoDevelop project, make sure to always open the `XIB` file from inside MonoDevelop.

See also

In this chapter:

- *Interface builder*
- *Creating the UI*
- *Adding actions*

In this book:

Chapter 2, User Interface: Views:

> ▸ *Adding and customizing views*

Adding actions

In this recipe, we discuss the concept of **Actions** and their usage with MonoTouch.

Getting ready

In this task, we will discuss how to use actions with the controls of the user interface. Create a new iPhone Single View Application project in MonoDevelop, and name it `ButtonInputAction`. Open `ButtonInputActionViewController.xib` in Interface Builder, and add the same controls, outlets, and connections as the ones from project `ButtonInput` from the previous task. Do not add any code in the project for now.

How to do it...

Adding actions to interface objects is similar to adding outlets.

1. In Interface Builder, *Ctrl*-drag from the button to the source code file. In the context window that will be shown, change the **Connection** field from **Outlet** to **Action**.
2. Enter `OnButtonTap` in the **Name** field, and select **Touch Up** Inside in the **Event** field, if it is not already selected.
3. Click on the **Connect** button, and save the document.
4. In the `ButtonInputActionViewController` class, add the following method:
    ```
    partial void OnButtonTap(NSObject sender){
       this.labelStatus.Text = "Button tapped!";
    }
    ```
5. The application is ready! Compile and run in the simulator.
6. Tap on the button, and see the text in the label change, just like in the previous application we created.

Development Tools

How it works...

Actions in Objective-C are the equivalent of control events in C#. They are responsible for delivering notification signals of various objects. In this example, instead of hooking up a handler on the `TouchUpInside` event of the button, we have added an action for it. As you may already have noticed, the method we added to act as a handler for the action was declared as `partial`. That is because MonoDevelop already declared a partial method declaration for us. This is the code that was produced when we saved the document in Interface Builder:

```
[Action ("OnButtonTap:")]
partial void OnButtonTap (MonoTouch.Foundation.NSObject sender);
```

The partial declaration of the method is marked with the `ActionAttribute`. This is another attribute from the `MonoTouch.Foundation` namespace that allows us to expose methods as Objective-C actions. You see that the string parameter passed in the attribute is exactly the same as the action name we entered in Interface Builder, with an appended colon (:) to it.

> Colons in Objective-C indicate the presence of parameters. For example, `doSomething` is different than `doSomething:`. Their difference is that the first one does not accept any parameters, while the second accepts one parameter.

The colon at the end of the action name indicates that there is one parameter; in this case, the parameter `MonoTouch.UIKit.NSObject` sender. This is what our application looks like when we have tapped on the button in the simulator:

There's more...

The previous example was created just to show how to implement actions in MonoTouch projects. Replacing an event with an action is basically at the discretion of the developer.

See also

In this chapter:

- *Interface builder*
- *Creating the UI*
- *Accessing the UI with outlets*

Compiling

In this recipe, we will discuss how to compile a project with MonoDevelop.

Getting ready

MonoDevelop provides many different options for compiling. In this task, we will discuss these options. We will be working with the project `ButtonInput` that we created earlier in this chapter.

How to do it...

1. With the project loaded in MonoDevelop, go to **Project | ButtonInput Options**.
2. In the window that appears, select **iPhone Build** from the **Build** section on the left pad. Select **Debug** as project configuration and **iPhoneSimulator** as a platform. In the **Linker behavior** field, select **Link all assemblies** from the combo box. In the **SDK version** field, select **Default**, if it is not already selected.
3. Now, go to **iPhone Application** on the left pad.

Development Tools

4. In the **Summary** tab, enter `Button Input` in the **Application name** field and `1.0` in the **Version** field. Select version **3.0** in the **Deployment Target** combo box. The **iPhone Application** options window is shown in the following screenshot:

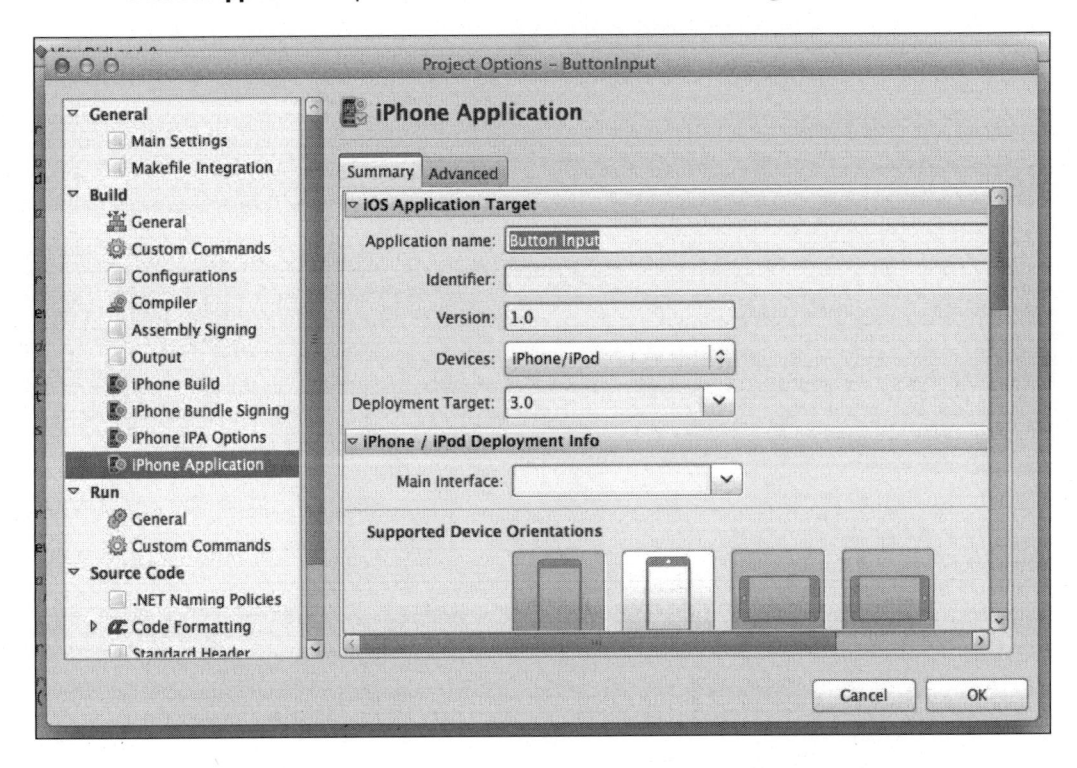

5. Click on the **OK** button, and compile the project by clicking on **Build | Build All** in the menu bar.

How it works...

We have set up some options for our project. Let's see what these options provide for compilation customization.

iPhone build options

The first option we set up regards the Linker. The **Linker** is a tool that was developed by the MonoTouch team and is provided in the SDK. Every time a MonoTouch project is compiled, the compiler does not only compile the project, but all the assemblies of the MonoTouch framework it needs, so that the final application will be able to run on the device (or the simulator). This actually means that every application comes with its own compiled version of the MonoTouch framework. Doing so means the final application bundle is quite large in size. This is where the Linker comes in. What it does is to strip down the assemblies of all the unused code so that the compiler will only compile what is needed and used by the application. This results in much smaller application bundles: a precious asset when it comes to mobile applications. Especially since Apple has a download limitation of 20 MB per file through the cellular network. The Linker options are the following:

- **Don't Link**: Use this option when debugging on the simulator. The Linker is turned off, and all the assemblies are compiled as they are. This provides faster compilation times.

- **Link SDK assemblies only**: Here, the Linker only strips down the MonoTouch Framework assemblies. The project assemblies remain intact. This option also effectively reduces the final size of the application.

- **Link all assemblies**: Here, the Linker is activated on all assemblies. it reduces the size a bit more. Care needs to be taken when using this option, if **Reflection** or **Serialization** is used in the code. Types and methods that are used through Reflection in the code are transparent to the Linker. If a situation like this exists in the code, decorate these types or methods with the `PreserveAttribute`. This attribute basically informs the Linker to be left out of the stripping down process.

In the SDK version field, we set the **iOS SDK version** that will be used to compile the application. Setting it to **Default** automatically selects the highest SDK version installed on the system.

iPhone application options

In the **iPhone Application** window of the **Build** section in the project options, we have set up three options. The first option is the **Application name**. This is the name of the application bundle that will be displayed on the simulator, the device, and on the App Store. As we can see here, we can normally add spaces to the name. The second option, **Version**, defines the version of the application. It is what will be displayed as the application's version when it is finally distributed through the App Store. The third option, **Deployment target**, is the minimum iOS version the application can be installed on.

There's more...

There are two more option windows. These are **iPhone Bundle Signing** and **iPhone IPA** options. They will be discussed thoroughly in the recipes of *Chapter 14, Deploying*.

Linker usage

> When compiling for the simulator, turning the Linker on is not suggested. That is because the compiler is not compiling the MonoTouch assemblies in the `iPhoneSimulator` platform; hence they are being used directly. Turning the Linker on only causes compilation to take more time to complete. It has no effect in reducing the final application bundle size.

Development Tools

See also

In this book:

Chapter 14, Deploying:

> ▶ Preparing our application for the App Store

Debugging our application

In this recipe, we will discuss information on debugging a MonoTouch application on the simulator.

Getting ready

MonoTouch, in combination with MonoDevelop, provides a debugger for debugging applications either on the simulator or on the device. In this task, we'll see how to use the debugger for debugging MonoTouch applications. Open MonoDevelop, and load the `ButtonInput` project. Make sure the debugger toolbar is activated by checking on **View | Toolbars | Debugger** in the menu bar. Also, set the project configuration to **Debug | iPhoneSimulator**.

How to do it...

1. MonoDevelop supports breakpoints. To activate a breakpoint on a line, click on the space on the left of the line number to set it. Set a breakpoint on the following line in the `Main.cs` file:

   ```
   this.labelStatus.Text = "Button tapped!";
   ```

   This is what a breakpoint in MonoDevelop looks like:

   ```
   24  // If you have defined a view, add it here:
   25  // window.AddSubview (navigationController.View);
   26
   27  // Create and hook a handler to our button's TouchUpInside event
   28  // through its outlet
   29  this.buttonTap.TouchUpInside += delegate(object sender, EventArgs e) {
   30      this.labelStatus.Text = "Button tapped!";
   31  };
   32
   33  window.MakeKeyAndVisible ();
   34
   ```

2. Compile and debug the project by clicking on the second button with the double gears icon from the left, or by clicking **Run | Debug** on the menu bar. MonoDevelop will display a message box with the message, **Waiting for debugger to connect....** When the simulator is open and the app is loaded, watch the information that is provided in the **Application Output** pad. Tap on the app button. Execution will pause, and MonoDevelop will highlight the breakpoint in yellow. Move the mouse over the `labelStatus` variable in the breakpoint line. MonoDevelop will then display a window with all the evaluated variable's members:

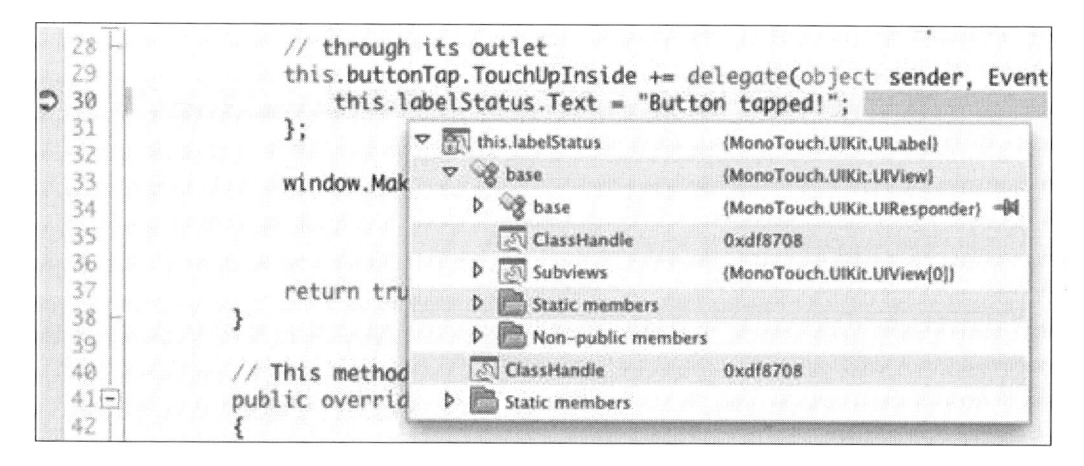

3. To stop debugging, click on the **stop** button on the toolbar, marked with a white (**X**) in a red circle.

How it works...

MonoTouch, in combination with MonoDevelop, uses a debugger called **Soft Debugger**. It is called this, because it depends on both the runtime and MonoDevelop combined to provide one unified debugging platform. When the debugging process starts, MonoDevelop begins listening for debugging information from the application. The same applies for debugging on both the simulator and the device. When the application executes, it starts sending information back to MonoDevelop, which then displays that information in the **Application Output** pad, which is automatically activated. A typical application output when debugging is the information on the assemblies that are loaded, the threads that begin execution, and the breakpoints, if any, that are available.

There's more...

The `Console.WriteLine()` method can also be used for debugging purposes. The debugger takes care of this and redirects the output of the method to MonoDevelop's **Application Output** pad.

Development Tools

Application performance when debugging

When compiling for debugging purposes, the compiler produces larger and slower code. That is because it generates extra code that is needed to provide the appropriate debugging information. That is why when debugging an application, the execution of the application is much slower than on simple running situations. Before producing a release copy of the application, remember to compile it with the **Release | iPhone project configuration** to avoid slow runtime execution.

Breakpoints in the FinishedLaunching method

One more reason not to have complicated code in the `FinishedLaunching` method is that in most cases, you will not be able to debug it. If you set a breakpoint in `FinishedLaunching`, application execution will pause, but iOS will terminate the application when the time limit is reached.

See also

In this book:

Chapter 14, Deploying:

- Creating profiles
- Debugging on other devices

2
User Interface: Views

In this chapter, we will cover the following:

- Adding and customizing views
- Receiving user input with buttons
- Using labels to display text
- Displaying images
- Displaying and editing text
- Using the keyboard
- Displaying progress
- Displaying content larger than the screen
- Navigating through content divided into pages
- Displaying a toolbar
- Creating a custom view

Introduction

An application's user interface is essential for providing the user with an easy way of communicating with a device, be it a computer, a mobile phone, or a tablet. On a mobile device, the user interface is not only essential but the only way to interact with the user. Developers have to cope with various limitations and restrictions when developing for mobile devices. The processing power does not match desktop CPUs and the screens are smaller, making the process of choosing what sort of information will be displayed each time somewhat more difficult.

User Interface: Views

In this chapter, we will discuss the key components of an iOS application's UI. We will see how to use and customize these components to create rich application user interfaces and discuss their similarities and differences they have with their desktop equivalents. Here is a list of these components:

- `UIView`: It is a customizable container, which is the base object of most iOS user interface controls
- `UIButton`: It is the equivalent of a `Button` in .NET world
- `UILabel`: It is the equivalent of a `Label` in .NET world
- `UIImageView`: It is a view that allows us to display and create basic animations with images
- `UITextView`: It is a view, which allows us to display editable text
- `UITextField`: It is similar to .NET's `TextBox` control
- `UIProgressView`: It displays known length progress
- `UIScrollView`: It provides the ability to display scrollable content
- `UIPageControl`: It provides navigation functionality to content, divided into different pages or screens
- `UIToolbar`: It provides a toolbar at the bottom of the screen that accepts customizable buttons

We will also talk about how to programmatically create instances of these components and use them efficiently.

Adding and customizing views

In this task, we will discuss how to add and customize a `UIView` with **Interface Builder**.

Getting ready

Adding views with Interface Builder is a simple task. Let's start by creating a new **iPhone Single View Application** project in MonoDevelop. Name the project `FirstViewApp`, and open the `FirstViewAppViewController.xib` file with Interface Builder.

How to do it...

1. To add a view to the project, drag-and-drop a `UIView` object from the **Library** pad onto the main view. Make sure it fits the entire window area.
2. To make the `UIView` accessible, create an outlet for it, and name it `subView`.

Chapter 2

> The concept of outlets and how to use them is discussed in detail in *Chapter 1, Accessing the UI with Outlets*.

3. Select the view that we just added and go to the **Inspector** pad. Select the **Attributes** tab, and in the **Background** drop-down list, select **Light Gray Color**.
4. Now, select the **Size** tab and reduce the view's height by 60 points.
5. Save the document.
6. Compile and run the application on the simulator. The result should look like the following image:

The gray portion of the simulator's screen is the view that we have just added.

How it works...

We have successfully created an application that contains one view. Of course, this application does not provide any functionality. It is only meant to show how to add a view and display it.

User Interface: Views

Views are the essential components of an iOS application interface. Every visual UI object inherits from the `UIView` class. The concept is somewhat different than a `Form` in .NET. A view manages content drawing, accepts other views as subviews, provides auto-sizing features, can accept touch events for itself and its subviews, and many of its properties can even be animated. Even `UIWindow` inherits from `UIView`. It is this class or its inheritors that iOS developers will use most frequently.

When a view, which is added with Interface Builder, is first instantiated at runtime, it sets its `Frame` property with values that are set through the **Inspector** window's **Size** tab. The `Frame` property is of type `RectangleF` and defines the location of the view in its superview's coordinate system, in our case the main window, and its size in points.

> In Objective-C, the `Frame` property of `UIView` is of the type `CGRect`. This type has not been bound in MonoTouch, and the more familiar `System.Drawing.RectangleF` was used instead.
>
> A superview is a view's parent view, while subviews are its child views. Views that have the same superview are described as siblings.

The default coordinate system in iOS originates from the top-left corner and extends towards the bottom and the right. The coordinate origin is always the same and cannot be changed programmatically.

The coordinate system of iOS is displayed in the following image:

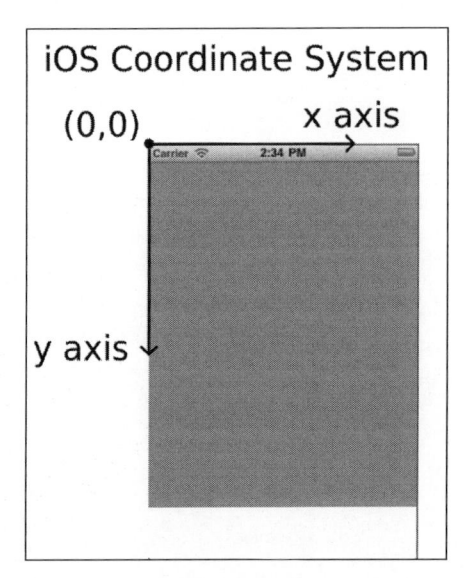

When the `Frame` property is set, it adjusts the `Bounds` property. The `Bounds` property defines the location of the view in its own coordinate system and its size in points. It is also of the type `RectangleF`. The default location for the `Bounds` property is (0,0), and its size is always the same as the view's `Frame` value. Both these properties' sizes are connected to each other, so when you change the size of the `Frame`, the size of the `Bounds` changes accordingly and vice versa. You can change the `Bounds` property to display different parts of the view. A view's `Frame` can exceed the screen in both location and position. That is to say that a view's frame with values (x = -50, y = -50, width = 1500, height = 1500) is perfectly acceptable.

There's more...

Another thing to note is that the `UIView` class inherits from `UIResponder`. The `UIResponder` class is responsible for responding to and handling events. When a view is added to another view, it becomes part of its responder chain. The `UIView` class exposes the properties and methods of `UIResponder`, and the ones we are interested in describing for now are the following two:

1. `IsFirstResponder` **property**: It returns a boolean value indicating whether the view is the first responder. Basically, it indicates if the view has focus.
2. `ResignFirstResponder()`: It causes the view to lose focus.

Adding views programmatically

If we would like to add a view programmatically, we would use the `UIView.AddSubview(UIView)` method:

```
this.View.AddSubview(this.subView);
```

The `AddSubview()` method adds its parameter, which is of the type `UIView`, to the list of the caller's subviews and sets its `Superview` parameter to the caller. A view will not be displayed unless it is added to a parent view with the `AddSubview()` method. Also, if a view already has a superview and it is added to another view with its `AddSubview()` method, then its `Superview` is changed to that of the new caller. What this means is that a view can only have only one superview each time.

> When adding a view as a subview with Interface Builder, it is not required to use the `AddSubview()` method to display the subview. It is required to call the `AddSubview()` method, however, when adding views programmatically.

For removing a view from its superview programmatically, call its `RemoveFromSuperview()` method. Calling this method on a view, which has no superview, does nothing. Care must be taken when we want to reuse the view we want to remove. We must keep a reference to it, or it might be released after the method is called.

User Interface: Views

View content layout

Another important property of `UIView` is `ContentMode`. `ContentMode` accepts values of the enumeration type `UIViewContentMode`. This property sets how the `UIView` will display its content. The default value of this property is `UIViewContentMode.ScaleToFill`, which scales the content to fit the exact view's size, distorting it if necessary.

See also

In this chapter:

- *Creating a custom view*

In this book:

Chapter 1, Accessing the UI with Outlets:

- *Creating the UI*
- *Accessing the UI with outlets*

Chapter 3, User Interface: View Controllers:

- *View controllers* and *views*

Receiving user input with buttons

In this recipe, we will learn how to use buttons to receive and respond to user input.

Getting ready

We used buttons in *Chapter 1, Accessing the UI with Outlets* to discuss how to use Interface Builder to add controls to the user interface. In this task, we will describe the `UIButton` class in more detail. Open the project `FirstViewApp` that we created in the previous task in MonoDevelop. Increase the main view's height to cover the entire screen in Interface Builder, and save the document.

Chapter 2

How to do it...

We will programmatically add a button in our interface that will change our view's background color when tapped.

1. Open the `FirstViewAppViewController.cs` file, and enter the following code in the class::

   ```
   UIButton buttonChangeColor;
   private void CreateButton (){
      RectangleF viewFrame = this.subView.Frame;
      RectangleF buttonFrame = new RectangleF (10f, viewFrame.Bottom -
        200f, viewFrame.Width - 20f, 50f);

      this.buttonChangeColor = UIButton.FromType
        (UIButtonType.RoundedRect);
      this.buttonChangeColor.Frame = buttonFrame;
      this.buttonChangeColor.SetTitle ("Tap to change view color",
        UIControlState.Normal);
      this.buttonChangeColor.SetTitle ("Changing color...",
        UIControlState.Highlighted);
      this.buttonChangeColor.TouchUpInside +=
        this.buttonChangeColor_TouchUpInside;
      this.subView.AddSubview (this.buttonChangeColor);
   }

   bool isRed;
   private void buttonChangeColor_TouchUpInside (object sender,
     EventArgs e){
      if (this.isRed) {
         this.subView.BackgroundColor = UIColor.LightGray;
         this.isRed = false;
      } else {
         this.subView.BackgroundColor = UIColor.Red;
         this.isRed = true;
      }
   }
   ```

2. And in the `ViewDidLoad()` method, add the following line:

   ```
   this.CreateButton ();
   ```

User Interface: Views

3. Compile and run the application on the simulator. When the button is tapped, the result should be similar to the following screenshot:

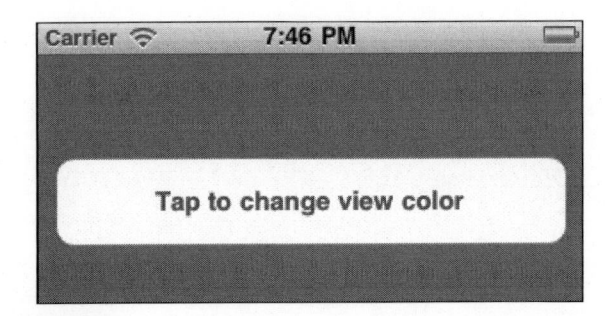

How it works...

In this task, we have added a button to the user interface that changes the background color of the superview. Furthermore, we have accomplished this without using Interface Builder at all.

Let's now see what the code does.

1. We create a field that will hold the button object:

   ```
   // A button to change the view's background color
   UIButton buttonChangeColor;
   ```

2. In the `CreateButton()` method, we create the button and set some properties.

   ```
   RectangleF viewFrame = this.subView.Frame;
   RectangleF buttonFrame = new RectangleF (10f, viewFrame.Bottom -
     200f, viewFrame.Width - 20f, 50f);
   ```

3. First, we assign the view's `Frame` to a new variable named `viewFrame`. Then, we create a new `RectangleF` object named `buttonFrame`, which will be assigned to the button's `Frame` property. Now that we have a frame for our button, we can initialize it, as shown in the following code snippet:

   ```
   //Create the button.
   this.buttonChangeColor = UIButton.FromType
      (UIButtonType.RoundedRect);
   this.buttonChangeColor.Frame = buttonFrame;
   ```

4. The button is initialized with the static method `UIButton.FromType(UIButtonType)`. This method takes one parameter of the type `UIButtonType` and returns predefined types of buttons that are included in iOS SDK. The `UIButtonType.RoundedRect` button enumeration value, used here, is the default type of iOS button with rounded corners. After the `buttonChangeColor` object is initialized, we set its `Frame` to the `RectangleF` value we created previously.

5. Now that we have provided initialization code for the button, we will set its titles (that's right, more than one):

   ```
   // Set the button's titles
   this.buttonChangeColor.SetTitle ("Tap to change view color",
     UIControlState.Normal);
   this.buttonChangeColor.SetTitle ("Changing color...",
     UIControlState.Highlighted);
   ```

   We call the `UIButton.SetTitle(string, UIControlState)` method twice. This method is responsible for setting the button's title for each given button state. The string parameter is the actual title that will be shown. The second parameter is an enumeration of the type `UIControlState` that indicates the different control states that apply to controls. These control states are:

   - `Normal`: The default idle state of an enabled control
   - `Highlighted`: The state of the control when a touch-up event occurs
   - `Disabled`: The control is disabled and does not accept any events
   - `Selected`: The control is selected. In most cases, this state does not apply. It is useful, however, when a selection state is required, such as in a `UISegmentedControl` object
   - `Application`: An additional control state values for application use
   - `Reserved`: For internal framework use

   So, with the method `UIButton.SetTitle(string, UIControlState)`, we have set the title that will be displayed when the button is in its default state and the title that will be displayed while it is being tapped.

6. After that, we set the button's handler for the `TouchUpInside` event, and add it as a subview to the `subView`:

   ```
   this.buttonChangeColor.TouchUpInside +=
     this.buttonChangeColor_TouchUpInside;
   this.subView.AddSubview (this.buttonChangeColor);
   ```

7. Inside the `buttonChangeColor_TouchUpInside` event, we change the background color of the view, according to the boolean field that we have declared:

   ```
   if (this.isRed) {
     this.subView.BackgroundColor = UIColor.LightGray;
       this.isRed = false;
   } else {
     this.subView.BackgroundColor = UIColor.Red;
       this.isRed = true;
   }
   ```

User Interface: Views

This is done by setting the view's `BackgroundColor` property to the appropriate `UIColor` class instance we want, as shown in the highlighted code previously. The `UIColor` object is a class with many different static methods and properties that allow us to create different color objects.

When you compile and run the application on the simulator, notice not only the view's color change when you tap the button, but also how the button's title changes while the mouse cursor (or finger on the device) is touching the button.

There's more...

In this task, we used the `UIButton.FromType(UIButtonType)` static method to initialize the button. A brief description of each of the enumeration flags of `UIButtonType` is as follows:

- `Custom`: It's a borderless transparent button. Use this flag when creating custom buttons with images as backgrounds. The button's title is not transparent.
- `RoundedRect`: It's the default type of button with rounded corners.
- `DetailDisclosure`: It's a round blue button that reveals additional information related to an item.
- `InfoLight`: It's a light-colored button with the letter (i), representing information display.
- `InfoDark`: It's the same as `InfoLight`, shown with dark color.
- `ContactAdd`: It's a round blue button with a white plus sign (+). Usually displayed to present contact information to add to an item.

Creating custom buttons

For creating custom buttons with the type `UIButtonType.Custom`, use the `UIButton` class' `SetBackgroundImage()` and `SetImage()` methods. They both accept one `UIImage` and one `UIControlState` parameters, so that different images for different control states can be set. When setting images for buttons, whether creating a custom button or not, be sure to set the `UIButton.ContentMode` property accordingly.

The functionality provided by the methods `SetImage` and `SetBackgroundImage` can also be accomplished in the corresponding **Image** and **Background** fields in the **Attributes** tab of the **Inspector** pad in Interface Builder. Select the state for which to set the desired image(s) from the drop-down list box, and set the path to the image file, as shown in the following screenshot:

Chapter 2

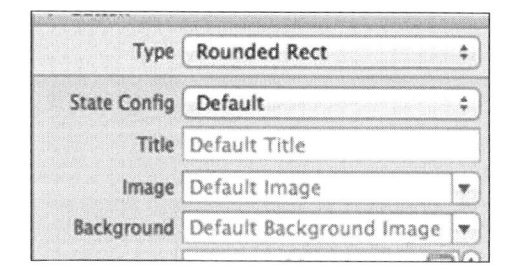

See also

In this chapter:

- *Adding and customizing views*
- *Displaying images*
- *Creating a custom view*

In this book:

Chapter 1, Development Tools:

- *Creating the UI,*
- *Accessing the UI with Outlets*

Using labels to display text

In this recipe, we will learn how to display informative text to the user with labels.

Getting ready

In this task, we will describe the `UILabel` class in more detail. Once again, all of the work will be done without the help of Interface Builder. Open the project `FirstViewApp` that we modified in the previous recipe in MonoDevelop.

How to do it...

We will programmatically create a label, which will display some static guidance text.

1. Open the file `FirstViewAppViewcontroller.cs`, and enter the following code in the class:

   ```
   UILabel labelInfo;
   private void CreateLabel (){
      RectangleF viewFrame = this.subView.Frame;
   ```

53

User Interface: Views

```
        RectangleF labelFrame = new RectangleF (10f, viewFrame.Y + 20f,
           viewFrame.Width - 20f, 100f);

        this.labelInfo = new UILabel (labelFrame);
        this.labelInfo.Lines = 3;
        this.labelInfo.TextAlignment = UITextAlignment.Center;
        this.labelInfo.BackgroundColor = UIColor.Clear;

        this.labelInfo.TextColor = UIColor.White;
        this.labelInfo.ShadowColor = UIColor.DarkGray;
        this.labelInfo.ShadowOffset = new SizeF (1f, 1f);

        this.labelInfo.Text = "Tap the button below to change the
           background color." +
           " Notice the button's title change while it is being tapped!";

        //this.labelInfo.AdjustsFontSizeToFitWidth = true;

        this.subView.AddSubview (this.labelInfo);
    }
```

2. And in the `FinishedLaunching()` method, add the following line:

   ```
   this.CreateLabel();
   ```

3. Compile and run the application on the simulator. The output should look like the following screenshot:

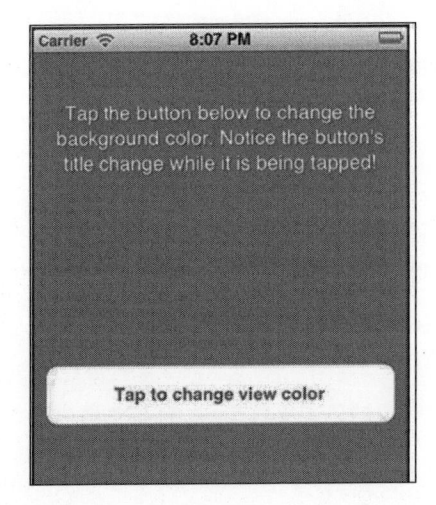

How it works...

We have successfully created a label and put some information text in it. Let's step through the code and see what actually goes on.

1. We first create the `labelInfo` field that will hold our `UILabel` object in the `FirstViewAppViewController` class.

   ```
   // A label that displays some text
   UILabel labelInfo;
   ```

2. We then create the method `CreateLabel()`, which will instantiate and customize the label. Like the button we created in the previous task, our label needs a frame. So, we create one, again depending on the view's `Frame` property:

   ```
   //Create the appropriate rectangles for the label's frame
   RectangleF viewFrame = this.subView.Frame;
   RectangleF labelFrame = new RectangleF (10f, viewFrame.Y + 20f,
      viewFrame.Width - 20f, 100f);
   ```

3. We just set its height to be higher than the button's, to 100 points. Now that we have a `Frame` for the label, we initialize it:

   ```
   //Create the label
   this.labelInfo = new UILabel (labelFrame);
   this.labelInfo.Lines = 3;
   this.labelInfo.TextAlignment = UITextAlignment.Center;
   this.labelInfo.BackgroundColor = UIColor.Clear;
   ```

   The `UILabel(RectangleF)` constructor is used, so that the `Frame` property will be set immediately upon initialization. The `Lines` property determines the total number of lines the text on the `label` text will be divided to. The `TextAlignment` property accepts values of the enumeration type `UITextAlignment`, which contains the usual text alignment flags: `Center`, `Left`, and `Right`. To make the `Frame` of the `label` completely invisible, so that only our text will be visible, we set the `BackgroundColor` property to the color `UIColor.Clear`.

4. The next part is quite interesting. Apart from being able to set the font color of the `label`, we can also set a shadow at the displayed text:

   ```
   // Set text color and shadow
   this.labelInfo.TextColor = UIColor.White;
   this.labelInfo.ShadowColor = UIColor.DarkGray;
   this.labelInfo.ShadowOffset = new SizeF (1f, 1f);
   ```

User Interface: Views

The `TextColor` property accepts `UIColor` values. To set a shadow for the text of the `label`, set a `UIColor` to the `ShadowColor` property. Then, set a `SizeF` structure to the `ShadowOffset` property. This property determines the exact location of the shadow. The `width` parameter of `SizeF` defines the horizontal placement of the shadow, and the `height` parameter defines the vertical placement. Negative values are acceptable. A negative value for `width` means that the shadow will be positioned towards the left, while a negative value for the `height` means that the shadow will be positioned above the text. The value we have set in the previous code means that the shadow will be displayed `1` point to the right and `1` point below the text.

5. We have prepared how the `label` will render its text. To assign the text the `label` will display, set its `Text` property:

   ```
   // Set text to be displayed
   this.labelInfo.Text = "Tap the button below to change the
     background color." +
     " Notice the button's title change while it is being tapped!";
   ```

6. As you can see, we have defined quite a long string for the `label` to display. Finally, add the `label` to the view to be displayed:

   ```
   this.mainView.AddSubview (this.labelInfo);
   ```

This code gives the result shown in the *How to do it* section of this task.

There's more...

In the previous code, there is also one more line of code, which is commented out:

```
//this.labelInfo.AdjustsFontSizeToFitWidth = true;
```

The `AdjustsFontSizeToFitWidth` property accepts a boolean value. If set to `true`, it instructs the `label` to automatically change the font size so that it can fit inside the width of the `label`. Setting this property to `true` has absolutely no effect if the `label` supports more than one line. So, just to see how this property works, uncomment it and set the `Lines` property to `1`. The result will look similar to the following:

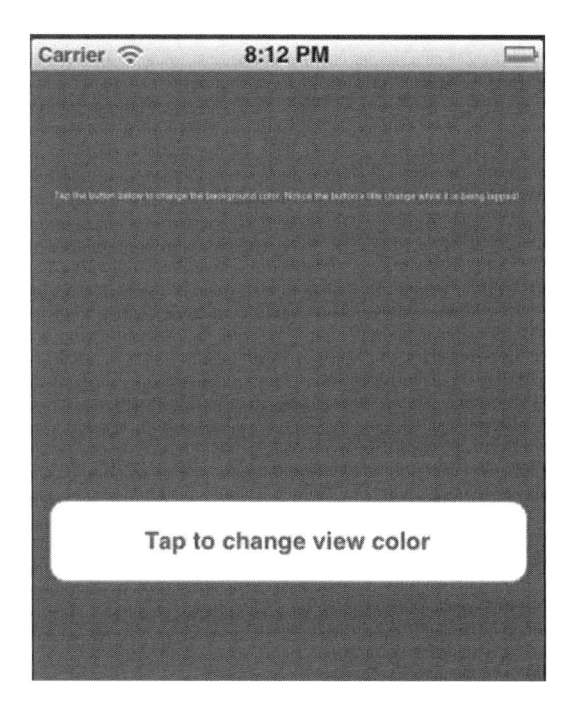

As you can see, the text on the `label` needs a magnifying glass to read, so it does not work for us properly here. The `AdjustsFontSizeToFitWidth` property, however, is very useful when there is limited space for the width of the `label` on the screen and we want our text to fit that space. To prevent a situation like this, set the `MinimumFontSize` property to the desired value. Just as its name suggests, the size of the font will not be smaller than this property's value.

UILabel fonts

Setting the font of the displayed text in a `label` is easy. Set its `Font` property with the `UIFont.FromName(string, float)` static method. The `string` parameter represents the name of the font to set and can include both the font family and style, while the `float` parameter determines its size. For example, to set the font of the `label` to `Helvetica Bold`, call the following method:

```
this.labelInfo.Font = UIFont.FromName("Helvetica-Bold", 17f);
```

User Interface: Views

If the font name is not found, the `FromName` static method returns `null`. Care must be taken for this, since when the `UILabel.Font` property is set to `null`, an exception will occur. The available styles for a font family can be determined by calling the `UIFont.FontNamesForFamilyName(string)` method, which returns a `string[]` containing all the available font styles. If the `Helvetica` font family is passed to this method, it will return a `string[]` with the following items:

```
Helvetica-BoldOblique
Helvetica
Helvetica-Bold
Helvetica-Oblique
```

See also

In this chapter:

- *Displaying and editing text*

In this book:

Chapter 1, Accessing the UI with Outlets:

- *Creating the UI*

Chapter 11, Graphics and Animation:

- *Display blinking text*

Displaying images

In this recipe, we will learn how to use the `UIImageView` class to display images on screen.

Getting ready

In this task, we will see how to bundle and display images in a project. An image file will be needed for display. The image file used here is named `Toroni.jpg`. Create a new **iPhone Single View Application** project in MonoDevelop, and name it `ImageViewerApp`.

How to do it...

1. Open the `ImageViewerAppViewController.xib` file in Interface Builder.
2. Add a `UIImageView` object on its view. Connect the `UIImageView` object with an outlet named `imageDisplay`.

3. Save the document.
4. Back in MonoDevelop, in the `ImageViewerAppViewController` class, enter the following code:

```
public override ViewDidLoad(){
  base.ViewDidLoad();
  this.imageDisplay.ContentMode =
    UIViewContentMode.ScaleAspectFit;
  this.imageDisplay.Image = UIImage.FromFile("Toroni.jpg");
}
```

5. Right-click on the project in the **Solution** pad and select **Add | Add Files...**. Select the image file you want to display, and click on **Open**.
6. Right-click on the image file you have just added, and click on **Build Action | Content**.
7. Finally, compile and run the application on the simulator. The image you added to the project should be displayed on the screen, as shown in the following Image:

User Interface: Views

How it works...

The `UIImageView` class is basically a view customized for displaying images. When adding an image in a project, its **Build Action** must be set to **Content** in the **Solution** pad, otherwise the image will not be copied into the application bundle.

The `ContentMode` property is very important when displaying images. It sets the way the `UIView` (`UIImageView`, in this case) object will display the image. We have set it to `UIViewContentMode.ScaleAspectFit`, so that it will be resized to fit the area of `UIImageView`, keeping the aspect ratio intact at the same time. If the `ContentMode` field was left at its default `Scale To Fill` value, the output would be something like the following Image:

To set the image that the `UIImageView` should display, we set its `Image` property with a `UIImage` object:

```
this.imageDisplay.Image = UIImage.FromFile("Toroni.jpg");
```

The `ContentMode` property accepts an enumeration type named `UIViewContentMode`. The values provided are:

- **ScaleToFill**: This is the default value of the base **UIView** object. It scales the content to fit the size of the view, changing the aspect ratio as necessary.
- **ScaleAspectFit**: It scales the content to fit the size of the view, maintaining its aspect ratio. The remaining area of the view's content becomes transparent.

- **ScaleAspectFill**: Scales the content to fill the size of the view, maintaining its aspect ratio. Some part of the content may be left out.
- **Redraw**: When a view's bounds are changed, its content is not redrawn. This value causes the content to be redrawn. Drawing content is an expensive operation in terms of CPU cycles, so think twice before using this value with large contents.
- **Center**: Places the content at the center of the view, keeping its aspect ratio.
- **Top**, **Bottom**, **Left**, **Right**, **TopLeft**, **TopRight**, **BottomLeft**, and **BottomRight**: Aligns the content in the view, with the corresponding value.

There's more...

The `UIImage` class is the object that represents image information. The file formats it supports are listed in the following table:

File Format	File Extension
Portable Network Graphics (PNG)	.png
Joint Photographic Experts Group (JPEG)	.jpg, .jpeg
Tagged Image File Format (TIFF)	.tiff, .tif
Graphic Interchange Format	.gif
Windows Bitmap Format	.bmp
Windows Icon Format	.ico
Windows Cursor	.cur
XWindow bitmap	.xbm

> Animated GIF image files are not supported by the `UIImageView` class. When an animated GIF is set to the `Image` property of a `UIImageView`, only its first frame will be displayed.

Using images for different screen sizes

Creating images for backgrounds provides developers with the ability to produce rich and elegant user interfaces for their applications. The preferred image file format for creating backgrounds for views is PNG. But, since the iPhone 4 was released, the screen resolution was increased. To support both screen resolutions in an application, the iOS SDK provides an easy solution. Just save the image in the higher resolution and add a `@2x` suffix to the filename, just before the extension. For example, the name of a higher resolution version of a file named `Default.png` would be `Default@2x.png`. Also, no extra code is required to use both files.

User Interface: Views

Just use the `UIImage.FromBundle(string)` static method, passing the filename without extension, and iOS takes care of loading the appropriate file, depending on the device the application is running on.

```
this.imageDisplay = UIImage.FromBundle("Default");
```

> The preceding only applies to PNG image files.

See also

In this chapter:

- *Adding and customizing views*

In this book:

Chapter 7, *Multimedia Resources*:

- *Loading an Image*

Displaying and editing text

In this recipe, we will learn how to display simple text blocks with editing functionality.

Getting ready

In this task, we will discuss the usage of `UITextView` and how to display editable text with it. Create a new **iPhone Single View Application** project in MonoDevelop, and name it `TextViewApp`.

How to do it...

1. Open `TextViewAppViewController.xib` in Interface Builder.
2. Add a UIButton near the top of its view and a UITextView below it. Connect both objects to their outlets.
3. Save the document.
4. Back in MonoDevelop, enter the following `ViewDidLoad` method in the `TextViewAppViewController` class:

   ```
   public override void ViewDidLoad (){
     base.ViewDidLoad ();
   ```

Chapter 2

```
      this.buttonFinished.Enabled = false;
      this.buttonFinished.TouchUpInside += delegate {
        this.myTextView.ResignFirstResponder();
      } ;
      this.myTextView.Delegate = new MyTextViewDelegate(this);
    }
    Add the following nested class:
    private class MyTextViewDelegate : UITextViewDelegate{
      public MyTextViewDelegate (TextViewAppViewController
        parentController){
        this.parentController = parentController;
      }
      private TextViewAppViewController parentController;

      public override void EditingStarted (UITextView textView){
        this.parentController.buttonFinished.Enabled = true;
      }

      public override void EditingEnded (UITextView textView){
        this.parentController.buttonFinished.Enabled = false;
    }

      public override void Changed (UITextView textView){
        Console.WriteLine ("Text changed!");
      }
    }//end void MyTextViewDelegate
```

5. Compile and run the application on the simulator.
6. Tap somewhere in the text view and the keyboard will appear. Type some text and then tap on the **Finished** button to hide the keyboard.

How it works...

The `UITextView` class provides an object that displays editable blocks of text. To respond to the events of our text view, we have implemented a class that inherits from `UITextViewDelegate` that will act as the text view's delegate:

```
    private class MyTextViewDelegate : UITextViewDelegate{
      public MyTextViewDelegate (TextViewAppViewController
        parentController){
        this.parentController = parentController;
      }
      private TextViewAppViewController parentController;
```

User Interface: Views

We declared a constructor that accepts a `TextViewAppViewController` object, so that we can have an instance of our controller available to access our controls.

Then, we override three methods of the `UITextViewDelegate` class:

```
public override void EditingStarted (UITextView textView){
  this.parentController.buttonFinished.Enabled = true;
}
public override void EditingEnded (UITextView textView){
  this.parentController.buttonFinished.Enabled = false;
}
public override void Changed (UITextView textView){
  Console.WriteLine ("Text changed!");
}
```

These methods are the handlers that will get called whenever a corresponding event is triggered. When tapping on the text, the `EditingStarted()` method gets called. We enable the **Finished** button in it. When we type some text in the text view, the `Changed()` method gets called, and we can see the output of the `Console.WriteLine()` method in MonoDevelop's **Application Output** pad. Finally, when we tap on the **Finished** button, the keyboard hides and the `EditingEnded()` method gets called that allows us to disable the button.

In the `ViewDidLoad` method, we assign a handler to the `TouchUpInside` event of the button:

```
this.buttonFinished.TouchUpInside += delegate {
  this.myTextView.ResignFirstResponder ();
};
```

We call the text view's `ResignFirstResponder()` method in it so that when the button is tapped, the text view will lose focus, causing the keyboard to hide. Then, we assign a new instance of the delegate that we created to the text view's `Delegate` property, passing the instance of the `TextViewAppViewController` object:

```
this.myTextView.Delegate = new MyTextViewDelegate (this);
```

There's more...

Delegates in Objective-C are somewhat different than delegates in C#. Although in both worlds their most common usage is to provide access to some form of event notification mechanism, in Objective-C this mechanism is a bit more complex. A C# delegate is much like a function pointer in C or C++ programming languages. It is an object that holds a reference to a method of a specific signature. On the other hand, an Objective-C delegate is a certain type of object that conforms to a specific protocol. It is basically an object that wraps one or more methods (and/or other members) that act as event handlers.

> An Objective-C protocol is similar to an interface in C#.

The concept of Delegate objects might seem confusing at first, but it is not difficult to comprehend. Regarding the event notification mechanism, MonoTouch simplifies things for .NET developers by providing events for most objects.

> The `UITextView` class is suitable for displaying simple blocks of text, without formatting. For displaying formatted text, use the `UIWebView` class instead.

See also

In this chapter:

- Using the keyboard

In this book:

Chapter 5, Displaying Data:

Displaying and formatting text

Using the keyboard

In this recipe, we will discuss some important aspects of the virtual keyboard usage.

Getting ready

In the previous two tasks, we discussed the types of text input available. In this task, we will discuss some of the things we can, or even must, do to use the keyboard effectively. Create a new **iPhone Single View Application** project in MonoDevelop, and name it `KeyboardApp`.

How to do it...

Follow these steps to create the project:

1. Open the `KeyboardAppViewController.xib` file in Interface Builder.
2. Add a `UITextField` object in the bottom-half portion of the view and connect it to an outlet.

User Interface: Views

3. Save the document.

4. Back in MonoDevelop, enter the following code in the `KeyboardAppViewController` class:

```
private NSObject kbdWillShow, kbdDidHide;
public override void ViewDidLoad(){
  base.ViewDidLoad();
  this.emailField.KeyboardType = UIKeyboardType.EmailAddress;
  this.emailField.ReturnKeyType = UIReturnKeyType.Done;
  this.kbdWillShow = NSNotificationCenter.DefaultCenter.
    AddObserver (UIKeyboard.WillShowNotification,
    delegate(NSNotification ntf) {
    RectangleF kbdBounds = UIKeyboard.FrameEndFromNotification
       (ntf);
    RectangleF textFrame = this.emailField.Frame;
    textFrame.Y -= kbdBounds.Height;
    this.emailField.Frame = textFrame;
  } );

  this.kbdDidHide = NSNotificationCenter.DefaultCenter.AddObserver
    (UIKeyboard.DidHideNotification, delegate(NSNotification ntf){
    RectangleF kbdBounds = UIKeyboard.FrameEndFromNotification
       (ntf);
    RectangleF textFrame = this.emailField.Frame;
    textFrame.Y += kbdBounds.Height;
    this.emailField.Frame = textFrame;
  } );

  this.emailField.ShouldReturn = delegate(UITextField textField) {
    return textField.ResignFirstResponder ();
  } ;
}
```

5. Compile and run the application on the simulator.

6. Tap on the text field and watch it moving upwards to avoid being hidden from the keyboard.

7. Tap the **Done** button on the keyboard and watch the text field returning to its original position when the keyboard hides.

How it works...

There are various types of keyboards in iOS. Since not all keys can be displayed at once due to the restricted screen size, it is good practice to set the appropriate type of keyboard, according to the text input we need the user to provide. In this project, we have set the keyboard to the **Email Address** type. We have also customized the type of the **Return** key by setting it to **Done**.

```
this.emailField.KeyboardType = UIKeyboardType.EmailAddress;
this.emailField.ReturnKeyType = UIReturnKeyType.Done;
```

When the keyboard is displayed, it is the developer's responsibility to make sure it does not obstruct essential UI elements. In this case, since we provide the user with the ability to enter some text input, we have to make sure that the text field is visible so the user will be able to see what is being typed. For this, we add two observers in the default notification center.

```
// Add observers for the keyboard
this.kbdWillShow = NSNotificationCenter.DefaultCenter.AddObserver
    (UIKeyboard.WillShowNotification, delegate(NSNotification ntf) {
```

An `NSNotificationCenter` provides a notification mechanism for various notifications.

We access the runtime's default notification center through the `NSNotificationCenter.DefaultCenter` static property. An observer is added with the `AddObserver()` method, which accepts two parameters. The first parameter represents an `NSString` value, which informs the notification center of what type of notification to watch. The `UIKeyboard` class contains pre-defined static properties with the types of keyboard notifications we need. The `UIKeyboard.WillShowNotification` is passed, stating that the observer will observe and inform when the keyboard will be ready to appear. The second parameter is of the type `Action<NSNotification>` and represents the handler that will be executed when the notification occurs. Inside the `anonymous()` method, we call the `UIKeyboard.FrameEndNotification(NSNotification)` method that returns the keyboard's bounds:

```
//Get the keyboard's bounds
RectangleF kbdBounds = UIKeyboard.FrameEndNotification (ntf);
```

Then, we store the text field's frame in a variable and reduce its Y position value so that the text field will move upwards:

```
// Get the text field's frame
RectangleF textFrame = this.emailField.Frame;

// Change the y position of the text field frame
textFrame.Y -= kbdBounds.Height;
```

User Interface: Views

When the new frame is set to the `emailField`, it will move to the new position:

```
this.emailField.Frame = textFrame;
```

The second observer is needed for moving the text field back to its original position. It is almost the same as the first observer, except for two differences. The `UIKeyboard.DidHideNotification` `NSString` is passed, instructing the observer to trigger the handler after the keyboard has been dismissed, and the `Y` value of the text field's frame is increased to make the text field return to its original position.

There's more...

The two fields of the type `NSObject` in the class hold information about the observers we added. For removing the two observers we have added here, add the following code:

```
NSNotificationCenter.DefaultCenter.RemoveObserver (this.kbdWillShow);
NSNotificationCenter.DefaultCenter.RemoveObserver (this.kbdDidHide);
```

> Care must be taken when developing an application that uses the keyboard and supports multiple interface orientations. If, for example, the keyboard appears in portrait orientation and the user changes to landscape orientation, both the keyboard's bounds and the text field's frame will be different and must be adjusted accordingly.

See also

In this chapter:

- *Displaying and editing text*

In this book:

Chapter 9, Interacting with Device Hardware:

- *Rotating the device*
- *Adjusting the UI*

Displaying progress

In this recipe, we will discuss how to display progress of a known length.

Getting ready

In this task, we will talk about the `UIProgressView` control. This control provides similar functionality to the **ProgressBar** in .NET. Create a **iPhone Single View Application** project in MonoDevelop, and name it `ProgressApp`.

How to do it...

Here are the steps for using the `UIProgressView` class. Note that in this recipe, we will add all controls programmatically, without the use of Interface Builder:

1. Add the following `using` directives in the `ProgressAppViewController` class file:

   ```
   using System.Drawing;
   using System.Threading;
   ```

2. Add the following fields:

   ```
   UILabel labelStatus;
   UIButton buttonStartProgress;
   UIProgressView progressView;
   float incrementBy = 0f;
   ```

3. Enter the following code in the `ViewDidLoad` override:

   ```
   // Initialize the label
   this.labelStatus = new UILabel (new RectangleF (60f, 60f, 200f,
     50f));
   this.labelStatus.AdjustsFontSizeToFitWidth = true;
   // Initialize the button
   this.buttonStartProgress = UIButton.FromType
     (UIButtonType.RoundedRect);
   this.buttonStartProgress.Frame = new RectangleF (60f, 400f, 200f,
     40f);
   this.buttonStartProgress.SetTitle ("Tap to start progress!",
     UIControlState.Normal);
   this.buttonStartProgress.TouchUpInside += delegate {
     // Disable the button
     this.buttonStartProgress.Enabled = false;
     this.progressView.Progress = 0f;
     // Start a progress
     new Action (this.StartProgress).BeginInvoke (null, null);
   } ;

   // Initialize the progress view
   this.progressView = new UIProgressView (new RectangleF (60f, 200f,
     200f, 50f));
   ```

User Interface: Views

```
// Set the progress view's initial value
this.progressView.Progress = 0f;

// Set the progress increment value
// for 10 items
this.incrementBy = 1f / 10f;

this.View.AddSubview(this.labelStatus);
this.View.AddSubview(this.buttonStartProgress);
this.View.AddSubview(this.progressView);
```

4. Add the following method in the class:

```
private void StartProgress (){
  while (this.progressView.Progress < 1){
    Thread.Sleep (1000);
    this.BeginInvokeOnMainThread (delegate {
      // Advance the progress
      this.progressView.Progress += this.incrementBy;
      // Set the label text
      this.labelStatus.Text = String.Format ("Current value: {0}",
        Math.Round ((double)this.progressView.Progress, 2));
      if (this.progressView.Progress == 1){
        this.labelStatus.Text = "Progress completed!";
        this.buttonStartProgress.Enabled = true;
      }
    });
  }
}
```

5. Compile and run the application on the simulator.
6. Tap on the button and watch the progress bar fill.

How it works...

The current value of `UIProgressView` is represented by its `Progress` property. Its acceptable value range is always from 0 to 1. So, when initializing it, we set it to 0 to make sure that the bar is not filled at all:

```
this.progressView.Progress = 0f;
```

Since the `UIProgressView` has a specific range, we need to assign the value we want it to be incremented by, depending on the number of items we need to process, in this case 10:

```
this.incrementBy = 1f / 10f;
```

Chapter 2

In the button's `TouchUpInside` handler, we disable the button and start our progress by asynchronously invoking a method:

```
this.buttonStartProgress.TouchUpInside += delegate {
  // Disable the button
  this.buttonStartProgress.Enabled = false;
  this.progressView.Progress = 0;
  // Start a progress
  new Action (this.StartProgress).BeginInvoke (null, null);
};
```

In the `StartProgress()` method, we start a loop that will process the work that needs to be done. Since the work executes in an asynchronous method, when we want to make changes to the controls, it must be done on the main UI thread by calling the `BeginInvokeOnMainThread()` method of `UIApplicationDelegate`, which accepts a parameter of the type `NSAction`. An `NSAction` can accept anonymous methods as well:

```
this.BeginInvokeOnMainThread (delegate {
  // Advance the progress
  this.progressView.Progress += this.incrementBy;
  // Set the label text
  this.labelStatus.Text = String.Format ("Current value: {0}",
    Math.Round ((double)this.progressView.Progress, 2));
  if (this.progressView.Progress == 1){
    this.labelStatus.Text = "Progress completed!";
    this.buttonStartProgress.Enabled = true;
  }
});
```

There's more...

The `UIProgressView` supports one more style other than the default. Set its `Style` property to `UIProgressViewStyle.Bar` so that the bar will look like the one in the Mail application when receiving new e-mails.

See also

In this chapter:

- *Receiving user input with buttons*

User Interface: Views

Displaying content larger than the screen

In this recipe, we will learn how to display content that extends beyond the screen's bounds.

Getting ready

In this task, we will discuss the `UIScrollView` control. Create an **iPhone Single View Application** project, and name it `ScrollApp`.

How to do it...

Here are the steps to create the project:

1. Open the `ScrollAppViewController.xib` file in Interface Builder.
2. Add a `UIScrollView` object on its view and connect it to an outlet. And save the document.
3. Back in MonoDevelop, add the following code in the `ScrollAppViewController` class:

   ```
   // Image view
   UIImageView imgView;
   public override void ViewDidLoad(){
     base.ViewDidLoad();
     this.imgView = new UIImageView (UIImage.FromFile
       ("Kastoria.jpg"));
     this.scrollContent.ContentSize = this.imgView.Image.Size;
     this.scrollContent.ContentOffset = new PointF (200f, 50f);
     this.scrollContent.PagingEnabled = true;
     this.scrollContent.MinimumZoomScale = 0.5f;
     this.scrollContent.MaximumZoomScale = 2f;
     this.scrollContent.ViewForZoomingInScrollView =
       delegate(UIScrollView scroll) {
       return this.imgView;
     };
     this.scrollContent.ZoomScale = 1f;
     this.scrollContent.IndicatorStyle =
       UIScrollViewIndicatorStyle.White;
     this.scrollContent.AddSubview (this.imgView);
   }
   ```

4. Finally, add an image to the project and set its **Build Action** to **Content**. An image larger than the simulator's screen, a size of **320x480** pixels, is preferable.

Chapter 2

5. Compile and run the application on the simulator. Tap-and-drag on the image to display different portions. By press *Alt* + mouse-click, you can simulate the pinch zooming function.

How it works...

The `UIScrollView` is capable of managing content that expands beyond the screen size. The size of the content the scroll view will display must be set in its `ContentSize` property:

```
this.scrollContent.ContentSize = this.imgView.Image.Size;
```

The `ContentOffset` property defines the position of the content inside the scroll view's bounds:

```
this.scrollContent.ContentOffset = new PointF (200f, 50f);
```

What this means is that the image's (x=200, y=50) point will be displayed at the origin (x=0, y=0) of the `UIScrollView`. To provide zooming functionality for the content, we first set the `MinimumZoomScale` and `MaximumZoomScale` properties that set the minimum and maximum zoom scale for the content. A value of `2` means the content will be double in size, while a value of `0.5` means the content will be half the size.

```
this.scrollContent.MinimumZoomScale = 0.5f;
this.scrollContent.MaximumZoomScale = 2f;
```

For the actual zooming operation, we need to set the `ViewForZoomingInScrollView` property, which accepts a delegate of the type `UIScrollViewGetZoomView` and returns a `UIView`. Here, the image view we created is returned, but another higher resolution image view can be used instead to provide better image quality when zooming. After the delegate is assigned, the initial zoom scale is set:

```
this.scrollContent.ViewForZoomingInScrollView = delegate(UIScrollView
    scroll) {
    return this.imgView;
};this.scrollContent.ZoomScale = 1f;
```

Finally, the scroll view's indicator style is set:

```
this.scrollContent.IndicatorStyle = UIScrollViewIndicatorStyle.White;
```

Indicators are the two lines that appear when scrolling or zooming: one on the vertical-right side and one on the horizontal-bottom side of the scroll view, which informs the user of the position of the content. Much like scroll bars.

User Interface: Views

There's more...

To provide a more pleasing scrolling and zooming effect to the user, the `UIScrollView` exposes the `Bounce` property. By default, it is set to `true`, but we have the option to disable it by setting it to `false`. Bouncing the content gives immediate feedback to the user that the bounds of the content have been reached, in either a horizontal or vertical direction. Furthermore, the `AlwaysBounceHorizontal` and `AlwaysBounceVertical` properties can be set individually. Setting one or both of these properties will make the scroll view always bounce the content in each respective direction, even if the content is equal to or smaller than the scroll view's bounds. Hence, no actual scrolling is needed.

UIScrollView events

The `UIScrollView` class exposes some very useful events:

- `Scrolled`: This event occurs while the content is being scrolled
- `DecelerationStarted`: This event occurs when the user has started scrolling the content
- `DecelerationEnded`: This event occurs when the user has finished scrolling and the content has stopped moving

> If a handler has been assigned to the `Scrolled` event, and the `ContentOffset` property is set, the event will be triggered.

See also

In this chapter:

- *Displaying images*
- *Displaying and editing text*
- *Navigating through content divided into pages*

Navigating through content divided into pages

In this recipe, we will learn how to use the `UIPageControl` class to provide page navigation.

Getting ready

The `UIPageControl` provides a simple visual representation of multiple pages or screens in an iOS app, indicated as dots. The dot that corresponds to the current page is highlighted. It is usually combined with the `UIScrollView`. Create a new **iPhone Single View Application** project in MonoDevelop, and name it `PageNavApp`. Add three image files in the project and set their **Build Action** to **Content.**

How to do it...

Here are the steps to create this project:

1. Open the `PageNavAppViewController.xib` file in Interface Builder.

2. Add a `UIPageControl` to the bottom of the view and `UIScrollView` above it. Resize the scroll view to take up all the remaining space of the view, and save the document.

3. Back in MonoDevelop, enter the following code in the `PageNavAppViewController` class:

```
UIImageView page1;
UIImageView page2;
UIImageView page3;
public override void ViewDidLoad(){
  base.ViewDidLoad();
  this.scrollView.DecelerationEnded +=
    this.scrollView_DecelerationEnded;
  this.pageControl.ValueChanged += this.pageControl_ValueChanged;
  this.scrollView.Scrolled += delegate {
    Console.WriteLine ("Scrolled!");
  } ;

  this.scrollView.PagingEnabled = true;
  RectangleF pageFrame = this.scrollView.Frame;
  this.scrollView.ContentSize = new SizeF (pageFrame.Width * 3,
    pageFrame.Height);
  this.page1 = new UIImageView (pageFrame);
  this.page1.ContentMode = UIViewContentMode.ScaleAspectFit;
  this.page1.Image = UIImage.FromFile ("Parga01.jpg");
  pageFrame.X += this.scrollView.Frame.Width;
  this.page2 = new UIImageView (pageFrame);
  this.page2.ContentMode = UIViewContentMode.ScaleAspectFit;
  this.page2.Image = UIImage.FromFile ("Parga02.jpg");
  pageFrame.X += this.scrollView.Frame.Width;
  this.page3 = new UIImageView (pageFrame);
```

User Interface: Views

```
      this.page3.ContentMode = UIViewContentMode.ScaleAspectFit;
      this.page3.Image = UIImage.FromFile ("Parga03.jpg");
      this.scrollView.AddSubview (this.page1);
      this.scrollView.AddSubview (this.page2);
      this.scrollView.AddSubview (this.page3);
}
```

4. Add the following methods in the class:

```
private void scrollView_DecelerationEnded (object sender,
  EventArgs e){
  float x1 = this.page1.Frame.X;
  float x2 = this.page2.Frame.X;
  float x = this.scrollView.ContentOffset.X;

  if (x == x1){
    this.pageControl.CurrentPage = 0;
  } else if (x == x2){
    this.pageControl.CurrentPage = 1;
  } else{
    this.pageControl.CurrentPage = 2;
  }
}

private void pageControl_ValueChanged (object sender,
  EventArgs e){
  PointF contentOffset = this.scrollView.ContentOffset;
  switch (this.pageControl.CurrentPage){
    case 0:
      contentOffset.X = this.page1.Frame.X;
      this.scrollView.SetContentOffset (contentOffset, true);
    break;

    case 1:
      contentOffset.X = this.page2.Frame.X;
      this.scrollView.SetContentOffset (contentOffset, true);
    break;

    case 2:
      contentOffset.X = this.page3.Frame.X;
      this.scrollView.SetContentOffset (contentOffset, true);
    break;

    default:
      // do nothing
```

Chapter 2

```
      break;
  }
}
```

5. Compile and run the application on the simulator. Scroll on the scroll view to change page. Likewise, tap or scroll on the page control to change page.

How it works...

The first thing we need to do is set the `UIScrollView.PagingEnabled` property to `true`, which is done as follows:

```
this.scrollView.PagingEnabled = true;
```

This property instructs the scroll view to perform scrolling at multiples of the scroll view's bounds, hence providing paging functionality. After that, the image views that will be displayed in different pages are prepared. Here, we take care of adjusting each image view's frame so that they will be positioned next to each other:

```
this.page1 = new UIImageView (pageFrame);
//...
pageFrame.X += this.scrollView.Frame.Width;
//...
pageFrame.X += this.scrollView.Frame.Width;
```

We have attached handlers for two events. The first one is the `UIScrollView.DecelerationEnded` event, which will adjust the page control's current page when the user scrolls the scroll view. The current page is determined by the scroll view's `ContentOffset` property:

```
float x = this.scrollView.ContentOffset.X;
if (x == x1) {
   this.pageControl.CurrentPage = 0;
// etc.
```

The second event we attach a handler to is the `UIPageControl.ValueChanged` event. In this handler, we make sure the content is scrolled when the user taps or drags on the page control. The scroll is performed when the `ContentOffset` property is set to the desired image view's `Frame.X` property, using the `UIScrollView.SetContentOffset(PointF, bool)` method:

```
case 0:
contentOffset.X = this.page1.Frame.X;
this.scrollView.SetContentOffset (contentOffset, true);
break;
// etc.
```

User Interface: Views

The second parameter of the `SetContentOffset()` method instructs the scroll view to animate while scrolling.

There's more...

In this recipe, different `UIImageView` objects have been used. Any kind of `UIView` objects can be used, according to the type of content we want to display.

Proper usage of the UIPageControl

Users expect that scrolling to other pages will occur when tapping or dragging on the page control. It is not good practice to use it for displaying page indexing only, without being a fully active control.

See also

In this chapter:

- *Displaying images*
- *Displaying content larger than the screen*

Displaying a toolbar

In this recipe, we will learn how to add and use toolbars in applications.

Getting ready

The `UIToolbar` class provides a toolbar that holds various buttons. It is the bar that resides at the bottom of views. Create a new **iPhone Single View Application** project in MonoDevelop, and name it `ToolbarApp`.

How to do it...

Here are the steps to create this project:

1. Open the `ToolbarAppViewController.xib` file in Interface Builder and add a `UIToolbar` object at the bottom of its view.
2. Select the button it contains by default and set its **Identifier** in the **Attributes Inspector** pad to **Save**.
3. Add a **Flexible Space Bar Button Item** object to the toolbar.

Chapter 2

4. Add another button on the toolbar, on the right side of the previous object, and set its **Identifier** to **Reply**.
5. Add a `UILabel` object on the view and connect all controls, apart from the flexible space item, to outlets.
6. Save the document.
7. Back in MonoDevelop, enter the following code in the `ToolBarAppViewController` class:

```
public override void ViewDidLoad (){
  base.ViewDidLoad ();
  this.barSave.Clicked += delegate {
    this.labelStatus.Text = "Button Save tapped!";
  } ;
  this.barReply.Clicked += delegate {
    this.labelStatus.Text = "Button Reply tapped!";
  } ;
}
```

8. Compile and run the application on the simulator. Tap on both of the toolbar's buttons and see the status string display on the label.

How it works...

The toolbar holds items of the type `UIBarButtonItem`. These items are special kinds of buttons and spacers. A `UIBarButtonItem` can have a custom type, or any of the predefined types that are listed in the **Identifier** attribute in Interface Builder. When the item is a button and the behavior it provides is included in these identifiers, it is recommended to use them. Each one of these identifiers basically provides a specific icon to the button, according to its intended usage, and the user is quite familiar with them since they are used by most iOS applications. Notice that the **Flexible Space Bar Button Item** we added to the toolbar is also a **UIBarButtonItem**, with a specific identifier. Its purpose is to keep two buttons apart, changing their in-between distance in situations where this is required, for example, when rotating the device at a landscape orientation and the toolbar resizes to fit the new width.

> Just rotating the device will not make the **UIToolbar** resize. This kind of behavior will be discussed in *Chapter 3, User Interface: View Controllers*.

This kind of bar button is displayed in Interface Builder, but not at runtime.

User Interface: Views

In the code, we add handlers to the bar buttons' `Clicked` event, whose purpose is quite familiar:

```
this.barSave.Clicked += delegate {
  this.labelStatus.Text = "Button Save tapped!";
};
```

It is being triggered when the user taps on the button.

There's more...

The `UIBarButtonItem` class has a `Style` property that determines the button's style. It can be used only when the button item's identifier is set to `Custom`.

Setting a UIToolbar's items programmatically

To set bar button items to a `UIToolbar`, use one of the overloads of its `SetItems()` method. An example for setting two bar button items in a `UIToolbar` is as follows:

```
UIBarButtonItem barSave = new
  UIBarButtonItem(UIBarButtonSystemItem.Save);
UIBarButtonItem barReply = new
  UIBarButtonItem(UIBarButtonSystemItem.Reply);
this.toolBar.SetItems(new UIBarButtonItem[] { barSave, barReply },
  true);
```

See also

In this book:

Chapter 3, User Interface: View Controllers:

> ▶ *Navigating through different view controllers*

Creating a custom view

In this recipe, we will learn how to override the `UIView` class and/or classes that derive from it, to create custom views.

Getting ready

So far, we have discussed many of the available views there are to create iOS applications. There will be many cases, however, that we will need to implement our own custom views. In this task, we will see how to create a custom view and use it.

Chapter 2

> Creating custom views is very useful when we want to capture touches or implement other custom behavior, such as drawing.

Create a new **iPhone Single View Application** project in MonoDevelop, and name it `CustomViewApp`.

How to do it...

Here are the steps to complete this project:

1. Add a new C# class file in the project, and name it `MyView`.
2. Implement it with the following code:

    ```csharp
    using System;
    using MonoTouch.UIKit;
    using MonoTouch.Foundation;
    using System.Drawing;

    namespace CustomViewApp{
      [Register("MyView")]
      public class MyView : UIView{
        private UILabel labelStatus;
        public MyView (IntPtr handle) : base(handle){
          this.Initialize ();
        }

        public MyView (RectangleF frame) : base(frame){
          this.Initialize ();
        }

        private void Initialize (){
          this.BackgroundColor = UIColor.LightGray;
          this.labelStatus = new UILabel (new RectangleF (0f, 400f,
            this.Frame.Width, 60f));
          this.labelStatus.TextAlignment = UITextAlignment.Center;
          this.labelStatus.BackgroundColor = UIColor.DarkGray;
          this.AddSubview (this.labelStatus);
        }

        public override void TouchesMoved (NSSet touches,
          UIEvent evt){
          base.TouchesMoved (touches, evt);
          UITouch touch = (UITouch)touches.AnyObject;
    ```

User Interface: Views

```
            PointF touchLocation = touch.LocationInView (this);
            this.labelStatus.Text = String.Format ("X: {0} - Y: {1}",
              touchLocation.X, touchLocation.Y);
          }
        }
      }
```

3. Open the `CustomViewAppViewController.xib` file in Interface Builder, and add a `UIView` object on the main view.
4. Connect it to an outlet and set its **Class** field in the **Identity Inspector** to `MyView`.
5. Save the document.
6. Compile and run the application on the simulator. Tap-and-drag on the view, and watch the touch coordinates being displayed in the label at the bottom of the screen.

How it works...

The first thing to note when creating custom views is to derive them from the `UIView` class and to decorate them with the `Register` attribute:

```
[Register("MyView")]
public class MyView : UIView
```

The `Register` attribute basically exposes our class to the Objective-C world. Note that the name we pass as its parameter must be the same name that we enter in the **Class** field in the **Identity Inspector**. It is important to create the following constructor that overrides the base class' `UIView(IntPtr)`.

```
public MyView (IntPtr handle) : base(handle) {}
```

This constructor is always being called when a view is initialized through native code. If we do not override it, an exception will occur upon initialization of the object when the runtime tries to recreate it if it has been removed when a memory warning is issued. The other constructor that is used in this example is just provided as guidance on what might be used if the view was initialized programmatically:

```
public MyView (RectangleF frame) : base(frame) {}
```

Both these constructors call the `Initialize()` method that performs the initialization we need, such as creating the label that will be used, set background colors, and so on.

Then, the `TouchesMoved` method is overridden. This is the method that is executed when the user drags a finger on the view. Inside the method, we retrieve the `UITouch` object from the method's `NSSet` parameter:

```
UITouch touch = (UITouch)touches.AnyObject;
```

> An `NSSet` object is a collection of data that are not in particular order. It is similar to an array. Its `AnyObject` parameter returns an object from the collection.

The `UITouch` object contains information about user touches. We retrieve the touch's current location from it:

```
PointF touchLocation = touch.LocationInView (this);
```

Its `LocationInView` method accepts a parameter of the type `UIView` that declares in which view's coordinate system the location will be calculated. In this case, we are interested in the coordinates of `MyView`.

There's more...

If we would like to initialize the custom view that we created programmatically, we would enter the following code:

```
MyView myView = new MyView(new RectangleF(0f, 0f, 320f, 480f));
```

See also

In this chapter:

- *Adding and customizing views*

In this book:

Chapter 3, User Interface: View Controllers:

- *View controllers and views*

3
User Interface: View Controllers

In this chapter, we will cover:

- Loading a view with a view controller
- Navigating through different view controllers
- Providing controllers in tabs
- Creating a table controller
- Modal view controllers
- Creating a custom view controller
- Using view controllers efficiently
- Combining different view controllers
- iPad view controllers
- Creating a user interface for different devices

Introduction

So far, we have discussed views and how to use them. In most cases of real-world application scenarios, views alone are not enough. Apple provides another base class, the `UIViewController`, which is responsible for managing views. A view controller can respond to device notifications, such as when the device rotates, or can provide different ways for displaying and dismissing multiple views or even other view controllers.

We will also see how to use the most common view controllers to create applications that manage multiple views.

User Interface: View Controllers

These view controllers are:

- `UIViewController`: This is the base class of all view controllers
- `UINavigationController`: This is the view controller that provides various ways of navigating through different view controllers
- `UITabBarController`: This is a view controller that displays multiple view controllers in a tab-like interface
- `UITableViewController`: This is a view controller that is used to display data in a list form
- **iPad-specific view controllers**: These are view controllers that only apply to the iPad device

Furthermore, we will discuss combining different controllers, how to create custom controllers and use them, and we will create an application that can be deployed in both the iPhone and iPad.

Loading a view with a view controller

In this recipe, we will learn how to use the `UIViewController` class to manage views.

Getting ready

Create a new iPhone empty project in MonoDevelop, and name it `ViewControllerApp`.

How to do it...

1. Add a new file to the project.
2. Right-click on the project in the **Solution** pad and select **Add | New File...**.
3. In the dialog box that will appear, select **iPhone View** with **Controller** from the **MonoTouch** section. Name it `MainViewController`, and click on the **New** button. MonoDevelop will create a new XIB file and will automatically open the `MainViewController.cs` source file. This file contains a class that overrides the `UIViewController`, and we can implement any code related to our view controller in it.
4. Open the `MainViewController.xib` file in Interface Builder.
5. Add a `UILabel` on the view.
6. Create and connect an outlet for it inside the `MainViewController` class, and name it `myLabel`.
7. Enter the text `View in controller!` in the label.
8. Save the XIB document.

9. Back in MonoDevelop, enter the following code in the `FinishedLaunching()` method:

   ```
   MainViewController mainController = new MainViewController ();
   window.RootViewController = mainController;
   ```

10. Compile and run the application on the simulator.

How it works...

When we add a new **iPhone View with Controller** file in a project, in this case `MainViewController`, MonoDevelop basically creates and adds three files:

1. `MainViewController.xib`: This is the XIB file that contains the controller.
2. `MainViewController.cs`: This is the C# source file that implements the class of our controller.
3. `MainViewController.designer.cs`: This is the auto-generated source file that reflects the changes we make to the controller in Interface Builder.

Notice that we do not need to add an outlet for the view, since this is taken care of by MonoDevelop. We initialize the controller through its class:

```
MainViewController mainController = new MainViewController ();
```

Then, we display its view through the controller's `View` by setting it as the `RootViewController` of our application's window:

```
window.RootViewController = mainController;
```

There's more...

The project we have just created only shows how we can add a controller with a view. Notice that we created the outlet for the label inside the `MainViewController` class, which acts as the file's owner object in the `XIB` file. To provide some functionality for the `MainViewController`, add the following method in the `MainViewController` class in the `MainViewController.cs` file:

```
public override void ViewDidLoad (){
  base.ViewDidLoad();
  this.myLabel.Text = "View loaded!";
}
```

This method overrides the `UIViewController.ViewDidLoad()` method, which is executed when the controller loads its view.

User Interface: View Controllers

UIViewController methods to override

The methods that the `UIViewController` class contains are the ones that we override to use its features. Some of these methods are:

- `ViewDidUnload()`: It is called when the view is unloaded
- `ViewWillAppear()`: It is called when the view is about to appear on the screen
- `ViewDidAppear()`: It is called when the view has been displayed
- `ViewWillDisappear()`: It is called when the view is about to disappear, for example, when another controller is about to be displayed
  `ViewDidDisappear()`: It is called when the view has disappeared

See also

In this chapter:

- *Navigating through different view controllers*

In this book:

Chapter 1, Development Tools:

- *Creating an iPhone project with MonoDevelop*
- *Accessing the UI with outlets*

Navigating through different view controllers

In this recipe, we will learn how to use the `UINavigationController` class to navigate among multiple view controllers.

Getting ready

The `UINavigationController` is a controller that provides a hierarchical navigation functionality with multiple view controllers. Create a new iPhone empty project in MonoDevelop, and name it `NavigationControllerApp`.

How to do it...

1. Add three new **iPhone View with Controller** files in the project, and name them `RootViewController`, `ViewController1`, and `ViewController2`.

___

Chapter 3

2. Add the following field in the `AppDelegate` class:

   ```
   UINavigationController navController;
   ```

3. In the same class, add the following code in the `FinishedLaunching` method, above the `window.MakeKeyAndVisible();` line:

   ```
   RootViewController rootController = new RootViewController();
   this.navController = new UINavigationController(rootController);
   window.RootViewController = this.navController;
   ```

4. Open the `RootViewController.xib` file in Interface Builder, and add two buttons with their corresponding outlets. Set their titles to `First View` and `Second View` respectively.

5. Save the document.

6. Open both the `ViewController1.xib` and `ViewController2.xib`, and add a button in each one with the title `Pop to root`. Do not forget to connect the buttons with outlets and save the documents.

7. Enter the following code in the `RootViewController` class:

   ```
   public override void ViewDidLoad () {
     this.buttonFirstView.TouchUpInside += delegate {
       ViewController1 cont1 = new ViewController1 ();
       cont1.Title = "Controller #1";
       this.NavigationController.PushViewController (cont1, true);
     };
     this.buttonSecondView.TouchUpInside += delegate {
       ViewController2 cont2 = new ViewController2 ();
       cont2.Title = "Controller #2";
       this.NavigationController.PushViewController (cont2, true);
     };
   }
   ```

8. In both `ViewController1` and `ViewController2` classes, enter the following:

   ```
   public override void ViewDidLoad () {
     this.buttonPop.TouchUpInside += delegate {
       this.NavigationController.PopToRootViewController (true);
     };
   }
   ```

9. Compile and run the application on the simulator. Tap on each of the buttons to see and navigate through the available views.

___

89

User Interface: View Controllers

How it works...

The `UINavigationController` preserves a stack of controllers. The `UIViewController` class has a property named `NavigationController`. In normal situations, this property returns null. But, if the controller is pushed into a navigation controller's stack, it returns the instance of the navigation controller it is being pushed in. So this way, at any point in the hierarchy of controllers, access to the navigation controller is provided. To display a controller, we call the `UINavigationController.PushViewController(UIViewController, bool)` method:

```
this.NavigationController.PushViewController (cont1, true);
```

Notice that the `RootViewController` is the topmost or root controller in the navigation stack. A navigation controller must have at least one view controller that will act as its root controller. We set it when we create the instance of the UINavigationController class:

```
this.navController = new UINavigationController(rootController);
```

To return to the root controller, we call the `PopToRootViewController(bool)` method inside the current controller:

```
this.NavigationController.PopToRootViewController (true);
```

The `bool` parameters in both the methods are used for transitioning between controllers with animation.

There's more...

In this simple example, we provided backward navigation to the root controller with buttons. Notice that there is an arrow-shaped button at the top bar. That bar is called the **navigation** bar, and is of the type `UINavigationBar`. The arrow-shaped button is called the **back** button and is of the type `UIBarButtonItem`. The back button, when it exists, always navigates to the previous controller in the navigation stack.

Managing navigation bar buttons

To change, add, and hide the buttons of the navigation bar, we can use the following methods of our currently displayed view controller's `NavigationItem` property:

- `SetLeftBarButtonItem`: It adds a custom button on the left of the navigation bar, replacing the default **Back** button
- `SetRightBarButtonItem`: It adds a custom button on the right side of the navigation bar
- `SetHidesBackButton`: It sets the visibility of the default **Back** button

To remove or hide the custom left or right buttons on the navigation bar, call the appropriate methods, passing `null` instead of a `UIBarButtonItem` object.

See also

In this chapter:

- *Modal view controllers*
- *Using view controllers efficiently*
- *Combining different view controllers*

In this book:

Chapter 11, Graphics and Animation:

- *Pushing view controllers with animation*

Providing controllers in tabs

In this recipe, we will learn how to display multiple view controllers in a tabbed interface.

Getting ready

The `UITabBarController` provides a way of displaying different view controllers on the same hierarchy level divided into a tab-like interface. Create a new iPhone empty project in MonoDevelop, and name it `TabControllerApp`.

How to do it...

Add two **iPhone View with Controller** files to the project. Name them `MainController` and `SettingsController`.

1. Open both controllers in Interface Builder, and set different background colors for their views and save the documents.

2. Add the following field in the `AppDelegate` class:

   ```
   UITabBarController tabController;
   ```

3. Enter the following code in the `FinishedLaunching()` method, above the `window.MakeKeyAndVisible();` line:

   ```
   MainController mainController = new MainController();
   SettingsController settingsController = new SettingsController();
   mainController.TabBarItem.Title = "Main";
   settingsController.TabBarItem.Title = "Settings";
   this.tabController = new UITabBarController();
   this.tabController.SetViewControllers(new UIViewController[] {
     mainController,
   ```

```
            settingsController
    } , false);
    window.RootViewController = this.tabController;
    this.tabController.ViewControllerSelected += delegate(object
      sender, UITabBarSelectionEventArgs e) {
      Console.WriteLine("Selected {0} controller.",
      e.ViewController.TabBarItem.Title);
    } ;
```

4. Compile and run the application on the simulator.
5. Tap on each of the tabs at the bottom of the screen, and see their respective views shown. The console output is displayed in the **Application Output** pad in MonoDevelop. The following screenshot shows the screen of the simulator, with the **Settings** tab selected:

How it works...

The `UITabBarController` displays one tab for each of the controllers it manages. That tab is of the type `UITabBarItem`, and it can accept both text and images. The `UITabBarController` class holds information about the controllers it contains. We can determine which controller was selected by the user through the `ViewControllerSelected` event:

```
this.tabBarController.ViewControllerSelected += new
  EventHandler<UITabBarSelectionEventArgs> (delegate(object sender,
  UITabBarSelectionEventArgs e) {
```

The `UITabBarSelectionEventArgs` object holds an instance of the selected controller in the property `ViewController`. By accessing the `UIViewController.TabBarItem` property, we can determine which controller was selected:

```
Console.WriteLine ("Controller {0} selected.",
  e.ViewController.TabBarItem.Title);
```

In this example, we output its `Title` property.

> Just like the `UIViewController` class' `NavigationController` property, where it returns the instance of the `UINavigationController` it is part of, the `TabBarItem` property will hold an instance only when the controller is part of a `UITabBarController`. In other cases it will return `null`.

When we initialize the tab controller, we set the controllers it will contain through the `SetViewControllers` method, passing an array of view controller objects:

```
this.tabController.SetViewControllers(new UIViewController[] {
  mainController,
  settingsController
});
```

There's more...

The controller can accept as many controllers as we want, but if we add six or more, four will be displayed with their tabs, while a fifth predefined **More** tab will represent all the remaining controllers. That is to keep the interface easily accessible by the user, by keeping the tabs to a specific size suitable for human fingers. When we add more than six controllers in a tab bar controller interface, by default the object provides an **Edit** button on top in the **More** tab, which allows the user to rearrange the order of controllers. If we want to exclude some controllers from this functionality, we have to remove it from the `CustomizableViewControllers` array.

User Interface: View Controllers

Useful UITabBarController properties

Some more useful properties of the `UITabBarController` class are as follows:

- `ViewControllers`: It returns an array containing all the controllers that the tab controller holds
- `SelectedIndex`: It returns the zero-based index of the selected tab
- `SelectedViewController`: It returns the currently selected controller

Important note on tab bar interfaces

Although we can add whatever type of controllers we want in a `UITabBarController`, we must not add a `UITabBarController` in another controller, such as a `UINavigationController`. We can, however, add a `UINavigationController` in a `UITabBarController`. This is because the tab bar interface is provided for implementing different controllers as different application modes and not hierarchical screens.

See also

In this chapter:

- *Using view controllers efficiently*
- *Combining different view controllers*

Creating a table controller

In this recipe, we will learn how to create and add a `UITableViewController` to a project.

Getting ready

The `UITableViewController` is used to display a `UITableView`. A `UITableView` provides an interface for displaying data in a list form. Create a new iPhone empty project in MonoDevelop, and name it `TableControllerApp`.

How to do it...

1. Add an **iPhone View Controller** to the project, and name it `TableController`.
2. Add the following code in the `FinishedLaunching` method of the `AppDelegate` class:

   ```
   TableController tableController = new TableController();
   window.RootViewController = tableController;
   ```

3. Change the inheritance of the `TableController` class from `UIViewController` to `UITableViewController`:

   `public partial class TableController : UITableViewController`

4. Open the `TableController.xib` in Interface Builder, and delete its view by selecting it and pressing backspace.
5. Drag-and-drop a `UITableView` in its place.
6. Right-click on the `UITableView` to show the outlet panel.
7. Click-and-drag from the **New Referencing Outlet** to the **File's Owner** object, as shown in the following screenshot:

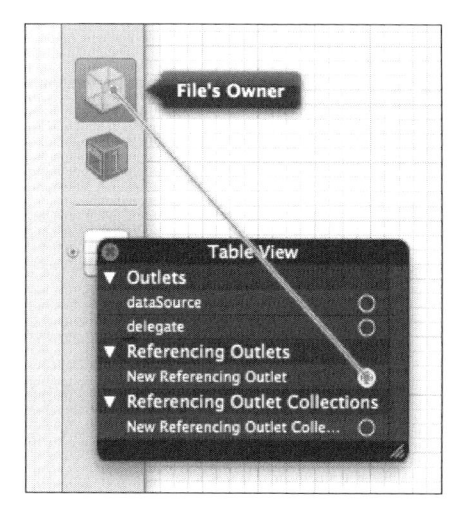

8. Select view from the small panel that will appear on the **File's Owner** object when you release the button. This connects the `UITableView` we have just added to the `view` outlet of the **File's Owner** object.
9. Save the document.

How it works...

When we add a `UITableView` in an Interface Builder document, its view is displayed with some predefined data. The data only appears at design time and not at runtime.

The `UITableViewController` contains a view of the type `UITableView`. This view is responsible for displaying the data and can be customized in many ways.

User Interface: View Controllers

There's more...

Apart from the `View` property, we can access the view of the `UITableViewController` through its `TableView` property. Both properties return the same object.

UITableViewController-specific property

The `UITableViewController` has one more property: `ClearsSelectionOnViewWillAppear`. When it is set to `true`, the controller will clear the selected row automatically whenever the view appears.

How to populate data with a `UITableView` is discussed thoroughly in *Chapter 5, Displaying Data*.

See also

In this chapter:

- *Modal view controllers*

In this book:

Chapter 5, Displaying Data:

- *Displaying data in a table*

Modal view controllers

In this recipe, we will discuss how to display view controllers modally.

Getting ready

A **Modal view controller** is any controller that is presented above other views or controllers. The concept is similar to displaying a **WinForm** as a dialog, which takes control of the interface and does not allow access to other windows of the application, unless it is dismissed. Create a new iPhone empty project in MonoDevelop, and name it `ModalControllerApp`.

How to do it...

1. Add two views with controllers to the project, and name them `MainController` and `ModalController`.
2. Open the `MainController.xib` file in Interface Builder, and add a button on its view with the title `Present`.

Chapter 3

3. Create and connect the appropriate outlet for the button. Save the document and open the `ModalController.xib` file.

4. Add a button on its view with the title `Dismiss`, and create the appropriate outlet for it. Set its view's background color to something other than white.

5. Save the document and enter the following code in the `MainController` class:

```
public override void ViewDidLoad (){
   this.buttonPresent.TouchUpInside += delegate {
      ModalController modal = new ModalController ();
      this.PresentModalViewController (modal, true);
   };
}
```

6. Similarly, override the `ViewDidLoad()` method in the `ModalController` class, and enter the following code in it:

```
this.buttonDismiss.TouchUpInside += delegate {
   this.DismissModalViewControllerAnimated (true);
};
```

7. Finally, add code to display the main controller in the `FinishedLaunching()` method:

```
MainController mainController = new MainController ();
window.RootViewController = mainController;
```

8. Compile and run the application on the simulator.

9. Tap on the **Present** button and watch the modal controller present itself on top of the main controller.

10. Tap on the **Dismiss** button to hide it.

How it works...

Each controller object has two methods that handle presenting and dismissing controllers modally. In our example, we call the `PresentModalViewController (UIViewController, bool)` method to present a controller:

```
this.buttonPresent.TouchUpInside += delegate {
   ModalController modal = new ModalController ();
   this.PresentModalViewController (modal, true);
};
```

Its first parameter represents the controller we want to display modally, and the second parameter determines if we want the presentation to be animated. To dismiss the controller, we call its `DismissModalViewControllerAnimated(bool)` method:

```
this.DismissModalViewControllerAnimated (true);
```

User Interface: View Controllers

It accepts only one parameter that toggles the animation for the dismissal.

There's more...

We can define the type of animation for a modal view controller presentation with the controller's `ModalTransitionStyle` property. Enter the following line of code before presenting the modal controller:

```
modal.ModalTransitionStyle = UIModalTransitionStyle.FlipHorizontal;
```

The main controller will flip to present the modal controller, giving the impression it is attached behind it.

Accessing a modal controller

Each controller that presents another controller modally provides access to its "child" controller through the `ModalController` property. If you need to access this property, make sure to do it before the `DismissModalViewControllerAnimated()` method is called.

How many modal controllers?

In theory, we can present an unlimited number of modal controllers. Of course, there are two restrictions on this:

1. **Memory is not unlimited**: View controllers consume memory, so the more view controllers we present, the worse performance we get.
2. **Bad user experience**: Presenting many controllers modally discomforts the user with repetition.

See also

In this chapter:

- *Navigating through different view controllers*
- *Providing controllers in tabs*

In this book:

Chapter 11, Graphics and Animation:

- *Pushing view controllers with animation*

Chapter 3

Creating a custom view controller

In this recipe, we will learn how to create a subclass of `UIViewController` and use it to derive view controllers contained in an `XIB` file.

Getting ready

In this task, we will see how to create a custom view controller that will act as a base controller, providing common functionality among its inheritors. The functionality we will add to our base controller to share with its inheritor classes will be to output the current touch position in the **Application Output** pad in MonoDevelop. Create a new iPhone empty project in MonoDevelop, and name it `CustomControllerApp`.

How to do it...

1. Add a new empty C# class in the project, and name it BaseController.
2. Enter the following code in the BaseController.cs file:

```
using System;
using System.Drawing;
using MonoTouch.Foundation;
using MonoTouch.UIKit;
public class BaseController : UIViewController{
  //Constructors
  public BaseController (string nibName, NSBundle bundle) :
    base(nibName, bundle){}
  public override void TouchesMoved (NSSet touches, UIEvent evt){
    base.TouchesMoved (touches, evt);
    // Capture the position of touches
    UITouch touch = (UITouch)touches.AnyObject;
    PointF locationInView = touch.LocationInView (this.View);
    Console.WriteLine ("Touch position: {0}", locationInView);
  }
}
```

3. Now, add an **iPhone View with Controller** file to the project, and name it `DerivedController`.
4. Change the class it inherits from `UIViewController` to `BaseController` in its class definition: `public partial class DerivedController : BaseController`.
5. Finally, add the derived controller's view to the main window:

```
DerivedController derivedController = new DerivedController();
window.RootViewController = derivedController;
```

99

User Interface: View Controllers

6. Compile and run the application on the simulator.
7. Click-and-drag the mouse pointer on the white surface, and watch MonoDevelop's **Application Output** pad displaying the current position of the pointer on the simulator's screen.

How it works...

What we have done here is create a base controller class that can be used in multiple MonoTouch projects. The functionality we have added to this controller is to respond to user touches. Any controller that inherits it will inherit the same functionality. The code we have added to create the `BaseController` class is fairly simple. The constructor we implemented is merely a copy of the constructors that MonoDevelop creates in the class implementations when we add new view controllers in a project. There is only one slight modification:

```
public BaseController (string nibName, NSBundle bundle) :
    base(nibName, bundle){}
```

This is the base constructor that will get called when we initialize the `DerivedController` class with the `new` keyword through our derived object's `DerivedController()` constructor.

```
derivedController = new DerivedController();
```

There's more...

The derived controller can also be added to another `XIB` file and used directly in code through outlets.

Subclassing view controllers from XIBs

If we would like to create a base controller that derives from a controller contained in an `XIB` file, the process is similar.

See also

In this chapter:

- *Loading a view with a controller*
- *Using view controllers efficiently*

In this book:

Chapter 2, User Interface: Views:

- *Adding and customizing views*

Chapter 3

Using view controllers efficiently

In this recipe, we will learn about the basic guidelines on efficient view controller usage.

Getting ready

Open the project `TabControllerApp` we created in the recipe *Providing controllers in tabs* earlier in this chapter.

How to do it...

1. Open the `MainController.xib` file in Interface Builder, and add a `UIButton` and a `UILabel`. Connect them with outlets.

2. Enter the following code in the `MainController` class:

   ```
   private Dictionary<int, string> cacheList;
   private Dictionary<int, string> cacheList;
   public override void DidReceiveMemoryWarning (){
     // Releases the view if it doesn't have a superview.
     base.DidReceiveMemoryWarning ();
     Console.WriteLine("Will clear cache in
       DidReceiveMemoryWarning...");
     // Release any cached data, images, and so on that aren't in
   use.
     this.cacheList.Clear();
   }
   public override void ViewDidLoad (){
     base.ViewDidLoad ();
     //any additional setup after loading the view,
       typically from a nib.
     this.cacheList = new Dictionary<int, string>() {
       {  0, "One" },
       {  1, "Two" },
       {  2, "Three" }
     } ;
     this.btnShowData.TouchUpInside += ButtonShowData_TouchUpInside;
   }
   public override void ViewDidUnload (){
     base.ViewDidUnload ();
     // Release any retained subviews of the main view.
     // e.g. myOutlet = null;
     this.lblOutput = null;
     this.btnShowData.TouchUpInside -= ButtonShowData_TouchUpInside;
     this.btnShowData = null;
   }
   ```

User Interface: View Controllers

```
        private void ButtonShowData_TouchUpInside (object sender,
          EventArgs e){
          foreach (KeyValuePair<int, string> eachItem
            in this.cacheList){
            this.lblOutput.Text += string.Format("Key: {0} - Value:
              {1}", eachItem.Key, eachItem.Value);
          }//end foreach
        }
      }
```

3. Compile and run the application on the simulator.
4. Tap on the button in the **Main** tab to display the contents of our list.
5. Switch to the **Settings** tab.
6. Click **Hardware | Simulate Memory Warning** in the menu bar of the simulator.
7. Watch the output in the **Application Output** of MainDevelop, and switch back to the **Main** tab.

How it works...

This project does not provide any useful functionality. Its main purpose is to show how to use view controllers properly.

When iOS needs more memory to perform various operations, it issues **memory warnings**. When a memory warning occurs, all UI objects that are handled by a controller and are not in use are purged from memory to free up more memory.

The simulator provides a way for developers to recreate such a scenario, with the **Hardware | Simulate Memory Warning** action we selected from the menu bar.

Since we were in the **Settings** tab, the contents of the `MainController` were purged from memory. Inside the `DidReceiveMemoryWarning` method, we clean up any non-UI objects, which otherwise would remain in memory:

```
    this.cacheList.Clear();
```

Next, in the `ViewDidUnload` method, we only need to release any UI objects that are retained by outlets. Note that this is where we unhook any handlers from events these objects might hold:

```
    this.lblOutput = null;
    this.btnShowData.TouchUpInside -= ButtonShowData_TouchUpInside;
    this.btnShowData = null;
```

When we select the **Main** tab again, the `ViewDidLoad` method will be called once more, after the view of the controller and all views and outlets it contains are loaded.

There's more...

When a memory warning occurs, instances of objects not related directly with the UI will remain in memory. In rare cases when there is not enough memory for specific tasks, the operating system might terminate our application if it occupies much of the available memory. To prevent such situations, we need to be careful to clean up all the objects and resources that are not needed, freeing up more memory for iOS.

> Never access a controller's view inside the `ViewDidUnload` method:
> ```
> public override ViewDidUnload()
> {
> base.ViewDidUnload();
> this.View = null; // Never do this.
> }
> ```
> That is because even when we request the return value of a view controller's `View` property, it causes the view to be loaded again, which in most cases will mean that no memory will be released.

See also

In this chapter:

- *Providing controllers in tabs*

In this book:

Chapter 1, Development Tools:

- *Interface builder*

Chapter 4, Data Management:

- *Creating files*
- *Creating an SQLite database*

Combining different view controllers

In this recipe, we will learn how to display a `UINavigationController` within a `UITabBarController`.

User Interface: View Controllers

Getting ready

Create a new iPhone empty project in MonoDevelop, and name it `CombinedControllerApp`.

How to do it...

These are the steps to create this project:

1. Add three iPhone View Controller files to the project, and name them `MainController`, `SettingsController`, and `AfterMainController`.

2. Add a `UIButton` on the view of `MainController` in Interface Builder, and save the document.

3. Enter the following code in the `MainController` class:

   ```
   public override void ViewDidLoad (){
     base.ViewDidLoad ();
     this.Title = "Main";
     this.buttonPush.TouchUpInside += delegate {
       this.NavigationController.PushViewController(new
         AfterMainController(), true);
     };
   }
   ```

4. Add the following fields in the `AppDelegate` class:

   ```
   UINavigationController navController;
   UITabBarController tabController;
   ```

5. Add the following code in the `FinishedLaunching` method of the `AppDelegate` class:

   ```
   MainController mainController = new MainController();
   SettingsController settingsController = new SettingsController();
   this.tabController = new UITabBarController();
   this.navController = new UINavigationController(mainController);
   this.tabController.SetViewControllers(new UIViewController[] {
     this.navController,
     settingsController
   }, false);
   navController.TabBarItem.Title = "Main";
   settingsController.TabBarItem.Title = "Settings";
   window.RootViewController = this.tabController;
   ```

6. Compile and run the application on the simulator. Tap the button in the `MainController` to push the `AfterMainController` in the navigation stack, and then switch between the **Main** and **Settings** tabs.

How it works...

The complete solution can be found in the `CombinedControllerApp` folder. What we have managed to do with this project is to provide a user interface with three different screens, which is not confusing for the user.

The tab bar contains two system-defined items, each representing a different view controller. We implemented the first item in the tab bar controller with a navigation controller. This way, we can provide more screens that are related with a specific part of our application (**Main** plus **AfterMain**), leaving another part of our application directly accessible at any time (**Settings**).

There's more...

The way this project combines three different controllers (a `UITabBarController`, a `UINavigationController`, and a `UIViewController`) is perfectly acceptable. We could even replace the second tab item with another navigation controller to provide even more screens for another section of the application, or even add another tab item.

However, as stated in the *Providing controllers in tabs* recipe in this chapter, it would not be acceptable if we added a `UITabBarController` inside a `UINavigationController`. If we want to provide tab-like behavior inside a navigation controller, we should use its `UIToolbar` to do so.

See also

In this chapter:

- *Navigating through different view controllers*
- *Providing controllers in tabs*
- *Creating a user interface for different devices*

iPad view controllers

In this recipe, we will discuss the controllers that are only available to the iPad.

Getting ready

Create a new iPad empty project, and name it `iPadControllerApp`.

User Interface: View Controllers

How to do it...

1. Add two iPad views with controllers to the project, and name them `FirstController` and `SecondController`. Set different colors for their background views. In `SecondController`, also add a `UIToolbar` on the top of its view, and connect it to an outlet.

2. Add the following fields in the `AppDelegate` class:

   ```
   UISplitViewController splitController;
   FirstController firstController;
   SecondController secondController;
   ```

   > The `UISplitViewController` class is available only to the iPad.

3. Add the following code in the `FinishedLaunching` method:

   ```
   this.firstController = new FirstController();
   this.secondController = new SecondController();
   this.splitController = new UISplitViewController();
   this.splitController.ViewControllers = new UIViewController[] {
     this.firstController,
     this.secondController
   };
   this.splitController.Delegate = new
     SplitControllerDelegate(this.secondController);
   window.RootViewController = this.splitController;
   ```

4. Add the following nested class in `AppDelegate`:

   ```
   private class SplitControllerDelegate :
     UISplitViewControllerDelegate{
     public SplitControllerDelegate (SecondController controller){
       this.parentController = controller;
     }//end ctor
     private SecondController parentController;
     public override void WillHideViewController (
       UISplitViewController svc, UIViewController aViewController,
       UIBarButtonItem barButtonItem, UIPopoverController pc){
       barButtonItem.Title = "First";
       this.parentController.SecToolbar.SetItems (new
         UIBarButtonItem[] { barButtonItem }, true);
     }
     public override void WillShowViewController (
       UISplitViewController svc, UIViewController aViewController,
       UIBarButtonItem button){
   ```

```
      this.parentController.SecToolbar.SetItems (new
        UIBarButtonItem[0], true);
    }
}
```

5. Add a property in the `SecondController` class, which returns the toolbar outlet that we created in *step 1*:

```
public UIToolbar SecToolbar{
  get { return this.secToolbar; }
}
```

6. Finally, compile and run the application in the simulator. Tap on the button in the toolbar to make the `FirstController` appear. The result should be similar to the following screenshot:

How it works...

The complete solution can be found in the `iPadControllerApp` folder. There are two iPad-specific controllers: `UISplitViewController` and `UIPopoverController`. Both of them are being used here, although the `UIPopoverController` is not used directly.

User Interface: View Controllers

The `UISplitViewController` helps to take full advantage of the iPad's larger screen. It provides a way of displaying two different views simultaneously on the same screen area. It does this by displaying one controller in full-screen in portrait orientation and the other controller smaller, in a popover. A **popover** is basically a view, which is displayed on top of other controllers (and their views), much like a modal view controller.

To provide access to both controllers in our project to the user, we have implemented a class that inherits from `UISpliViewControllerDelegate` and assigned it to our split controller inside the `FinishedLaunching()` method. The `Delegate` object we created overrides two methods. In the first method, we assign a button to the toolbar:

```
public override void WillHideViewController
   (UISplitViewController svc, UIViewController aViewController,
   UIBarButtonItem barButtonItem, UIPopoverController pc){
   barButtonItem.Title = "First";
   this.parentController.SecToolbar.SetItems (new UIBarButtonItem[] {
      barButtonItem }, true);
}
```

The `WillHideViewController()` method is executed whenever the `UISplitViewController` changes orientation from landscape to portrait, and its smaller controller is about to be hidden. So, to display it, we provide a button on the full-screen controller's toolbar. When we tap on that button, the other controller will appear in a popover. When the orientation changes from portrait to landscape, the smaller controller appears besides the larger controller, without the need for a popover. So, we no longer need the button on the toolbar, hence we override the `WillShowViewController` to remove the button from the toolbar. We do this by assigning an empty `UIBarButtonItem[]` array:

```
public override void WillShowViewController
   (UISplitViewController svc, UIViewController
   aViewController, UIBarButtonItem button){
   this.parentController.SecToolbar.SetItems (new
      UIBarButtonItem[0], true);
}
```

There's more...

When the device rotates, the interface does not respond automatically. To instruct the view controller to rotate its views, we override the `ShouldAutorotateToInterfaceOrientation(UIInterfaceOrientation)` method **in both the controllers of the split view controller**:

```
public bool ShouldAutorotateToInterfaceOrientation(UIInterfaceOrientat
ion toInterfaceOrientation){
   return true;
}
```

iPad-specific controller usage

Although all other controllers are available to both the iPhone and the iPad, these two controllers cannot be used on the iPhone. An exception will occur in this case.

See also

In this chapter:

- *Creating a user interface for different devices*

In this book:

Chapter 9, Interacting with Device Hardware:

- *Rotating the device*

Creating a user interface for different devices

In this recipe, we will learn how to create an application that will support both the iPhone and the iPad.

Getting ready

Create a new Universal empty project in MonoDevelop, and name it `UniversalApp`.

How to do it...

1. Add a new **iPhone View Controller** to the project, and name it `MainController`.
2. Open it in Interface Builder, and add a label and an outlet for it on the view.
3. Enter the text `Running on an iPhone!` in the label.
4. Change the background of the view to a color other than white. Do the same for the label, and save the document.
5. Add the following code in the `MainViewController` class:

   ```
   public override void ViewDidLoad (){
     base.ViewDidLoad ();
     if (UIDevice.CurrentDevice.UserInterfaceIdiom ==
       UIUserInterfaceIdiom.Pad){
       this.View.Frame = new RectangleF (0f, 0f, 768f, 1024f);
       this.labelMessage.Text = "Running on an iPad!";
     }
   }
   ```

User Interface: View Controllers

6. Add the following code in the `FinishedLaunching()` in the `AppDelegate` class:

   ```
   MainController mainController = new MainController();
   window.RootViewController = mainController;
   ```

7. Compile and run the application on the simulator.

8. Read the message of the label, stating that it is running on an iPhone. Terminate the execution in MonoDevelop, and click on **Run | Run With | iPad Simulator x.x** (where **x.x** is the corresponding iOS version installed on the system, here **5.0**) on the menu bar.

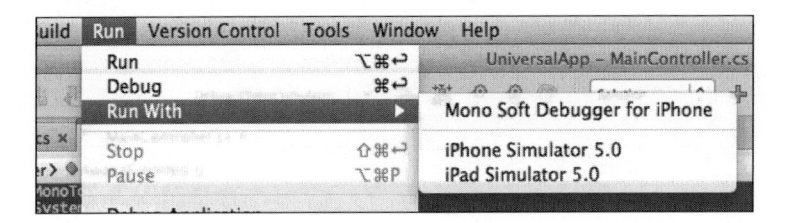

9. Read the message stating that the application is running on an iPad!

How it works...

When we create a universal project in MonoDevelop, the basic difference lies in the application settings file (`Info.plist`), where the application is declared to support both the iPhone and the iPad.

The fact that we have added an **iPhone View with Controller** does not prevent us from using the same controller for both devices. Remember, all controllers are available for all devices, except for the ones discussed in the previous recipe.

Inside the `ViewDidLoad` method, we check which device the application is running on, by checking the `UserInterfaceIdiom` property of the `UIDevice.CurrentDevice` static property, and provide a frame for the view that is sized to the iPad screen's dimensions {768, 1024}.

   ```
   if (UIDevice.CurrentDevice.UserInterfaceIdiom ==
      UIUserInterfaceIdiom.Pad)
   ```

There's more...

This takes care of sizing the views contained in a project according to which device the application is running on. But, it does not guarantee that all the controls will be sized and positioned correctly. To avoid cluttered user interfaces, we have to make sure to adjust the `Autosizing` property of our controls and views so that they will be resized and positioned correctly on different screens.

See also

In this chapter:

- *Using view controllers efficiently*
- *iPad view controllers*

In this book:

Chapter 1, Development Tools:

- *Creating an iPhone project with MonoDevelop*
- *Interface builder*

4
Data Management

In this chapter, we will cover the following topics:

- Creating files
- Creating an SQLite database
- Inserting and updating data
- Querying an SQLite database
- Using an already existing SQLite database
- Storing data with serialization
- Storing data with XML
- Managing XML data with LINQ to XML

Introduction

Almost every application needs to have permanent data storage on the filesystem. In this chapter, we will discuss different ways of storing data. We will see how to create an SQLite database and manage data with it from within an iPhone application. Also, we will learn how to use an already existing database in a project.

SQLite (`http://www.sqlite.org`) is a self-contained transactional database system. Each database is saved in a standalone file, and there is no database server. In iOS, SQLite support is native.

Next, we will see how to serialize and save objects to the filesystem and how to use XML files with LINQ to XML.

Data Management

Creating files

In this recipe, we will learn how to create files on the filesystem of iOS devices.

Getting ready

Create a new **iPhone Single View Application** project in MonoDevelop. Name it `FileCreationApp`. Open the `FileCreationAppViewController.xib` file, and add a `UILabel` and a `UIButton` on its view.

How to do it...

Enter the following code in the `FileCreationAppViewController` class:

```
public override void ViewDidLoad(){
    string filePath = Path.Combine (Environment.GetFolderPath
        (Environment.SpecialFolder.Personal), "MyFile.txt");
    using (StreamWriter sw = new StreamWriter (filePath)){
        sw.WriteLine ("Some text in file!");
    }
    this.btnShow.TouchUpInside += delegate {
        using (StreamReader sr = new StreamReader (filePath)){
            this.labelMessage.Text = sr.ReadToEnd ();
        }
    }
};
```

How it works...

As one can see from this code, we can use standard classes from the `System.IO` namespace, just like in desktop applications. The first thing we do is to set a path for the file we will save. We do this in the following line:

```
string filePath = Path.Combine (Environment.GetFolderPath
    (Environment.SpecialFolder.Personal), "MyFile.txt");
```

In iOS, we do not have access to the whole filesystem, not even inside the application bundle. An exception will occur if we try to write inside a folder we do not have access to. So, we use the static `Environment.GetFolderPath(SpecialFolder)` method and retrieve the `Personal` special folder, which corresponds to our application's `Documents` folder. Note the use of `Path.Combine(string, string)`, which combines two strings and returns a path. After that, we create a new instance of the `StreamWriter` class and write some text in the file with its `WriteLine(string)` method.

Chapter 4

```
using (StreamWriter sw = new StreamWriter (filePath)){
  sw.WriteLine ("Some text in file!");
}
```

To retrieve the text from the file, we create a new instance of the `StreamReader` class and read the text with its `ReadLine` method:

```
using (StreamReader sr = new StreamReader (filePath)){
  this.labelMessage.Text = sr.ReadToEnd ();
}
```

There's more...

If we want to write or read binary data, we can use the `FileStream` class.

Documents Folder

An application's `Documents` folder is relevant to the application alone. If the application is uninstalled from the device, its contents are also removed. We have both read and write access in this folder.

See also

In this chapter:

- *Storing data with serialization*

Creating an SQLite database

In this recipe, we will learn how to create an SQLite database file.

Getting ready

Create a new **iPhone Single View Application** in MonoDevelop, and name it `CreateSQLiteApp`. Add a `UILabel` and a `UIButton` on its view.

How to do it...

1. Add a reference to the project to the assembly `Mono.Data.Sqlite` and the corresponding `using` directive on the namespace:

   ```
   using Mono.Data.Sqlite;
   ```

115

Data Management

2. Enter the following method in the `CreateSQLiteAppViewController` class:

```
private void CreateSQLiteDatabase (string databaseFile){
  try{
    if (!File.Exists (databaseFile)){
      SqliteConnection.CreateFile (databaseFile);
      using (SqliteConnection sqlCon = new SqliteConnection
        (String.Format ("Data Source = {0};", databaseFile))){
        sqlCon.Open ();
        using (SqliteCommand sqlCom = new SqliteCommand
          (sqlCon)){
          sqlCom.CommandText = "CREATE TABLE Customers (ID
            INTEGER PRIMARY KEY, FirstName VARCHAR(20), LastName
            VARCHAR(20))";
          sqlCom.ExecuteNonQuery ();
        }
        sqlCon.Close ();
      }
      this.lblMessage.Text = "Database created!";
    } else {
      this.lblMessage.Text = "Database already exists!";
    }
  } catch (Exception ex) {
    this.lblMessage.Text = String.Format ("Sqlite error: {0}",
      ex.Message);
  }
}
```

3. And add the following code in the `ViewDidLoad` method:

```
string sqlitePath = Path.Combine (Environment.GetFolderPath
  (Environment.SpecialFolder.Personal), "MyDB.db3");
this.btnCreate.TouchUpInside += delegate {
  this.CreateSQLiteDatabase (sqlitePath);
};
```

How it works...

iOS provides native support for SQLite databases.

1. We can access SQLite databases with Mono's `Mono.Data.Sqlite` namespace, as follows:

```
using Mono.Data.Sqlite;
```

2. Inside the `CreateSQLiteDatabase` method, we first check if the file already exists:

   ```
   if (!File.Exists (databaseFile))
   ```

3. Then, we can continue with the creation of the database. We first create the file with the `SqliteConnection.CreateFile(string)` static method, as follows:

   ```
   SqliteConnection.CreateFile (databaseFile);
   ```

4. We connect to the newly created file by initializing an `SqliteConnection` object and calling its `Open()` method. The connection string for an SQLite database is `Data Source =`, followed by the filename of the database:

   ```
   using (SqliteConnection sqlCon = new SqliteConnection
      (String.Format ("Data Source = {0};", databaseFile)))
   sqlCon.Open();
   ```

5. To create a table in the database, an `SqliteCommand` object is initialized. We pass a standard SQL string to its `CommandText` property, and call the `ExecuteNonQuery()` method to execute the SQL:

   ```
   sqlCom.CommandText = "CREATE TABLE Customers (ID INTEGER PRIMARY
      KEY, FirstName VARCHAR(20), LastName VARCHAR(20))";
   sqlCom.ExecuteNonQuery ();
   ```

There's more...

Note the usage of a try-catch block. It is provided to display a message to the user if something goes wrong with the creation of the database.

SQL table creation

In this task, we have created a simple table for our database, with the name `Customers`. It contains three fields. `FirstName` and `LastName` are of type `VARCHAR(20)`, while `ID` is of type `INTEGER` and is also the `PRIMARY KEY` of the table.

Apart from using SQL commands for creating tables, we can create an SQLite database with various commercial or free GUI tools. A simple search on the Internet will yield various results.

See also

In this chapter:

- *Querying an SQLite database*
- *Inserting and updating data*
- *Using an already existing database*

Data Management

Inserting and updating data

In this recipe, we will learn how to write data to the database.

Getting ready

For this task, we will extend the project `CreateSQLiteApp` that we created in the previous task.

How to do it...

1. Add two more buttons on the view.
2. Inside the `CreateSQLiteAppViewController` class, create two methods that will connect to the database file using the code from the previous task. The difference here lies in the usage of the `SqliteCommand` object:

```
using (SqliteCommand sqlCom = new SqliteCommand (sqlCon)){
  // INSERT statement
  sqlCom.CommandText = "INSERT INTO Customers (FirstName,
    LastName) VALUES (@firstName, @lastName)";
  sqlCom.Parameters.Add (new SqliteParameter ("@firstName",
    "John"));
  sqlCom.Parameters.Add (new SqliteParameter ("@lastName",
    "Smith"));
  //UPDATE statement
  //sqlCom.CommandText = "UPDATE Customers SET FirstName = 'James'
    WHERE LastName = @lastName";
  //sqlCom.Parameters.Add (new SqliteParameter ("@lastName",
    "Smith"));
  sqlCom.ExecuteNonQuery ();
}
```

How it works...

To insert and update data in an SQLite table, we use the common `INSERT` and `UPDATE` statements respectively. The highlighted parts of the code indicate the usage of SQLite parameters. Both statements are executed on the database at the `sqlCom.ExecuteNonQuery();` line. The `ExecuteNonQuery` has a return value of type `int` that indicates the number of rows in the table that were affected. So, if we called the method like the following in our example, we would get the output 1, indicating that one row was affected:

```
Console.WriteLine(sqlCom.ExecuteNonQuery());
```

There's more...

Since we have used the project from the previous task, where we provided code for creating the database file, we should add the following code on the beginning of each of our methods that perform the data operations:

```
if (!File.Exists (databaseFile)) {
  this.lblMessage.Text = "Database file does not exist. Tap the
    appropriate button to create it.";
  return;
}
```

This is to make sure that we will not have an exception if the user taps on the **insert** or **update** button while there is no database file.

SQLite performance

Although SQLite offers great performance and portability, it relies to a great extent on its host filesystem, regardless of which platform it is stored on. If you want to perform multiple concurrent `INSERT` or `UPDATE` statements, consider using an `SqliteTransaction`. Apart from the benefit in performance, by batching multiple statements together, a transaction provides a way of rolling back the operation if a problem occurs.

See also

In this chapter:

- Creating files
- Creating an SQLite database
- Querying an SQLite database

Querying an SQLite database

In this recipe, we will learn how to retrieve data from an SQLite database.

Getting ready

Once again, we will use the `CreateSQLiteApp` project. Upon completion of this task, the project will be a full SQLite management application.

Data Management

How to do it...

1. Add another button on the view.
2. Inside the `CreateSQLiteAppViewController` class, add a method that will handle the query. The part that performs the query is the following:

```
using (SqliteCommand sqlCom = new SqliteCommand (sqlCon)){
  sqlCom.CommandText = "SELECT * FROM Customers WHERE LastName =
    @lastName";
  sqlCom.Parameters.Add (new SqliteParameter ("@lastName",
    "Smith"));
  using (SqliteDataReader dbReader = sqlCom.ExecuteReader ()){
    if (dbReader.HasRows){
      while (dbReader.Read ()){
        this.lblMessage.Text += String.Format ("ID: {0}\n",
          Convert.ToString (dbReader["ID"]));
        this.lblMessage.Text += String.Format ("First name:
          {0}\n", Convert.ToString (dbReader["FirstName"]));
        this.lblMessage.Text += String.Format ("Last name: {0}\n",
          Convert.ToString (dbReader["LastName"]));
      }
    }
  }
}
```

How it works...

To perform a query on an SQLite database, we create a simple SELECT statement and assign it to the `CommandText` property of the `SqliteCommand` object:

```
sqlCom.CommandText = "SELECT * FROM Customers WHERE LastName =
  @lastName";
```

The asterisk (*) after the SELECT word indicates that we want to retrieve all the fields of the table. The simplest way to execute the SQL query is by using the `SqliteDataReader` class:

```
using (SqliteDataReader dbReader = sqlCom.ExecuteReader ())
```

The `SqliteCommand.ExecuteReader()` method performs the query on the table and creates an `SqliteDataReader` object. Now that we have our object, we first check if the table contains any rows:

```
if (dbReader.HasRows)
```

If the above returns `true`, we begin advancing through each row by passing the `SqliteDataReader.Read()` method in a `while` loop:

```
while (dbReader.Read ())
```

We can now retrieve each field's value by passing the name of each field as an index on the `SqliteDataReader` instance:

```
this.lblMessage.Text += String.Format ("ID: {0}\n", Convert.ToString
    (dbReader["ID"]));
//...
```

Since the indexed `dbReader` variable returns an object of the type `System.Object`, we use the `Convert.ToString(object)` static method to convert it to a string.

There's more...

The SQLite database is not thread-safe. If we want to perform queries on a database while another thread might be executing `INSERT` or `UPDATE` statements, it would be better to provide some sort of synchronization mechanism.

Query performance

Although devices running the iOS platform are performing better than some older desktop computers, their resources are still limited in comparison. When querying data from large databases, consider narrowing the results to the data that is needed at that particular time with the SQL `WHERE` statement. Also, if no sorting is required, avoid using `ORDER BY` statements.

See also

In this chapter:

- *Creating an SQLite database*
- *Inserting and updating data*
- *Using an already existing SQLite database*

Using an already existing SQLite database

In this recipe, we will discuss how to include an already existing SQLite database file in our project.

Data Management

Getting ready

It is always easier to create databases with some kind of frontend. In this task, we will see how to integrate an existing SQLite database with an iPhone project. Create a new **iPhone Single View Application** project, and name it `SqliteIntegrationApp`.

How to do it...

1. Add a `UIButton` and a `UILabel` on the view in Interface Builder. Connect them with the appropriate outlets. Make sure the label is tall enough for six lines, and set its **# Lines** field in the **Inspector** tab.

2. In MonoDevelop, right-click on the project in the **Solution** pad, and click **Add Files....**

3. On the dialog box that will be shown, navigate to the path where the database file resides and select it. The file will be added in the project.

4. Right-click on it and select **Build Action | Content**.

5. Enter the following methods in the `SqliteIntegrationAppViewController` class:

    ```
    private string CopyDatabase (){
       string docPath = Environment.GetFolderPath
         (Environment.SpecialFolder.Personal);
       string databaseFile = "CustomersDB.db3";
       string databasePath = Path.Combine (docPath, databaseFile);
       if (!File.Exists (databasePath)){
          File.Copy (databaseFile, databasePath);
       }
       return databasePath;
    }
    private void QueryData (object sender, EventArgs e)
    { //... }
    ```

    The functionality of the `QueryData` method is the same as the method that performs the query in the previous task. The main difference is that in this project, it will act as the button's `TouchUpInside` event handler.

6. Add a field of type `string` that will hold the database path:

    ```
    private string database;
    ```

7. And, finally, in the `ViewDidLoad` method:

    ```
    this.database = this.CopyDatabase ();
    this.buttonQuery.TouchUpInside += this.QueryData;
    ```

8. Compile and run the application. Tap on the button, and watch the contents of the database being displayed in the label.

How it works...

What we have done here is a combination of various practices discussed in previous tasks. When we want to add various files in a project, it is important that we set their **Build Action** to **Content**. Any file that is marked as **Content** is being copied as-is in the application bundle. In this case, the file is an SQLite database, hence we will need write access to it at runtime. We need to copy it in the application's **Documents** folder. This is what the `CopyDatabase()` method does, at this point:

```
if (!File.Exists (databasePath)){
  File.Copy (databaseFile, databasePath);
}
```

It is important to check if the file already exists so that it will not be overwritten the next time the application is executed.

There's more...

If you get an `SqliteException`, the first thing to check is if for some reason the database file was not copied to the correct folder.

See also

In this chapter:

- *Creating files*
- *Creating an SQLite database*

Storing data with serialization

In this recipe, we will discuss using .NET serialization to store C# objects.

Getting ready

Create a new **iPhone Single View Application** project in MonoDevelop. Name it `SerializationApp`.

How to do it...

1. Add two buttons and a label on the view in Interface Builder. Add the following using directives in the `SerializationAppViewController.cs` file:

    ```
    using System.IO;
    using System.Runtime.Serialization.Formatters.Binary;
    ```

Data Management

2. Add the following methods in the `AppDelegate` class:

```
private void Serialize (){
    CustomerData custData = new CustomerData ();
    custData.ID = 1;
    custData.FirstName = "John";
    custData.LastName = "Smith";
    using (MemoryStream ms = new MemoryStream ()){
        BinaryFormatter bf = new BinaryFormatter ();
        bf.Serialize (ms, custData);
        ms.Seek (0, SeekOrigin.Begin);
        this.objBuffer = new byte[ms.Length];
        ms.Read (this.objBuffer, 0, this.objBuffer.Length);
    }
    this.labelOutput.Text = "Customer data serialized.\n";
}
private void DeserializeAndDisplay (){
    if (null != this.objBuffer){
        CustomerData custData = null;
        using (MemoryStream ms = new MemoryStream (this.objBuffer)){
            ms.Seek (0, SeekOrigin.Begin);
            BinaryFormatter bf = new BinaryFormatter ();
            custData = (CustomerData)bf.Deserialize (ms);
        }
        this.labelOutput.Text += String.Format ("ID: {0}\n
            \tFirst name: {1}\n\tLast name: {2}", custData.ID,
            custData.FirstName, custData.LastName);
    } else {
        this.labelOutput.Text = "Buffer is null!";
    }
}
```

The complete code can be found in the `SerializationApp` project.

How it works...

Serialization with MonoTouch works the same as in desktop C# applications. The `CustomerData` class indicated in the highlighted code is a simple object that contains one integer and two string properties.

1. To serialize the object, we first initialize a `MemoryStream`:

    ```
    using (MemoryStream ms = new MemoryStream ())
    ```

―― Chapter 4

2. We then use the `BinaryFormatter` class to serialize the object and store it into the stream:

   ```
   BinaryFormatter bf = new BinaryFormatter ();
   bf.Serialize (ms, custData);
   ```

3. After the serialization, we reset the stream's position to its beginning, and read the data from it into a byte array:

   ```
   ms.Seek (0, SeekOrigin.Begin);
   this.objBuffer = new byte[ms.Length];
   ms.Read (this.objBuffer, 0, this.objBuffer.Length);
   ```

4. To deserialize the object from the buffer, the process is similar, but in the reverse order. After the `MemoryStream` initialization, we reset the stream's position to its beginning and use the `Deserialize` method of the `BinaryFormatter`. It returns an object of type `System.Object`, so we need to cast it to the type of our object:

   ```
   ms.Seek (0, SeekOrigin.Begin);
   BinaryFormatter bf = new BinaryFormatter ();
   custData = (CustomerData)bf.Deserialize (ms);
   ```

There's more...

One important thing to remember when serializing objects with MonoTouch is to decorate the objects that will be serialized with the `PreserveAttribute`. This attribute instructs the linker to avoid stripping the object of unused members, keeping it intact. The `CustomerData` class in this task is declared as follows:

```
[Preserve()]
[Serializable()]
public class CustomerData
```

Serializable objects

This is a.simple example to display the use of binary serialization in an iOS application. Objects can be customized for serialization by inheriting the `ISerializable` C# interface.

When creating an object that will be used for serialization, do not forget to mark it with the `SerializableAttribute`. An exception will occur when trying to serialize objects that are not marked with this attribute.

See also

In this chapter:

▶ *Storing data with XML*

Data Management

In this book:

Chapter 1, Development Tools:

- Compiling

Storing data with XML

In this recipe, we will discuss how to store data with XML serialization.

Getting ready

Create a new **iPhone Single View Application** project in MonoDevelop, and name it `XMLDataApp`.

How to do it...

1. Add a `UIButton` and a `UILabel` on the view. Add the class `CustomerData` from the previous task to the project. Add the following `using` directives in the `XMLDataAppViewController.cs` file:

    ```
    using System.Xml.Serialization;
    using System.Xml;
    using System.Text;
    ```

2. Add the following method in the `XMLDataAppViewController` class:

    ```
    private void CreateXML (){
      CustomerData custData = new CustomerData ();
      custData.ID = 1;
      custData.FirstName = "John";
      custData.LastName = "Smith";
      this.sb = new StringBuilder ();
      XmlSerializer xmlSer = new XmlSerializer (typeof(CustomerData));
      xmlSer.Serialize (XmlWriter.Create (sb), custData);
      this.labelOutput.Text = sb.ToString ();
    }
    ```

The complete solution can be found in the `XMLDataApp` project.

How it works...

In this example, we are using the `XmlSerializer` class to serialize an object to XML. The `StringBuilder` object will hold the XML data:

```
this.sb = new StringBuilder ();
XmlSerializer xmlSer = new XmlSerializer (typeof(CustomerData));
```

To initialize the `XmlSerializer`, we use its `XmlSerializer(System.Type)` constructor, passing as a parameter the type of the object we want to serialize: `(typeof(CustomerData))`. We than call its `Serialize(XmlWriter, object)` method, which will perform the actual serialization and store the output XML to the `StringBuilder`, through the `XmlWriter` class, as follows:

```
xmlSer.Serialize (XmlWriter.Create (sb), custData);
```

When you compile and run the application, you will see the output XML in the label.

There's more...

There are two main advantages in using XML to store data:

1. The output is pure text, as opposed to binary serialization, which makes it human readable.
2. Data can be transmitted or received to and from different types of applications, websites, and so on that are not necessarily written in C#.

Deserialization

To deserialize our object from XML, we would use the following line:

```
custData = (CustomerData)xmlSer.Deserialize (new StringReader
   (sb.ToString ()));
```

See also

In this chapter:

- *Storing data with serialization*
- *Managing XML data with LINQ to XML*

Managing XML data with LINQ to XML

In this recipe, we will learn how to manage XML data using **Language INtegrated Query** (**LINQ**).

Getting ready

In this task, we are going to use the project `XMLDataApp` from the previous task. Open it in MonoDevelop.

Data Management

How to do it...

1. Add another `UIButton` on the view. Add a reference to the `System.Xml.Linq` assembly and the following `using` directive in the `XMLDataAppViewController.cs` file:

   ```
   using System.Linq.Xml;
   ```

2. Enter the following method in the `XMLDataAppViewController` class:

   ```
   private void ReadXML () {
     if (null != sb) {
       XDocument xDoc = XDocument.Parse (this.sb.ToString ());
       var query = from s in xDoc.Descendants()
       select new CustomerData() {
          ID = Convert.ToInt32(s.Element("ID").Value),
          FirstName = s.Element("FirstName").Value,
          LastName = s.Element("LastName").Value
       };
       CustomerData custData = query.FirstOrDefault();
       if (null != custData) {
         this.labelOutput.Text = String.Format("ID: {0}\n\t
           FirstName: {1}\n\tLastName: {2}", custData.ID,
           custData.FirstName, custData.LastName);
       }
     }
   }
   ```

How it works...

LINQ is very versatile and straightforward in querying XML data.

1. The first thing we do is create an `XDocument` from our XML data:

   ```
   XDocument xDoc = XDocument.Parse (this.sb.ToString ());
   ```

2. After this, we create a query on its `Descendants()` method, which returns an `IEnumerable<XElement>` object. Each `XElement` object corresponds to an XML element.

3. Using the information of each `XElement` returned, we construct our `CustomerData` object in the `select` statement:

   ```
   var query = from s in xDoc.Descendants()
   select new CustomerData() {
     ID = Convert.ToInt32(s.Element("ID").Value),
     FirstName = s.Element("FirstName").Value,
     LastName = s.Element("LastName").Value
   };
   ```

4. To retrieve the created object, we call the extension method `FirstOrDefault()` on the query:

```
CustomerData custData = query.FirstOrDefault();
```

There's more...

The XML in this example contains only one object of the type `CustomerData`. If there were more, we could narrow down the results, providing a `where` statement:

```
var query = from s in xDoc.Descendants()
  where s.Element("FirstName").Value == "John"
  select new CustomerData() {
  ID = Convert.ToInt32(s.Element("ID").Value),
  FirstName = s.Element("FirstName").Value,
  LastName = s.Element("LastName").Value
};
```

Anonymous types in LINQ

In MonoTouch, we can also use C#'s powerful feature of anonymous types in queries, for example, `select new { ID = ... }`

See also

In this chapter:

- *Storing data with serialization*
- *Storing data with XML*

5
Displaying Data

In this chapter, we will cover the following topics:

- Providing lists
- Displaying data in a table
- Customizing rows
- Editing a table: deleting rows
- Editing a table: inserting rows
- Table indexing
- Searching through the data
- Creating a simple web browser
- Displaying local content
- Displaying formatted text
- Displaying documents

Introduction

In the previous chapter, we discussed about some of the available options for data management in an iOS application. In this chapter, we will discuss various ways of displaying data to the user.

Specifically, we will see how to use the following controls:

- `UIPickerView`: This is the control that provides similar functionality to a list box.
- `UITableView`: This is a very customizable view for displaying data. One of the most used controls in iOS applications.

Displaying Data

- `UISearchBar` **and** `UISearchDisplayController`: These are a combination of controls that provide an easy-to-use interface for searching through data.
- `UIWebView`: This brings web browser functionality to applications.
- `QLPreviewController`: This displays various document formats.

Furthermore, we will learn how to provide indexing in tables, to make large volumes of data easily accessible to the user. We will also discuss some of the available ways to display formatted text, even **Portable Document Format** (**PDF**), and other documents.

Also, starting from this chapter, all code examples will use a default view controller named `MainController`, unless otherwise stated.

Providing lists

In this recipe, we will learn how to use the `UIPickerView` class.

Getting ready

The `UIPickerView` class provides us with a control whose functionality is similar to a listbox, specifically designed for human fingers touching the screen. Its main difference to a common listbox is that each column can have its own number of rows. To get started, create a new iPhone project and name it `PickerViewApp`.

How to do it...

1. Open the `MainController.xib` file in Interface Builder.
2. Add a `UILabel` and a `UIPickerView` on the main View.
3. Save the document.
4. Back in MonoDevelop, create a nested class in the `MainController` class that inherits from `UIPickerViewModel`:

   ```
   private class PickerModelDelegate : UIPickerViewModel
   ```

5. Add the following constructor and fields in the nested class:

   ```
   public PickerModelDelegate (MainController controller) {
     this.parentController = controller;
     this.transportList = new List<string>() { "On foot", "Bicycle",
       "Motorcycle", "Car", "Bus" };
     this.distanceList = new List<string>() { "0.5",     "1", "5",
       "10", "100" };
     this.unitList = new List<string>() { "mi", "km" };
     this.transportSelected = this.transportList[0];
     this.distanceSelected = this.distanceList[0];
   ```

Chapter 5

```
        this.unitSelected = this.unitList[0];
    }
    private MainController parentController;
    private List<string> transportList;
    private List<string> distanceList;
    private List<string> unitList;
    string transportSelected;
    string distanceSelected;
    string unitSelected;
```

6. You will now need to override four methods from the `UIPickerViewModel` class:
    - `int GetComponentCount (UIPickerView picker)`
    - `int GetRowsInComponent (UIPickerView picker, int component)`
    - `string GetTitle (UIPickerView picker, int row, int component)`
    - `void Selected (UIPickerView picker, int row, int component)`

7. Finally, set the model object created to the picker view's `Model` property inside the controller's `ViewDidLoad` method:

    `this.picker.Model = new PickerModelDelegate (this);`

The complete code can be found in the `PickerViewApp` project.

How it works...

The `UIPickerViewModel` class does not exist in `Objective-C`. MonoTouch provides this class as a wrapper around the native protocols `UIPickerViewDataSource` and `UIPickerViewDelegate` and contains both of these class' methods for us to override. This is extremely helpful, since we only have to implement and assign one class instead of two for our picker view. Both of these protocols are at the same time available as classes in MonoTouch.

Inside the constructor, we initialize the lists that will hold the data to be displayed in the picker. The four classes we need to override are responsible for displaying the data:

1. `int GetComponentCount (UIPickerView picker)`: This returns the number of columns we want the picker view to display.
2. `int GetRowsInComponent (UIPickerView picker, int component)`: This returns the number of rows each component will display.
3. `string GetTitle (UIPickerView picker, int row, int component)`: This returns the text of each row.

Displaying Data

4. `void Selected (UIPickerView picker, int row, int component)`: This returns the action to take when the user selects an item from any component/row combination in the picker view.

We use the lists we have assigned in the constructor to display the data. For example, the `GetTitle` method is implemented as follows:

```
switch (component) {
case 0:
   return this.transportList[row];
case 1:
   return this.distanceList[row];
default:
   return this.unitList[row];
}
```

When we run the application and select anything from the picker, the result will be similar to the following screenshot:

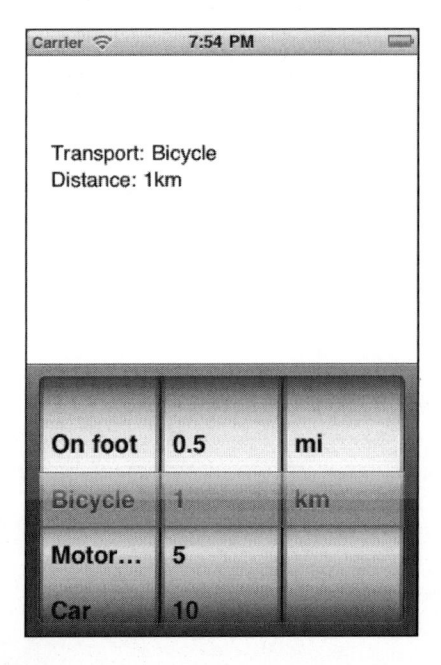

There's more...

We can programmatically select the initial selection of the picker view by calling the method `Select (int, int, bool)`. The first two parameters reflect the row and component index respectively, while the `bool` parameter toggles the selection animation. The only thing to remember with this method is to call it after we have assigned the picker's `Model` property. An exception will occur otherwise.

More information on UIPickerView customization

Apart from the options presented, we also have the option of setting the width of each component. To do this, we override the `GetComponentWidth(UIPickerView, int)` method, which returns a float that represents the width for each component.

We can also set custom views as items in the picker view, instead of plain text. This can be done by overriding the `GetView(UIPickerView, int, int, UIView)` method and returning the view we want to be displayed in each position in the `UIPickerView` control.

Date and time selection

There is a control named `UIDatePicker` that is similar to the `UIPickerView` and is specifically customized for displaying and selecting date and time values. Note that although its user interface is the same as the picker view, it does not inherit the `UIPickerView` class. It just uses an instance of it as a sub-view.

See also

In this chapter:

- *Displaying data in a table*

Displaying data in a table

In this recipe, we will learn how to use the `UITableView` class to display data.

Getting ready

The `UITableView` class, along with the `UITableViewCell` object, provides an interface for displaying data on the screen in multiple rows, but on a single column. To get started, create a new project in MonoDevelop, and name it `TableViewApp`.

How to do it...

1. Add a view with controller to the project, and name it `TableController`.
2. Change the `TableController` class' inheritance from `UIViewController` to `UITableViewController`:

   public partial class TableController : UITableViewController

3. Open the `TableController.xib` file in Interface.
4. Delete the document's `UIView`, and add a `UITableView` in its place.
5. Connect the outlet named view of the `TableController` to the table view added.

Displaying Data

6. Save the document.

7. Back in MonoDevelop, create the following nested class inside the `TableController` class:

```
private class TableSource : UITableViewSource{
  public TableSource (){
    this.cellID = "cellIdentifier";
    this.tableData = new Dictionary<int, string> () {
      {0, "Music"},
      {1, "Videos"},
      {2, "Images"}
    };
  }
  private string cellID;
  private Dictionary<int, string> tableData;
  public override int RowsInSection (UITableView tableview, int
    section){
    return this.tableData.Count;
  }
  public override UITableViewCell GetCell (UITableView tableView,
    NSIndexPath indexPath){
    int rowIndex = indexPath.Row;
    UITableViewCell cell =
      tableView.DequeueReusableCell (this.cellID);
    if (null == cell){
      cell = new UITableViewCell (UITableViewCellStyle.Default,
        this.cellID);
    }
    cell.TextLabel.Text = this.tableData[rowIndex];
    return cell;
  }
}
```

8. Override the controller's `ViewDidLoad` method, and add the following line of code:

```
this.TableView.Source = new TableSource ();
```

The complete code can be found in the `TableViewApp` project.

How it works...

The nested class that we created acts as the data source of the `UITableView`. It inherits from the MonoTouch `UITableViewSource` class:

```
private class TableSource : UITableViewSource
```

> Like the `UIPickerView`, in the example discussed in the previous recipe, the `UITableViewSource` class does not exist in `Objective-C`. It is merely a wrapper object offered by MonoTouch around `UITableViewDelegate` and `UITableViewSource` protocols.

In its constructor, we initialize two variables. A string that will act as the cells' identifier and a generic `Dictionary` for our data source.

```
this.cellID = "cellIdentifier";
this.tableData = new Dictionary<int, string> () {
   {0, "Music"},
   {1, "Videos"},
   {2, "Images"}
};
```

To make the `TableSource` class work, we need to override two methods. The first method, named `RowsInSection`, which returns the number of rows the table shall display. Here, we return the number of items in our data source object:

```
return this.tableData.Count;
```

The second method, `GetCell`, returns the `UITableViewCell` object that will be displayed in the table.

> The `UITableViewCell` class represents a single row and manages its content in a `UITableView`.

To be more efficient, the table view creates its cell objects when they are needed. For this reason, we need to get a previously used `UITableViewCell` from the table through its `DequeueReusableCell` method:

```
UITableViewCell cell = tableView.DequeueReusableCell (this.cellID);
```

If no cells exist for the particular cell identifier, the method returns `null`. Hence, we create the cell that will be used:

```
cell = new UITableViewCell (UITableViewCellStyle.Default,
   this.cellID);
```

Then, we assign the text that the particular cell will display and return it:

```
cell.TextLabel.Text = this.tableData[rowIndex];
return cell;
```

Displaying Data

By default, the `UITableViewCell` class contains two labels that can be used to display text. The main label can be accessed through the `TextLabel` property and the secondary label through the `DetailTextLabel` property. Note that when using a cell with the `Default` style, the `DetailTextLabel` property cannot be used and will return `null`.

There's more...

To provide functionality when the user selects a particular row, we need to override the `RowSelected` property in the class that acts as a `UITableViewSource`. By default, when the user taps on a row, the cell is highlighted with a blue color to indicate the selection. To de-select the row, we use the `UITableView.DeselectRow(NSIndexPath, bool)` method:

```
public override void RowSelected (UITableView tableView, NSIndexPath indexPath){
  tableView.DeselectRow (indexPath, true);
}
```

UITableView styles

The `UITableView` can be created with two different styles. The default style is `Plain`. The other style that can be used is the `Grouped` style. This style is being used in many iOS native applications, such as the `Settings` application.

Also, the `UITableView` supports display of data divided into different sections. We must explicitly return the number of rows that each section will have in the `RowsInSection` override if we want to use different sections.

See also

In this chapter:

- Providing lists
- Customizing rows

In this book:

Chapter 3, User Interface: View Controllers:

- Creating a table controller

Customizing rows

In this recipe, we will cover some of the different options available for customizing the display of content in table cells.

Chapter 5

Getting ready

Create a new project in MonoDevelop in the same manner the project in the previous recipe was created. Name it `CustomRowsApp`.

How to do it...

1. Copy and paste the `TableSource` class from the project in the previous task, inside the `TableController` class.

2. Perform the following changes in the `GetCell` override:
    ```
    int rowIndex = indexPath.Row;
    string cellID = this.tableData[rowIndex];
    UITableViewCell cell = tableView.DequeueReusableCell (cellID);
    if (null == cell){
       cell = new UITableViewCell (this.cellStyles[rowIndex], cellID);
    }
    cell.TextLabel.Text = this.tableData[rowIndex];
    if (rowIndex > 0){
       cell.DetailTextLabel.Text = String.Format ("Details for {0}",
          cellID);
    }
    return cell;
    ```

3. Remove the `cellID` field and add a new one:
    ```
    private Dictionary<int, UITableViewCellStyle> cellStyles;
    ```

4. Initialize it in the constructor, as follows:
    ```
    this.cellStyles = new Dictionary<int, UITableViewCellStyle>() {
       {0, UITableViewCellStyle.Default},
       {1, UITableViewCellStyle.Subtitle},
       {2, UITableViewCellStyle.Value1},
       {3, UITableViewCellStyle.Value2}
    };
    ```

5. Add another `KeyValuePair` in the data source object:
    ```
    {3, "Recordings"}
    ```

Displaying Data

6. Compile and run the application on the simulator. The output should be something similar to the following, as explained in the following screenshot:

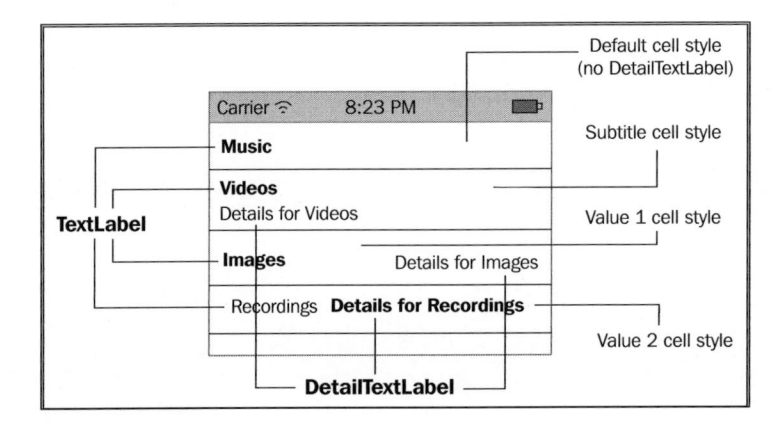

```
                                              Default cell style
                                              (no DetailTextLabel)
            Carrier 📶    8:23 PM       🔋
            Music                             Subtitle cell style
            Videos
            Details for Videos                Value 1 cell style
TextLabel
            Images
                          Details for Images
            Recordings  Details for Recordings
                                              Value 2 cell style
                     DetailTextLabel
```

How it works...

A table cell can have four different cell styles, which are represented by the `UITableViewCellStyle` enumeration. Its values are:

1. `Default`: This is the default cell style. Only the `TextLabel` property can be used to display text.
2. `Subtitle`: This is a style that provides the `DetailTextLabel` as a sub-title to the `TextLabel`.
3. `Value1`: This is a style that displays both `TextLabel` and `DetailTextLabel` text in the same size, with different colors and aligned to the sides of the cell.
4. `Value2`: This is a style that displays the `TextLabel` text smaller than the `DetailTextLabel` text. This style is used in the native `Contacts` application, in the contact details screen.

To easily use all available styles, we have added all the values of the `UITableViewCellStyle` enumeration in a `Dictionary`:

```
private Dictionary<int, UITableViewCellStyle> cellStyles;
```

Now that we use different cell styles, hence different cells, we need one cell identifier for each string. To avoid declaring another list or more fields in the class, we use the data source for this reason:

```
int rowIndex = indexPath.Row;
string cellID = this.tableData[rowIndex];
UITableViewCell cell = tableView.DequeueReusableCell (cellID);
```

Chapter 5

To create each cell with a specific style, we extract the `UITableViewCellStyle` value from the `cellStyles` field, according to the current row:

```
cell = new UITableViewCell (this.cellStyles[rowIndex], cellID);
```

To set the `DetailTextLabel` text for each cell, we just make sure we are not trying to set it on a cell with `Default` style, as the first one in this example:

```
if (rowIndex > 0) {
  cell.DetailTextLabel.Text = String.Format ("Details for {0}",
    cellID);
}
```

There's more...

Further customization can be done in a `UITableViewCell`. All views a cell contains, including the `TextLabel` and `DetailTextLabel`, are sub-views to the cell's view, which is exposed through its `ContentView` property. We can create custom views and add them as sub-views to it.

Other useful properties of the UITableViewCell class

Apart from adding text in the default labels, the `UITableViewCell` contains some other properties, whose values we can set, to add more default items in a cell:

- `ImageView`: This property accepts a `UIImageView`. We can use it to display an image in a cell, on its left side.
- `AccessoryView`: This property accepts any instance of `UIView`. Its position defaults to the right of the cell, in the place of the cell's `Accessory`, which is located at the right side of the cell.
- `Accessory`: This property accepts values of the type `UITableViewCellAccessory`. It provides predefined views for the cell's accessory, such as a `DetailDisclosureButton` or a `Checkmark`.

See also

In this chapter:

- *Displaying data in a table*
- *Editing data in a table*

141

Displaying Data

Editing a table: deleting rows

In this recipe, we will discuss how to delete rows from a `UITableView`, with appropriate feedback to the user.

Getting ready

Create a new project in MonoDevelop, and name it `EditingTableDataApp`.

How to do it...

1. Add a view controller to the project, and convert it to a `UITableViewController` as described in the *Displaying data in a table* section in this chapter, and name it `TableController`.

2. Add a `UINavigationController` in the `AppDelegate` class. Initialize it, setting the `TableController` as its root controller:

   ```
   TableController tableController;
   UINavigationController navController;
   //...
   this.tableController = new TableController();
   this.navController = new
     UINavigationController(this.tableController);
   window.RootViewController = this.navController;
   ```

3. Back in MonoDevelop, add three fields in the TableController class: `List<string> tableData`, `UIBarButtonItem buttonEdit`, and `UIBarButtonItem buttonDone`. Override the class' `ViewDidLoad` method, as follows:

   ```
   public override void ViewDidLoad (){
     base.ViewDidLoad ();
     this.buttonEdit = new UIBarButtonItem ("Edit",
       UIBarButtonItemStyle.Bordered, this.ButtonEdit_Clicked);
     this.buttonDone = new UIBarButtonItem
       (UIBarButtonSystemItem.Done, this.ButtonDone_Clicked);
     this.NavigationItem.SetRightBarButtonItem (this.buttonEdit,
       false);
     this.tableData = new List<string>() {"Music", "Videos", "Images"
       };
     this.TableView.Source = new TableSource(this.tableData);
   }
   ```

―― Chapter 5

4. Create a proper table view source for the table, which accepts the `tableData` generic `List` as an argument in its constructor. Create the handler method `ButtonEdit_Clicked`, and enter the following code in it:

   ```
   this.TableView.SetEditing (true, true);
   this.NavigationItem.SetRightBarButtonItem (this.buttonDone, true);
   ```

5. Create the handler method `ButtonDone_Clicked`, and enter the following code in it:

   ```
   this.TableView.SetEditing (false, true);
   this.NavigationItem.SetRightBarButtonItem (this.buttonEdit, true);
   ```

6. Finally, override the `CommitEditingStyle` method of the table source:

   ```
   public override void CommitEditingStyle (UITableView tableView,
     UITableViewCellEditingStyle editingStyle,
     NSIndexPath indexPath) {
     int rowIndex = indexPath.Row;
     if (editingStyle == UITableViewCellEditingStyle.Delete) {
       this.tableData.RemoveAt (rowIndex);
       tableView.DeleteRows (new NSIndexPath[] { indexPath },
         UITableViewRowAnimation.Left);
     }
   }
   ```

How it works...

The first thing we do here is make use of the navigation bar to add buttons that will handle the table's edit mode. When the view loads, we set the edit button with the `SetRightBarButtonItem` method:

```
this.NavigationItem.SetRightBarButtonItem (this.buttonEdit, false);
```

Inside the `ButtonEdit_Clicked` method, we set the table to editing mode. Then, we change the button in the navigation bar so that the user can exit from editing:

```
this.TableView.SetEditing (true, true);
this.NavigationItem.SetRightBarButtonItem (this.buttonDone, true);
```

The `SetEditing` method enables or disables the table's editing mode. When a table view is in editing mode, a round red icon with the minus (-) symbol appears on the left side of each cell. When the user taps the icon, a confirmation red **Delete** button appears in the cell. To actually delete the row when the user confirms deletion by tapping on the **Delete** button, we must implement the `CommitEditingStyle` method in the table source:

```
if (editingStyle == UITableViewCellEditingStyle.Delete){
  this.tableData.RemoveAt (rowIndex);
  tableView.DeleteRows (new NSIndexPath[] { indexPath },
    UITableViewRowAnimation.Left);
}
```

Displaying Data

The first thing we need to do is check if the method was called as a result of the user tapping the `Delete` button. This is done by checking the `editingStyle` parameter, highlighted in this code. Then, we delete the data of the row from the data source and the row from the table with the `DeleteRows` method.

There's more...

The table view provides another, more direct way to the user for deleting rows. This can be accomplished by swiping the finger on the cell we want to delete. In this case, only the **Delete** button is shown. We still need to implement the `CommitEditingStyle` method in the table source to actually remove the row from the table.

The fact that a navigation controller was used in this recipe doesn't mean it is the only way to accomplish the function of deleting rows. It is, however, a combination of view controllers that will be used most of the time, in real-world application scenarios.

Row removal animations

The `UITableViewRowAnimation` enumeration used in the `DeleteRows` method represents the type of animation a row will be removed by. It contains various values (`Left`, `Right`, `Middle`, `Fade`, `Top`, `Bottom`, and `None`) for animating the row. Note that to accomplish the best result, the type of animation should be used according to the position of the row in the data source. For example, if the row to be removed is the last one on the table, it is best to use `UITableViewRowAnimation.Bottom` so that the row that should be removed will move downwards. If the row to be removed is the first one in the data source, it is best to use `UITableViewRowAnimation.Top` so the row that should be removed will move upwards. The rest of the options are more suitable for the intermediate rows, between the first and last.

See also

In this chapter:

- *Displaying data in a table*
- *Editing a table: Inserting rows*

In this book:

Chapter 3, User Interface: View Controllers:

- *Navigating through different view controllers*

Editing a table: inserting rows

In this recipe, we will learn how to provide the user with the ability to insert rows in a `UITableView`.

Getting ready

For this task, we will use the project `EditingTableDataApp` from the previous task. Open it in MonoDevelop.

How to do it...

1. Add another `UIBarButtonItem` field in the `TableController` class, and initialize it in the `ViewDidLoad` method:

    ```
    this.buttonAdd = new UIBarButtonItem (UIBarButtonSystemItem.Add,
       this.ButtonAdd_Clicked);
    ```

2. Add the handler method `ButtonAdd_Clicked`:

    ```
    private void ButtonAdd_Clicked (object sender, EventArgs e){
       this.tableData.Add ("Recordings");
       this.TableView.ReloadData ();
    }
    ```

3. In the `ButtonEdit_Clicked` method, add the following line:

    ```
    this.NavigationItem.SetLeftBarButtonItem (this.buttonAdd, true);
    ```

4. Also add the following line in the `ButtonDone_Clicked` method:

    ```
    this.NavigationItem.SetLeftBarButtonItem (null, true);
    ```

5. Compile and run the app on the simulator.
6. Tap the **Edit** button, and see the add button appear on the leftside in the navigation bar. Tap it and see the new row is added to the table.

How it works...

A system-default **Add** button is used here. When the user taps on the button, a new row is added in the table. The button is added in the edit button's `Clicked` handler as the left button in the navigation bar. To remove it, we call the same method, passing as the `UIBarButtonItem` parameter, which is a `null` value inside the `ButtonDone_Clicked` method:

```
this.NavigationItem.SetLeftBarButtonItem (this.buttonAdd, true);
this.NavigationItem.SetLeftBarButtonItem (null, true);
```

Displaying Data

This way, when the user disables the editing mode, the `add` button will disappear. Next, all we need to do to add a row is add the data to the data source and force the table to reload, which is done as follows:

```
this.tableData.Add ("Recordings");
this.TableView.ReloadData ();
```

There's more...

This is the simplest way of inserting rows in a table. It is not the most efficient though. Calling the `UITableView.ReloadData` method causes the `UITableView` to reload everything, which will degrade performance if the table contains a large number of rows. To avoid this, you can replace the `ReloadData` call in this example with the following line:

```
this.TableView.InsertRows (new NSIndexPath[] {
   NSIndexPath.FromRowSection(this.tableData.Count - 1, 0) },
   UITableViewRowAnimation.Right);
```

The `InsertRows` method causes the table view to reload only the part of its contents that are needed, in this case the last item in the data source. Note that with this method, we can also specify in which section of the table the cell will be inserted.

Row re-ordering

Another useful feature of the `UITableView` class is that of re-ordering rows. To demonstrate this, add the following method overrides in the table source:

```
public override bool CanMoveRow (UITableView tableView, NSIndexPath indexPath){
   return true;
}
public override void MoveRow (UITableView tableView, NSIndexPath sourceIndexPath, NSIndexPath destinationIndexPath){
   string itemToMove = this.tableData[sourceIndexPath.Row];
   this.tableData.Remove (itemToMove);
   this.tableData.Insert (destinationIndexPath.Row, itemToMove);
}
```

Returning `true` in the `CanMoveRow` method enables re-ordering for all cells. This is indicated by a grip appearance icon displaying on the right side in each cell. When the user touches and drags the icon, the cell can be moved to another position. Inside the `MoveRow` method is where the actual re-ordering occurs. The only thing that needs to be done is to remove and re-insert the item in the data source in the desired index, using the `sourceIndexPath` and `destinationIndexPath` parameters.

See also

In this chapter:

- *Displaying data in a table*
- *Editing a table: deleting rows*

Table indexing

In this recipe, we will learn how to provide an index in a table, allowing the user to browse through the rows of a `UITableView` quicker.

Getting ready

Create a new project in MonoDevelop, and name it `TableIndexApp`. Add a `UITableViewController` as shown in the previous tasks in this chapter, and implement the `TableSource` class.

How to do it...

In the table source class, override and implement the following methods:

```
public override int NumberOfSections (UITableView tableView){
  return this.tableData.Count;
}
public override string TitleForHeader (UITableView tableView,
  int section){
  return Convert.ToString (this.tableData[section][0]);
}
public override string[] SectionIndexTitles (UITableView tableView){
  return this.tableData.Select
    (s => Convert.ToString (s[0])).Distinct ().ToArray ();
}
```

How it works...

The table source created in this task contains many different sections. For simplicity, each section contains one row. The `NumberOfSections` method returns the total number of sections the table will display.

Displaying Data

To set a title for each section, we must override the `TitleForHeader` method:

```
public override string TitleForHeader (UITableView tableView,
   int section){
   return Convert.ToString (this.tableData[section][0]);
}
```

This implementation returns the first letter of each string in the data source. To provide the index, we override the `SectionIndexTitles` method:

```
public override string[] SectionIndexTitles (UITableView tableView){
   return this.tableData.Select
      (s => Convert.ToString (s[0])).Distinct ().ToArray ();
}
```

Here, it returns the first letter of each item in the data source. The result of this project will be similar to the following:

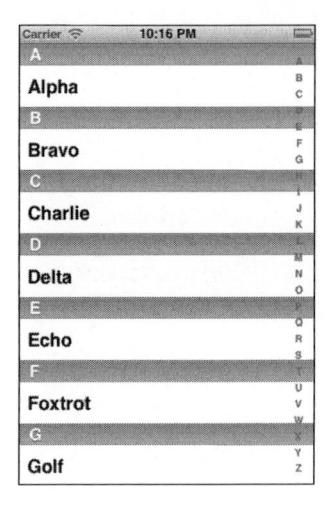

When the user touches somewhere on the index, the table view will automatically scroll to that specific section.

There's more...

Indexing should be applied on tables with a `Plain` style. Applying an index in tables with a `Grouped` style set is not advisable, because the index will not be easily distinguished.

A good example of a native iOS application with an index on a table can be found in the native `Contacts` application.

See also

In this chapter:

- *Displaying data in a table*
- *Searching through the data*

Searching through the data

In this recipe, we will learn how to provide search functionality for the content in a table view.

Getting ready

Create a new project in MonoDevelop, and name it `SearchTableApp`. Add a `UITableViewController`, and name it `TableController`.

How to do it...

1. Open the `TableController.xib` file in Interface Builder.
2. Add a **Search Bar** and **Search Display Controller** in the `UITableView`. Note that after this action, some outlets are created and connected automatically. We need most of them, so we leave them as they are and save the document.
3. Back in MonoDevelop, implement a class that will act as a delegate object for the search display controller:

```
private class SearchDelegate : UISearchDisplayDelegate{
  public SearchDelegate (TableController controller){
    this.parentController = controller;
  }
  private TableController parentController;
  public override bool ShouldReloadForSearchString (
    UISearchDisplayController controller, string forSearchString){
    this.parentController.filterDataList =
      this.parentController.tableData
    .Where (s => s.ToLower ().Contains
      (forSearchString.ToLower ()))
    .ToList ();
    this.parentController.filterDataList.Sort (delegate
      (string firstStr, string secondStr) {
      return firstStr.CompareTo (secondStr);
    });
    return true;
  }
}
```

Displaying Data

4. Override the `ViewDidLoad` method and assign the source and delegate objects in it:

   ```
   this.TableView.Source = new TableSource (this);
   this.SearchDisplayController.SearchResultsSource =
     new TableSource(this);
   this.SearchDisplayController.Delegate = new SearchDelegate(this);
   ```

5. You can find the complete code in the `SearchTableApp` project. The result will be the common iOS search bar above the table, similar to the following screenshot:

How it works...

The `UISearchDisplayController` class provides a convenient way of search through data. It contains a `UISearchBar` that accepts input from the user and a `UITableView` that is used to display the results. After we add a search controller in a view controller, we can access it through that controller's `SearchDisplayController` property. To trigger the results table, we must implement a `UISearchDisplayDelegate` and override its `ShouldReloadForSearchString`, which returns a boolean value:

   ```
   private class SearchDelegate : UISearchDisplayDelegate
   ```

Inside the `ShouldReloadForSearchString` method override, we search our data source saving the filtered results in a new data source, according to its `forSearchString` parameter:

   ```
   this.parentController.filterDataList =
     this.parentController.tableData
   .Where (s => s.ToLower ().Contains (forSearchString.ToLower ()))
   .ToList ();
   ```

We then sort the results alphabetically and return `true`, so that the search controller's table will reload its data:

   ```
   this.parentController.filterDataList.Sort (delegate(
     string firstStr, string secondStr) {
     return firstStr.CompareTo (secondStr);
   });
   return true;
   ```

The search controller's table view also needs a source object. In this example, we set it to the same object that we created for our table:

```
this.TableView.Source = new TableSource (this);
this.SearchDisplayController.SearchResultsSource =
  new TableSource(this);
```

Since we are using instances of the same object, we need to modify some things in it to display data according to which table calls it. So, for example, the RowsInSection method looks like the following:

```
public override int RowsInSection (UITableView tableview,
  int section){
  if (tableview.Equals (this.parentController.TableView)){
    return this.parentController.tableData.Count;
  } else{
    return this.parentController.filterDataList.Count;
  }
}
```

This way, we return the number of rows according to which table calls the method. Similarly, we need to set each cell's text label inside the GetCell method:

```
if (tableView.Equals (this.parentController.TableView)){
  cell.TextLabel.Text = this.parentController.tableData[rowIndex];
} else{
  cell.TextLabel.Text =
    this.parentController.filterDataList[rowIndex];
}
```

There's more...

When the user taps on the search bar, the keyboard appears, setting the search controller active. To de-activate it, we can hook on the search bar's SearchButtonClicked event. This event will get triggered when the user taps on the keyboard's **Search** button:

```
this.SearchDisplayController.SearchBar.SearchButtonClicked +=
  delegate {
    this.SearchDisplayController.SetActive(false, true);
  };
```

The SetActive method is what we can use to enable or disable the search controller.

Displaying Data

Providing search functionality to other controllers.

Although this example uses a `UISearchDisplayController` in a `UITableViewController`, it does not mean that it is the only way it can be used. We can use a search controller with whatever kind of `UIViewController` we want. The only extra thing we need to do in this case is set the search controller's `SearchContentsController` property to the view controller it belongs to. This is being taken care of automatically by Interface Builder when we add a `UISearchDisplayController` in a `UITableViewController`, but not with other controllers.

See also

In this chapter:

- *Displaying data in a table*
- *Table indexing*

Creating a simple web browser

In this recipe, we will discuss displaying online content with the `UIWebView` class.

Getting ready

Create a new project in MonoDevelop, and name it `WebBrowserApp`.

How to do it...

1. Open the `MainController.xib` file in Interface Builder, and add a `UIWebView` object on the main View.
2. Create and connect an outlet for it with the name `webView`.
3. Save the document.
4. Override the `ViewDidAppear` method in the `MainController` class:

   ```
   public override void ViewDidAppear (bool animated){
      NSUrl url = new NSUrl ("http://software.tavlikos.com");
      NSUrlRequest urlRequest = new NSUrlRequest (url);
      this.webView.LoadRequest (urlRequest);
   }
   ```

5. Compile and run the application on the simulator. Watch the website load on the screen!

How it works...

The `UIWebView` class is iOS SDK's web browser control. To load web content, we just have to call its `LoadRequest` method, which accepts a parameter of the type `NSUrlRequest`. The `NSUrlRequest` object contains the URL we want it to load:

```
NSUrl url = new NSUrl ("http://software.tavlikos.com");
```

There's more...

The `UIWebView` class contains some very useful events:

- `LoadStarted`: It is triggered when the control has started loading content
- `LoadFinished`: It is triggered when the content has finished loading successfully
- `LoadError`: It is triggered when loading of the content has failed

Scaling content

Another important feature of the `UIWebView` is the automatic scaling of content. It can be activated by setting its `ScalePageToFit` property to `true`.

See also

In this chapter:

- *Displaying local content*
- *Displaying formatted text*
- *Displaying documents*

Displaying local content

In this recipe, we will discuss displaying local HTML files.

Getting ready

Create a new project in MonoDevelop, and name it `LocalContentApp`.

How to do it...

1. Add a `UIWebView` on the main view of `MainController`, and save the document.
2. Add a new folder to the project, and name it `html_content`.

Displaying Data

3. Add your content to that folder through MonoDevelop. Don't forget to set each file's **Build Action** to **Content**.
4. Override the `ViewDidAppear` method in the `MainController` class, and enter the following code:

   ```
   NSUrl fileUrl = NSUrl.FromFilename (
       "./html_content/T-Shirts.html");
   NSUrlRequest urlRequest = new NSUrlRequest (fileUrl);
   this.webView.ScalesPageToFit = false;
   this.webView.LoadRequest (urlRequest);
   ```

5. Compile and run the application on the simulator.
6. View your HTML content displayed on the screen.
7. Zoom in to view the content larger, just like you would do for online content.

How it works...

The process of displaying local content is the same as displaying online content. The `NSUrl` class has a static method that creates an instance, based on a file path:

```
NSUrl fileUrl = NSUrl.FromFilename ("./html_content/T-Shirts.html");
```

There's more...

The `UIWebView` is a very powerful control. It can be used to display everything the Safari browser on iOS can. This includes HTML, plain text, images, and PDF documents.

Navigating through content

You can also navigate through the history of `UIWebView` with its `GoBack()` and `GoForward()` methods.

UIWebView supported files

The `UIWebView` control can be used to display other types of files as well. These file types are:

- **Excel (.xls)**
- **Keynote (.key.zip)**
- **Numbers (.numbers.zip)**
- **Pages (.pages.zip)**
- **PDF (.pdf)**
- **PowerPoint (.ppt)**

- Word (.doc)
- Rich Text Format (.rtf)
- Rich Text Format Directory (.rtfd.zip)
- Keynote '09 (.key)
- Numbers '09 (.numbers)
- Pages '09 (.pages)

See also

In this chapter:

- *Creating a simple web browser*
- *Displaying documents*

Displaying formatted text

In this chapter, we will learn how to use the `UIWebView` class to display formatted text.

Getting ready

In this task, we will work on the `LocalContentApp` project discussed previously. Open it in MonoDevelop.

How to do it...

1. Comment out the previous code in the `ViewDidAppear` method, and add the following:

   ```
   string htmlString = "<html><head></head><body>
     <span style=\"font-weight: bold;\">This</span> " +
     "<span style=\"text-decoration: underline;\">is</span>
     <span style=\"font-style: italic;\">some formatted</span> " +"
     <span style=\"font-weight: bold;
     text-decoration: underline;\">text!</span><br></body></html>";
   this.webView.LoadHtmlString (htmlString, null);
   ```

2. Compile and run the application on the simulator.
3. Watch how the HTML string is displayed.

How it works...

As discussed in *Chapter 2, User Interface: Views*, the `UITextView` can be used to display large blocks of text and edit it, but it cannot display formatted text. The `UIWebView` can do this by passing our HTML-formatted text as a parameter to the `LoadHtmlString` method:

```
this.webView.LoadHtmlString (htmlString, null);
```

The second parameter is of the type `NSUrl`. Since we have created our HTML string in-code and there are no external references to other files, we don't need it, and so we just pass `null`.

There's more...

If we would like to reference external files inside our HTML string, we should set the `NSUrl` parameter of `LoadHtmlString` to the path that contains the files, thus setting the base directory for the HTML. For example, consider the following HTML string, which references a file inside the `html_content` folder of the application bundle:

```
string htmlString =
  "<img style=\"width: 215px;\" src=\"tshirts_s.jpg\">";
```

If we were to pass it to the `LoadHtmlString` to display the image, we should have also set the `baseUrl` parameter:

```
this.webView.LoadHtmlString (htmlString, new NSUrl (
  "./html_content", true));
```

The `bool` parameter of the `NSUrl` constructor indicates that the URL string of the first parameter is a path to a directory and should be treated like one.

> Although the `UIWebView` can display a wide variety of content, it cannot be used to edit it.

Allowing specific links

The `UIWebView` also provides control on how links that the user taps on be treated. To do this, we can assign a handler to its `ShouldStartLoad` property. It accepts delegates of the type `UIWebLoaderControl`.

See also

In this chapter:

- *Creating a simple web browser*
- *Displaying local content*

Chapter 5

In this book:

Chapter 2, User Interface: Views:

- *Displaying and editing text*

Displaying documents

In this recipe, we will discuss how to easily display various documents of different formats with the `QLPreviewController` class.

Getting ready

Create a new project in MonoDevelop, and name it `DocumentPreviewApp`. Add a view with controller, and name it `MainController`.

How to do it...

1. Open the `MainController.xib` file in Interface Builder and add a `UIButton`.
2. Save the document.
3. Add a folder named `docs` to the project and put some document files in it. The project `DocumentPreviewApp` contains three different documents: a `PDF`, a `DOCX`, and an `XLSX`.
4. Enter the following `using` directive in the `MainController.cs` file:

   ```
   using MonoTouch.QuickLook;
   ```

5. Create the following nested class inside the `MainController` class:

   ```
   private class PreviewDataSource : QLPreviewControllerDataSource{
     public PreviewDataSource (List<PreviewItem> items){
       this.previewItems = items;
     }
     private List<PreviewItem> previewItems;
     public override int PreviewItemCount (
       QLPreviewController controller){
       return this.previewItems.Count;
     }
     public override QLPreviewItem GetPreviewItem (
       QLPreviewController controller, int index){
       return this.previewItems[index];
     }
   }
   ```

157

Displaying Data

6. Enter the following code in the `ViewDidLoad` override of the `MainController`:

```
this.previewItems = new List<PreviewItem>() {
  new PreviewItem("PDF", NSUrl.FromFilename("docs/pdfdoc.pdf")),
  new PreviewItem("DOCX", NSUrl.FromFilename("docs/text.docx")),
  new PreviewItem("XLSX",
    NSUrl.FromFilename("docs/spreadsheet.xlsx"))
};
this.previewController = new QLPreviewController();
this.previewController.DataSource = new
  PreviewDataSource(this.previewItems);
this.buttonPreviewDocs.TouchUpInside += delegate {
  this.PresentModalViewController(this.previewController, true);
};
```

How it works...

The `QLPreviewController` class provides a very convenient way of displaying multiple document formats at once. It is a controller that can be displayed either by pushing it in a navigation controller stack, or by presenting it modally.

To define the documents that we want it to display, we have to create a `QLPreviewControllerDataSource` class and assign it to its `DataSource` property:

```
private class PreviewDataSource : QLPreviewControllerDataSource
```

The `QLPreviewControllerDataSource` contains two methods we need to override: `PreviewItemCount`, which returns the number of items the controller has to display, and `GetPreviewItem`, which returns the actual item. This item is of the type `QLPreviewItem`, and we have to implement a method that inherits it:

```
private class PreviewItem : QLPreviewItem
```

In this class, we have to override two properties, both of which represent the information of the item to be previewed. These are `ItemTitle` and `ItemUrl`.

When the controller calls the `PreviewItemCount` method and it returns a number more than 1, it adds a `UIToolbar` with two arrow buttons that allows the user to navigate through the documents. When the `GetPreviewItem` method is called, it sets the current title to its `ItemTitle` property and loads the document according to the `ItemUrl` property. If the button is tapped in this application, the result will be similar to the following:

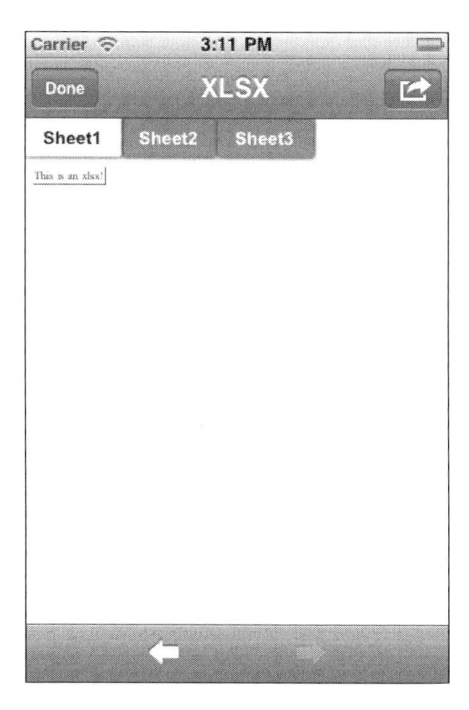

This screenshot displays the `QLPreviewController` after navigating to the last document that is a file of the type `XLSX`.

There's more...

The controller contains a system-default **Done** button on its navigation bar. If the button is tapped, the controller is automatically dismissed. We can hook on its `WillDismiss` and/or `DidDismiss` events to provide extra behavior.

See also

In this chapter:

- *Displaying local content*
- *Displaying formatted text*

6
Web Services

In this chapter, we will cover:

- Consuming web services
- Invoking web services
- Consuming WCF services
- Reading JSON data

Introduction

Providing online information to the user is a crucial part of mobile development. In this chapter, we will discuss developing applications that communicate with web services to provide information. We will see how to consume and invoke web services, based on SOAP. We will also discuss how to use WCF web services and how to parse the popular JSON data format from a web server.

All examples in this chapter use the xsp lightweight web server that ships with the Mono Framework, so there is no need to have a live web service up and running online to make use of the provided code.

Consuming web services

In this recipe, we will learn how to use a SOAP web service in a MonoTouch project.

Getting ready

Create a new project in MonoDevelop, and name it `WebServiceApp`. This chapter's code contains a web service project, named `MTWebService`. This is the web service that will be used.

Web Services

How to do it...

1. To use the `MTWebService` web service, we need a web server. Mono Framework provides the xsp lightweight web server for testing purposes.

2. Open a terminal and type the following command to get to the web service's directory, replacing `<code_directory>` with the path the downloaded code is in:

   `cd <code_directory>/CH06_code/MTWebService/MTWebService`

3. Run the xsp web server by typing `xsp4` in the prompt. You will see an output similar to the following:

   ```
   xsp4
   Listening on address: 0.0.0.0
   Root directory: /Users/dtavlikos/projects/CH06_code/MTWebService/MTWebService
   Listening on port: 8080 (non-secure)
   Hit Return to stop the server.
   ```

   The web server is up and running.

4. Now, we need to add a web reference to the web service in the project. Right-click on the project in the **Solution** pad and select **Add | Add Web Reference**.

5. In the dialog that will be shown, add the information provided in the following screenshot:

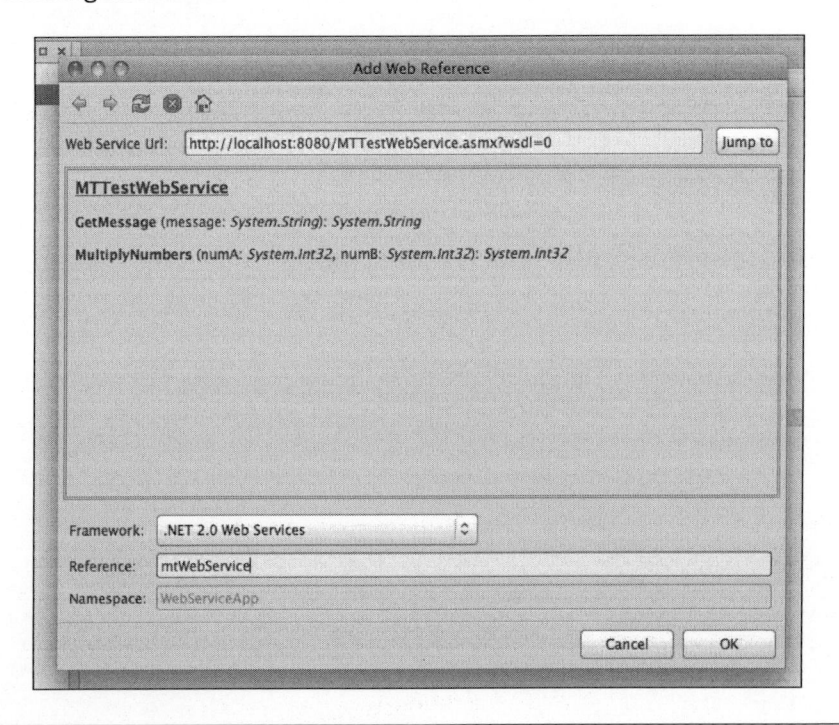

6. After adding the web reference to the **MTTestWebService** web service, add a button and a label on the view of `MainController`. Override the `ViewDidLoad` method of the `MainController` class, and enter the following code in it:

   ```
   this.buttonFetchData.TouchUpInside += delegate {
     using (MTTestWebService webService = new MTTestWebService()){
       this.lblMessage.Text = webService.GetMessage ("Hello
       Web Service!");
     }
   } ;
   ```

7. Finally, provide a `using` directive for our web service's namespace:

   `using WebServiceApp.mtWebService;`

8. Compile and run the application on the simulator.
9. Tap the button to invoke the web service, and notice the output message in the label.

How it works...

MonoTouch can consume web services just like a .NET desktop application. The `xsp` lightweight web server is installed by default when installing the Mono Framework, which is a requirement for the MonoTouch installation. When running the `xsp4` command in the terminal without any parameters, it sets its base directory to the current directory by default and starts listening on the `8080` port. If the web server is started, the web service description can be viewed by entering `http://localhost:8080/MTTestWebService.asmx` in a browser:

Web Services

The link that needs to be entered in the **Web Service Url** field of the web reference dialog can be found by clicking on the **Service Description** link in the service description page, and then by clicking on the **Download** link above the web service's WSDL description.

We then set the **Framework** value to **.NET 2.0 Web Services**, and provide a **Reference** name, which will reflect the namespace of the web reference. To make use of the web service within our code, we instantiate it, and then just call the method we are interested in:

```
this.lblMessage.Text = webService.GetMessage ("Hello Web Service!");
```

There's more...

Apart from using a local hosted web service, there are also numerous sample web services on the Internet. A simple search will yield many results.

XSP shutdown

To shutdown the `xsp` web server, just press the *return* key in the terminal where it was executed from.

See also

In this chapter:

- *Invoking web services*
- *Consuming WCF services*

Invoking web services

In this recipe, we will discuss how to properly use web services with MonoTouch.

Getting ready

Create a new project in MonoDevelop, and name it `WebServiceApp2`. Start the `xsp` web server, and add a web reference in the project to the `TTestWebService` web service, as described in the previous task.

How to do it...

1. Add a label and a button on the view of `MainController`.
2. In the `MainController` class in MonoDevelop, override the `ViewDidLoad` method, and enter the following code in it:

Chapter 6

```
    this.buttonInvoke.TouchUpInside += delegate {
      int a = 5;
      int b = 12;
      MTTestWebService webService = new MTTestWebService ();
      webService.MultiplyNumbersCompleted +=
        MultiplyNumbers_CompletedHandler;
      webService.MultiplyNumbersAsync (a, b);
      UIApplication.SharedApplication.
        NetworkActivityIndicatorVisible = true;
      this.lblMessage.Text = String.Format (
        "Multiplying {0} by {1}", a, b);
    } ;
```

3. Finally, add the following method:

```
    private void MultiplyNumbers_CompletedHandler (
      object sender, MultiplyNumbersCompletedEventArgs args){
      UIApplication.SharedApplication.
        NetworkActivityIndicatorVisible = false;
      this.InvokeOnMainThread (delegate {
        this.lblMessage.Text = String.Format (
          "Multiplication result: {0}", args.Result);
      } );
    }
```

4. Compile and run the application on the simulator.
5. Tap on the button and see the result from the web service being displayed on the label.

How it works...

As you may already have noticed, the application from the previous task froze while it was communicating with the web service, until it received the result. In this task, we use the asynchronous invocation so that the user interface will not freeze while the application is contacting the web service.

We want to be notified when our application receives a response from the web service, but we also need its result. Prior to calling the web method that we are interested in, we subscribe to the web service object's `MultiplyNumbersCompleted` event, as the highlighted code shows in the `ViewDidLoad` override. This event is part of the class that was created by MonoDevelop when we added the web reference, and every web method has a corresponding event. We then call the web method asynchronously by accessing the `MultiplyNumbersAsync` method. This call returns instantly. The next call is interesting:

```
    UIApplication.SharedApplication.NetworkActivityIndicatorVisible =
      true;
```

Web Services

Through the `UIApplication.SharedApplication` static property, we have access to some application-wide components, such as the status bar that is displayed on the screen. It is recommended to provide some sort of information to the user when a process is pending. The status bar contains an activity indicator, which is what is displayed when the device connects to the Internet in native iOS applications. Hence, the user is accustomed to this control and knows that when it is displayed, the device connects to receive data. By setting the `NetworkActivityIndicatorVisible` property to `true`, the network indicator is activated and displayed.

When a call to a web method is completed, the appropriate event is triggered. Inside the `MultiplyNumbers_CompletedHandler` method, we first make sure to hide the network indicator to inform the user that the application is no longer connected. We can access the result of the web method through the `MultiplyNumbersCompletedEventArgs.Result` property.

In this example, we want to display the result in the label directly, from within our handler. Because the web method was asynchronously called, the handler will most likely be executed on a different thread than the main thread. So, we wrap the assignment of the result to the label to an anonymous method and execute it on the main thread, as shown in the highlighted code of the handler implementation.

There's more...

The web service object contains a more common set of asynchronous invocation that we can use. It follows the `BeginInvoke` – `EndInvoke` pattern, with the methods renamed according to the web method of the service. In this case, these methods are named `BeginMultiplyNumbers` and `EndMultiplyNumbers`.

Error handling

The `MultiplyNumbersCompletedEventArgs` class also contains an `Error` property. It returns a value of the type `System.Exception`, and if something went wrong, for example, due to lack of network connection, it will contain the appropriate information. If no error occurred, the `Error` property will return `null`. It is advisable to always check this property first, before proceeding to retrieving the result of the web method:

```
if (null != args.Error) {
   // Something went wrong, handle appropriately.
}
```

See also

In this chapter:

- *Consuming WCF services*

Chapter 6

Consuming WCF services

In this recipe, we will learn how to consume WCF services with MonoTouch.

Getting ready

For this project, we will need a running WCF service. A WCF service can be found in the code download of this chapter. To start the service, open a terminal and go to the project's directory. Start the service by running the `start_wcfservice.sh` shell script:

```
cd <code_directory>/CH06_code/
  WcfService/WcfService
```

```
./start_wcfservice.sh
```

After the service is started, create a new project in MonoDevelop, and name it `WcfServiceApp`.

How to do it...

1. Add the references to the `System.Runtime.Serialization` and `System.ServiceModel` to the project and their corresponding `using` directives in the `MainController.cs` file.

2. MonoTouch does not yet provide full support for WCF services. To generate a proxy for the client, we will need to use the `slsvcutil` tool on a Windows machine. Run the following command in the terminal under Windows:

   ```
   "c:\Program Files\Microsoft SDKs\Silverlight\v3.0\Tools\slsvcutil
   /noconfig http://192.168.1.18:8080/WcfService.svc?wsdl"
   ```

   This command will produce a C# source file named `service.cs`. Add this file to the MonoDevelop project.

3. Add a label and a button on the view of `MainController`. Override the `ViewDidLoad` method of the `MainController` class, and enter the following code in it:

   ```
   this.buttonFetchData.TouchUpInside += delegate(
     object sender, EventArgs e) {
   WcfTestServiceClient client = new WcfTestServiceClient (
     new BasicHttpBinding (), new EndpointAddress (
     "http://192.168.1.18:8080/WcfTestService.svc"));
   client.GetBookInfoCompleted +=
     WcfTestServiceClient_GetBookInfoCompleted;
   client.GetBookInfoAsync ();
   UIApplication.SharedApplication.
     NetworkActivityIndicatorVisible = true;
   } ;
   ```

Web Services

4. Finally, add the following event handler:

```
private void WcfTestServiceClient_GetBookInfoCompleted (
  object sender, GetBookInfoCompletedEventArgs e){
  this.InvokeOnMainThread (delegate {
    UIApplication.SharedApplication.
      NetworkActivityIndicatorVisible = false;
    this.labelResult.Text = String.Format ("Book title:
      {0}\nAuthor: {1}", e.Result.Title, e.Result.Name);
  } );
}
```

5. Compile and run the application on the simulator.
6. Tap on the button and watch the data returned from the service populate in the label.

How it works...

MonoTouch relies on Mono Framework's support on WCF services, which is not complete. However, the fact alone that WCF services can be used in iOS applications makes MonoTouch more appealing to .NET developers.

For instance, there is no tool to create the client proxy on a Mac, so we will have to have access to a Windows machine to do this, with the **Silverlight Service Model Proxy Generation Tool** (**slsvcutil.exe**). The source file this tool generates allows us to consume the WCF service in our project. It basically does what MonoDevelop does automatically when we add a web reference to an ASMX web service, like in the two previous tasks.

> It is important to use the **Silverlight version 3.0** `slsvcutil` to create the client proxy.

Apart from Mono Framework's support, there is another limitation: dynamic code generation is not allowed on iOS. This makes any code that relies on the `System.Reflection.Emit` namespace unusable. In fact, the `System.Reflection.Emit` namespace is not available at all in MonoTouch.

After copying the produced file on the Mac, we add it to the project and we are ready to use the WCF service. The previous highlighted code shows how to instantiate the service object. Note that the default constructor of the service object cannot be used, since MonoTouch does not support the `System.Configuration` namespace.

The actual communication occurs by calling the method's asynchronous implementation, after setting a handler to its corresponding completion event. Note that in this case, there is no alternative of using synchronous invocations, or `BeginInvoke` - `EndInvoke` pattern:

```
client.GetBookInfoCompleted +=
  WcfTestServiceClient_GetBookInfoCompleted;
client.GetBookInfoAsync ();
```

Chapter 6

The result returned from the service can be retrieved through the specified `EventArgs` derivative's `Result` property:

```
this.labelResult.Text = String.Format (
   "Book title: {0}\nAuthor: {1}", e.Result.Title, e.Result.Name);
```

There's more...

When debugging a project that consumes WCF services, remember to set the address of the machine the service is running on, instead of `localhost` or `127.0.0.1`. That is because when we run the application on the device, the application will fail to connect to the service.

More information on MonoDevelop's WCF support

There is an option of adding a WCF web reference through MonoDevelop in the **Add Web References** window shown in the *Consuming Web Services* recipe. However, it is not yet complete.

WCF service creation

The object returned from the `WcfService` service and the actual service itself were created completely on a Mac with MonoDevelop. Since there is no WCF project template, the **Empty Project** template was used.

See also

In this chapter:

- *Consuming web services*

Reading JSON data

In this recipe, we will learn how to read **JavaScript Object Notation** (**JSON**) data.

Getting ready

Create a new project in MonoDevelop, and name it `JsonDataApp`. Add a button and a label on the view of the `MainController`.

169

Web Services

How to do it...

1. Add a reference to the project to the `System.Json` assembly.
2. Add the following `using` directives in the `MainController.cs` file:

   ```
   using System.Json;
   using System.Net;
   using System.IO;
   ```

3. Enter the following method:

   ```
   private JsonValue GetJsonObject (){
     string responseString = string.Empty;
     Uri uri = new Uri ("http://192.168.1.18:8080/mtjson.txt");
     HttpWebRequest request = new HttpWebRequest (uri);
     request.Method = "GET";
     HttpWebResponse response =
       request.GetResponse () as HttpWebResponse;
     using (StreamReader sr =
       new StreamReader(response.GetResponseStream())) {
       responseString = sr.ReadToEnd ();
     }
     response.Close ();
     return JsonValue.Parse (responseString);
   }
   ```

4. Attach a handler to the button's `TouchUpInside` event, and enter the following code in it:

   ```
   JsonValue json = this.GetJsonObject ();
   this.labelResponse.Text = String.Format ("File name: {0}\n
     Description: {1}", json ["filename"], json ["description"]);
   ```

5. Finally, run the `xsp` server in the project's directory. The file "`mtjson.txt`" contains data in JSON format.

How it works...

JSON is a specific text format that is human-readable and easy to implement. Many popular websites use this format to distribute data. Its main advantage is that it is language-independent. The structure of JSON is based on name/value pairs and arrays. The JSON data object used in this task is fairly simple:

```
{
  "filename":"mtjson.txt",
  "description":"a sample json object"
}
```

To read the data from the web server, we simply create an `HttpWebRequest` object, setting its `Method` property to `HTTP GET`:

```
HttpWebRequest request = new HttpWebRequest (uri);
request.Method = "GET";
```

We then need to get the response from the server. We do this by retrieving the request's response object and read the data from its underlying stream with a `StreamReader`:

```
HttpWebResponse response = request.GetResponse () as HttpWebResponse;
using (StreamReader sr =
  new StreamReader(response.GetResponseStream())) {
  responseString = sr.ReadToEnd ();
}
```

The `responseString` variable now contains the raw JSON data shown previously. For parsing JSON data, MonoTouch provides the `JsonValue` class. To create a `JsonValue` object, we use its `Parse` static method, passing it as the string containing the JSON data:

```
return JsonValue.Parse (responseString);
```

To access the data that the `JsonValue` object has parsed, we use indexers:

```
this.labelResponse.Text = String.Format ("File name:
  {0}\nDescription: {1}", json ["filename"], json ["description"]);
```

There's more...

If a name that does not exist in the JSON object is passed, an exception will occur. If the names of the JSON object are not known, we can use integers to retrieve the data:

```
//json[0], json[1] etc...
```

The `JsonValue` class inherits from the `IEnumerable` interface.

Serialization

The `System.Json` namespace provides objects for simple parsing of JSON data. It does not provide JSON serialization functionality. We can, however, create a `JsonObject` from a set of `KeyValuePair<string, JsonValue>` objects. To create the previous JSON object, we would write something like the following:

```
JsonObject obj = new JsonObject (new KeyValuePair<string, JsonValue>
  ("filename", JsonValue.Parse ("\"mtjson.txt\"")),
  new KeyValuePair<string, JsonValue>("description",
  JsonValue.Parse("\"a sample json object\"")));
```

Web Services

See also

In this chapter:

- *Consuming web services*

7
Multimedia Resources

In this chapter, we will cover:

- Selecting images and videos
- Capturing media with the camera
- Playing video
- Playing music and sounds
- Recording with the microphone
- Managing multiple album items directly

Introduction

One of the most important features of today's smartphones and tablets is their ability to capture and manage multimedia resources. Be it photos, videos, or audio, an application targeted at these devices that can handle multimedia effectively is very important.

In this chapter, we will learn how to manage media stored on the device. We will also see how to use the device's multimedia capturing devices (camera and microphone) to capture content and create an application that will provide a rich experience to the user.

More specifically, we will discuss:

- `UIImagePickerController`: This is a controller that not only provides access, through a user interface, to the saved photos and videos on the device, but also a camera interface for capturing
- `MPMoviePlayerController`: This is a controller that allows us to play and stream video files
- `MPMediaPickerController`: This is the default user interface for accessing the saved content, managed by the native iPod application

Multimedia Resources

- `MPMusicPlayerController`: This is the object responsible for playing the iPod content
- `AVAudioPlayer`: This is the class that allows us to play sound files
- `AVAudioRecorder`: This is the class that allows us to use the microphone to record audio
- `ALAssetsLibrary`: This is the class that provides access to the device's available assets and their metadata

Selecting images and videos

In this recipe, we will learn how to provide the user with the ability to import images and videos from the device album.

Getting ready

Create a new project in MonoDevelop, and name it `ImagePickerApp`.

How to do it...

1. Add a `UIImageView` and a `UIButton` on the main view of `MainController`.
2. Override the `ViewDidLoad` method of the `MainController` class, and enter the following code in it:

   ```
   this.imagePicker = new UIImagePickerController();
   this.imagePicker.FinishedPickingMedia +=
     this.ImagePicker_FinishedPickingMedia;
   this.imagePicker.Canceled += this.ImagePicker_Cancelled;
   this.imagePicker.SourceType =
     UIImagePickerControllerSourceType.PhotoLibrary;
   this.buttonChoose.TouchUpInside += delegate {
     this.PresentModalViewController(this.imagePicker, true);
   };
   ```

3. Implement the handler methods for the `FinishedPickingMedia` and `Canceled` events:

   ```
   private void ImagePicker_FinishedPickingMedia (object sender,
     UIImagePickerMediaPickedEventArgs e) {
     UIImage pickedImage =
       e.Info[UIImagePickerController.OriginalImage] as UIImage;
     this.imageView.Image = pickedImage;
     this.imagePicker.DismissModalViewControllerAnimated(true);
   }
   ```

```
private void ImagePicker_Cancelled (object sender, EventArgs e){
   this.imagePicker.DismissModalViewControllerAnimated(true);
}
```

4. Compile and run the application on the simulator.
5. Tap on the button to present the image picker, and select an image by tapping on its thumbnail. The image will be displayed in the image view. The `UIImagePickerController` is displayed in the following screenshot:

Multimedia Resources

How it works...

The `UIImagePickerController` is a special view controller that iOS provides for selecting images and videos that are saved on the device album, or from the camera.

> By default, the iOS simulator does not have images stored in its album. To add images to the simulator, uncomment the method `AddImagesToAlbum` of the downloaded project source code and call it once, passing as a parameter the physical path on your computer that contains images.

After initializing the image picker object, we need to subscribe to its `FinishedPickingMedia` event, which provides us with the media the user has selected. In the handler we assign to it, we get the selected image:

```
UIImage pickedImage = e.Info[UIImagePickerController.OriginalImage]
    as UIImage;
```

The `Info` property returns an `NSDictionary` object that contains various information about the picked media. We retrieve the image passing the constant `UIImagePickerController.OriginalImage` as a key. Because the values of the dictionary are of the type `NSObject`, we cast the return value to a `UIImage`. After we assign the image to the `UIImageView` to be displayed, we dismiss the controller:

```
this.imagePicker.DismissModalViewControllerAnimated(true);
```

The `Canceled` event is triggered when the user taps on the controller's **Cancel** button. We must subscribe to it to dismiss the controller, because it will not be dismissed automatically when the user taps on the **Cancel** button.

There's more...

We can define the source of images/videos the image picker will read from, through its `SourceType` property. In this example, we use `UIImagePickerController.PhotoLibrary` because the simulator does not support the camera hardware.

Picking videos

The `UIImagePickerController` displays only images by default. To support videos, its `MediaType` property must be set. It accepts a `string[]`, with the specified media names:

```
this.imagePicker.MediaTypes = new string[] { "public.image",
    "public.movie" };
```

To determine the media type the user has picked, we check the `MediaType` key of the dictionary in the `FinishedPickingMedia` handler. If it is a video, we get its URL with the `MediaUrl` key:

```
if (e.Info[UIImagePickerController.MediaType].ToString() ==
  "public.movie"){
  NSUrl mediaUrl = e.Info[UIImagePickerController.MediaURL] as NSUrl;
  // Do something useful with the media url.
}
```

See also

In this chapter:

- *Capturing media with the camera*
- *Managing album items directly*

Capturing media with the camera

In this recipe, we will learn how to use the device camera for capturing media.

Getting ready

Open the project `ImagePickerApp`, discussed in the previous task.

> The camera functionality is not available on iOS simulator. This example can only run on the device. Refer to *Chapter 14, Deploying* for More Information.

How to do it...

1. Inside the `ViewDidLoad` method, replace the following line:

   ```
   this.imagePicker.SourceType =
     UIImagePickerControllerSourceType.PhotoLibrary;
   ```

   with this code block:

   ```
   if (UIImagePickerController.IsSourceTypeAvailable(
     UIImagePickerControllerSourceType.Camera)){
     this.imagePicker.SourceType =
       UIImagePickerControllerSourceType.Camera;
   } else{
     this.imagePicker.SourceType =
       UIImagePickerControllerSourceType.PhotoLibrary;
   }
   ```

Multimedia Resources

2. In the `FinishedPickingMedia` handler, add the following code before the dismissal of the image picker:

   ```
   pickedImage.SaveToPhotosAlbum(delegate(
     UIImage image, NSError error) {
     if (null != error){
       Console.WriteLine("Image not saved! Message: {0}",
         error.LocalizedDescription);
     }
   } );
   ```

3. Compile and run the application on the device.
4. Tap the button to open the camera and take a picture. The picture will be saved to the device album.

How it works...

Before presenting the camera viewfinder, we have to make sure that the device the application is running on actually has the appropriate hardware. We do this by calling the static `IsSourceTypeAvailable` method of the `UIImagePickerController` class:

```
if (UIImagePickerController.IsSourceTypeAvailable(
  UIImagePickerControllerSourceType.Camera))
```

If it returns `true`, we set the source type to `Camera`:

```
this.imagePicker.SourceType =
  UIImagePickerControllerSourceType.Camera;
```

This will cause the image picker controller to start the camera device instead of loading the device albums.

When the user takes a photo (or video), it is not automatically saved on the device. To save it, we use the `SaveToPhotosAlbum` method of the `UIImage` class. This method accepts a delegate of type `UIImage.SaveStatus`, which will report an error if something goes wrong:

```
if (null != error){
  Console.WriteLine("Image not saved! Message: {0}",
    error.LocalizedDescription);
}
```

There's more...

The camera view can also be customized. To disable the default camera controls, set the `ShowsCameraControls` property to `false`. Then, pass a custom view with the controls you want to the `CameraOverlayView` property. To trigger the shutter of the camera, call the `TakePicture` method.

Image editing

The camera supports a simple editing function, after capturing an image. This editing function allows the user to select a specific part of the image and even zoom to a specific area. To present the editing controls, set the `AllowsEditing` property to `true`. The edited image can be retrieved from the dictionary in the `FinishedPickingMedia` handler, passing the `UIImagePickerController.EditedImage` key. The editing interface is shown in the following screenshot:

See also

In this chapter:

- *Selecting images and videos*

Multimedia Resources

Playing video

In this recipe, we will learn how to display a video player interface and play video files.

Getting ready

Create a new project in MonoDevelop and name it `PlayVideoApp`.

How to do it...

1. Add a button on the main view of `MainController`.
2. Add a video file to the project, and set its **Build Action** to **Content**.
3. Enter the following `using` directive in the `MainController.cs` file:

   ```
   using MonoTouch.MediaPlayer;
   ```

4. Override the `ViewDidLoad` method of the `MainController` class, and enter the following code:

   ```
   this.moviePlayer = new MPMoviePlayerController(
     new NSUrl("videos/video.mov"));
   this.moviePlayer.View.Frame = this.View.Bounds;
   this.View.AddSubview(this.moviePlayer.View);
   this.playbackStateChanged =
     NSNotificationCenter.DefaultCenter.AddObserver(
     MPMoviePlayerController.PlaybackStateDidChangeNotification,
     this.MoviePlayer_PlaybackStateChanged);
   this.finishedPlaying =
     NSNotificationCenter.DefaultCenter.AddObserver(
     MPMoviePlayerController.PlaybackDidFinishNotification,
     this.MoviePlayer_FinishedPlayback);
   this.buttonPlay.TouchUpInside += delegate {
     this.moviePlayer.Play();
   };
   ```

5. Enter the following methods in the `MainController` class:

   ```
   private void MoviePlayer_PlaybackStateChanged(NSNotification ntf){
     Console.WriteLine("Movie player load state changed: {0}",
       this.moviePlayer.PlaybackState);
   }
   private void MoviePlayer_FinishedPlayback(NSNotification ntf){
     Console.WriteLine("Movie player finished playing.");
   }
   ```

6. Compile and run the application on the simulator.

Chapter 7

7. Tap on the button and the video will load and start playing. Watch the messages displayed in the **Application Output** in MonoDevelop.

How it works...

The `MPMoviePlayerController` plays video files stored locally or streamed from the network. We initialize it with the constructor that accepts an `NSUrl` parameter:

```
this.moviePlayer = new MPMoviePlayerController(
    new NSUrl("videos/video.mov"));
```

The `NSUrl` object maps to the local file we have added to the project.

After creating the instance, we define a frame for its view and add it to our view:

```
this.moviePlayer.View.Frame = this.View.Bounds;
this.View.AddSubview(this.moviePlayer.View);
```

The highlighted code adds observers to the default notification center, so that we will be notified when the state of the playback changes or has finished. Then, we call its `Play` method and the view of the `MPMoviePlayerController` is displayed, and the video starts playing.

Inside the `MoviePlayer_PlaybackStateChanged` method, we output the `PlaybackState` property:

```
Console.WriteLine("Movie player load state changed: {0}", this.
moviePlayer.PlaybackState);
```

This property informs us of the status of the playback, such as `Paused`, `Playing`, `SeekingForward`, `SeekingBackward`, and so on.

There's more...

Apart from the ones used in this example, we can add observers for more notifications of an `MPMoviePlayerController`, some of which are:

- `DidEnterFullscreenNotification`: This notifies that the user has tapped the full-screen control, and the controller has entered `fullscreen` mode.
- `DidExitFullscreenNotification`: This notifies that the controller has left `fullscreen` mode.
- `DurationAvailableNotification`: This notifies that the controller has received information on the duration of the video.
- `LoadStateDidChangeNotification`: This notification is useful for network playback and is triggered when the controller has finished preloading the media in the buffer.

Multimedia Resources

- `NaturalSizeAvailableNotification`: This notification is triggered when the dimensions of the movie frame are made available. The size can be retrieved through the player's `NaturalSize` property.
- `NowPlayingMovieDidChangeNotification`: This notification is triggered when the video content of the player has changed. The current content is available through its `ContentUrl` property.

Wireless streaming

Starting with iOS version 4.3, the `MPMoviePlayerController` can be used to stream video to Apple's AirPlay-enabled devices. To enable it, set its `AllowsAirPlay` property to `true`. When the `MPMoviePlayerController` is displayed, it will present an interface that will allow the user to select the devices it detects.

See also

In this chapter:

- *Playing music and sounds*

Playing music and sounds

In this recipe, we will learn how to play simple audio files and songs stored on the device.

Getting ready

Create a new project in MonoDevelop, and name it `PlayMusicApp`.

> This example will not work on the simulator. You will also need at least one song stored on the device.

How to do it...

1. Add three buttons on the view of `MainController`.
2. Add the following `using` directive in the `MainController.cs` file:
   ```
   using MonoTouch.MediaPlayer;
   ```
3. Add two fields in the class:
   ```
   private MPMusicPlayerController musicPlayerController;
   private MPMediaPickerController mediaPicker;
   ```

4. Override the `ViewDidLoad` method of the `MainController` class, and enter the following code:

   ```
   this.mediaPicker =
     new MPMediaPickerController(MPMediaType.Music);
   this.mediaPicker.ItemsPicked += MediaPicker_ItemsPicked;
   this.mediaPicker.DidCancel += MediaPicker_DidCancel;
   this.musicPlayerController =
     MPMusicPlayerController.ApplicationMusicPlayer;
   this.buttonSelectSongs.TouchUpInside += delegate {
     this.PresentModalViewController(this.mediaPicker, true);
   };
   this.buttonPlay.TouchUpInside += delegate {
     this.musicPlayerController.Play();
   };
   this.buttonStop.TouchUpInside += delegate {
     this.musicPlayerController.Stop();
   };
   ```

5. Add the following methods:

   ```
   private void MediaPicker_ItemsPicked (
     object sender, ItemsPickedEventArgs e){
     this.musicPlayerController.SetQueue(e.MediaItemCollection);
     this.DismissModalViewControllerAnimated(true);
   }
   private void MediaPicker_DidCancel (object sender, EventArgs e){
     this.mediaPicker.DismissModalViewControllerAnimated(true);
   }
   ```

6. Compile and run the application on the device.
7. Tap the **Select songs** button, and select one or more songs.

How it works...

The `MPMediaPickerController` provides the same user interface as the native iPod application. The `MPMusicPlayerController` is responsible for playing the songs stored on the device.

We first initialize the media picker, passing the type of media we want it to look for in its constructor:

```
this.mediaPicker =
  new MPMediaPickerController(MPMediaType.Music);
```

Multimedia Resources

After that, we subscribe to its `ItemsPicked` and `DidCancel` events so that we can capture feedback from the user:

```
this.mediaPicker.ItemsPicked += MediaPicker_ItemsPicked;
this.mediaPicker.DidCancel += MediaPicker_DidCancel;
```

The highlighted code shows how to initialize the music player object. The option demonstrated here, `MPMusicPlayerController.ApplicationMusicPlayer`, creates an instance that is specific only to the application. The other option available, `MPMusicPlayerController.iPodMusicPlayer`, creates an instance that allows media to be played even if the application is in the background, similar to the iPod application.

In the `MediaPicker_ItemsPicked` handler, we set the songs that were picked by the user to the music player, through its `SetQueue` method:

```
this.musicPlayerController.SetQueue(e.MediaItemCollection);
```

After that, we dismiss the modal media picker controller. Playing and stopping songs is achieved through the `Play()` and `Stop()` methods respectively of `MPMusicPlayerController`.

There's more...

The `MPMusicPlayerController` holds information on the currently playing item. This information can be accessed through its `NowPlayingItem` property. It is of the type `MPMediaItem` and holds various types of information of the currently playing media. The following example gets the title of the song that is being played:

```
Console.WriteLine(this.musicPlayerController
    .NowPlayingItem.ValueForProperty(MPMediaItem.TitleProperty));
```

Playing sound files

The `MPMusicPlayerController` is an object that is specifically designed to manage and play items and playlists stored on the device's iPod library.

For playing simple sound files, MonoTouch provides another wrapper to iOS' class, `AVAudioPlayer`. The following is an example of its most simple usage:

```
using MonoTouch.AVFoundation;
//...
AVAudioPlayer audioPlayer = AVAudioPlayer.FromUrl(
    new NSUrl("path/to/sound file"));
audioPlayer.Play();
```

See also

In this chapter:

- *Playing video*

Recording with the microphone

In this recipe, we will learn how to use the device's microphone to record sounds.

Getting ready

Create a new project in MonoDevelop, and name it `RecordSoundApp`.

> This example will not work on the simulator.

How to do it...

1. Add two buttons on the view of `MainController`.
2. Enter the following `using` directives in the `MainController.cs` file:

   ```
   using System.IO;
   using MonoTouch.AVFoundation;
   using MonoTouch.AudioToolbox;
   ```

3. Override the `ViewDidLoad` method, and add the following code in it:

   ```
   string soundFile = Path.Combine(Environment.GetFolderPath(
     Environment.SpecialFolder.Personal), "sound.wav");
   NSUrl soundFileUrl = new NSUrl(soundFile);
   NSDictionary recordingSettings = NSDictionary.FromObjectAndKey(
     AVAudioSettings.AVFormatIDKey, NSNumber.FromInt32((int)
     AudioFileType.WAVE));
   NSError error = null;
   this.audioRecorder = AVAudioRecorder.ToUrl(
     soundFileUrl, recordingSettings, out error);
   this.buttonStart.TouchUpInside += delegate {
     this.audioRecorder.Record();
   } ;
   this.buttonStop.TouchUpInside += delegate {
     this.audioRecorder.Stop();
     AVAudioPlayer player = AVAudioPlayer.FromUrl(soundFileUrl);
     player.Play();
   } ;
   ```

Multimedia Resources

4. Compile and run the application on the device.
5. Tap the **Start recording** button to start recording audio, for example, say something to record your voice.
6. Tap the **Stop recording** button to stop recording and listen to the playback.

How it works...

The `AVAudioRecorder` class provides the recording functionality. It does this by streaming the captured audio directly to the filesystem. To initialize an instance of `AVAudioRecorder`, we use its static `ToUrl` method:

```
this.audioRecorder = AVAudioRecorder.ToUrl(
   soundFileUrl, recordingSettings, out error);
```

If the file that corresponds to the `NSUrl` variable already exists, it will be overwritten.

The `recordingSettings` variable is of type `NSDictionary` and contains the settings for the output sound file. We must provide at least some minimal settings to the `AVAudioRecorder` upon initialization. Here, we set the sound format to plain wav:

```
NSDictionary recordingSettings = NSDictionary.FromObjectAndKey(
   AVAudioSettings.AVFormatIDKey, NSNumber
   .FromInt32((int)AudioFileType.WAVE));
```

To instruct the recorder to start recording, we just call its `Record()` method:

```
this.audioRecorder.Record();
```

When the user taps on the **Stop recording** button, the recording stops, and the saved sound starts playing with the `AVAudioPlayer`:

```
this.audioRecorder.Stop();
AVAudioPlayer player = AVAudioPlayer.FromUrl(soundFileUrl);
player.Play();
```

There's more...

The `AVAudioRecorder` class also provides sound metering options. To enable sound metering, set its `MeteringEnabled` property to `true`. We can then output the peak power in decibels on a specific channel. To do this for the first channel of our recording, add the following code right after the `Record()` method call:

```
ThreadPool.QueueUserWorkItem(delegate {
   while (this.audioRecorder.Recording) {
     this.audioRecorder.UpdateMeters();
     Console.WriteLine(this.audioRecorder.PeakPower(0));
   }
} );
```

———Chapter 7

The `PeakPower` method accepts the zero-based index of the channel and returns the peak of the channel in decibels. Call `UpdateMeters()` right before calling the `PeakPower` method to get the most recent reading.

Note that enabling metering on the recorder uses CPU resources. Do not enable it if you do not intend on using the metering values.

Record for a pre-defined amount of time

To record audio for a pre-defined amount of time, without the need for the user to stop the recording, call the `RecordFor(double)` method. Its parameter specifies the amount of time in seconds for which to record.

See also

In this chapter:

- *Playing music and sounds*

Managing multiple album items directly

In this recipe, we will discuss programmatically accessing the device's photo album.

Getting ready

Create a new project in MonoDevelop, and name it `ManageAlbumApp`.

> This example works on the simulator. At least one image must exist in the photo album.

How to do it...

1. Add a button on the main view of `MainController`.
2. Enter the following using directive in the `MainController.cs` file:
   ```
   using MonoTouch.AssetsLibrary;
   ```
3. Override the `ViewDidLoad` method, and enter the following code in it:
   ```
   this.buttonEnumerate.TouchUpInside += delegate {
     this.assetsLibrary = new ALAssetsLibrary();
     this.assetsLibrary.Enumerate(ALAssetsGroupType.All,
       this.GroupsEnumeration, this.GroupsEnumerationFailure);
   } ;
   ```

Multimedia Resources

4. Add the following methods in the class:

   ```
   private void GroupsEnumeration(ALAssetsGroup assetGroup,
      ref bool stop) {
      if (null != assetGroup) {
         stop = false;
         assetGroup.SetAssetsFilter(ALAssetsFilter.AllPhotos);
         assetGroup.Enumerate(this.AssetEnumeration);
      }
   }
   private void AssetEnumeration(ALAsset asset, int index,
      ref bool stop) {
      if (null != asset) {
         stop = false;
         Console.WriteLine("Asset url: {0}",
            asset.DefaultRepresentation.Url.AbsoluteString);
      }
   }
   private void GroupsEnumerationFailure(NSError error) {
      if (null != error) {
         Console.WriteLine("Error enumerating asset groups! Message:
            {0}", error.LocalizedDescription);
      }
   }
   ```

5. Compile and run the application.
6. Tap the **Enumerate assets** button, and watch the URLs of saved photos being displayed in the **Application Output** pad.

How it works...

The `ALAssetsLibrary` class provides access to the album items of the device. These items are represented by the `ALAsset` class and are divided into groups, represented by the `ALAssetGroup` class.

The first thing we need to do is to enumerate the asset groups. To do this, call the `Enumerate` method:

```
this.assetsLibrary.Enumerate(ALAssetsGroupType.All,
   this.GroupsEnumeration, this.GroupsEnumerationFailure);
```

The first parameter is of the type `ALAssetGroupTypes` and instructs the assets library on which asset groups to enumerate. Passing `ALAssetGroupTypes.All` means we want to enumerate all asset groups. The other two parameters are delegate types. The `GroupsEnumeration` method is where we read the group's data, while the `GroupsEnumerationFailure` will occur if an error occurs. When the `Enumerate` method is called for the first time, the user is asked to grant access to the application for accessing the device's assets. If the user denies access, the failure method will be triggered. The next time the `Enumerate` method gets called, the access message appears again.

The signature of the `GroupsEnumeration` method is the following:

```
private void GroupsEnumeration(ALAssetsGroup assetGroup,
    ref bool stop)
```

The `assetGroup` parameter contains the group's information.

Note the `stop` parameter, which is declared as a `ref`. When the enumeration occurs, the method is being triggered once to return the first group and does not get called for the second time, no matter how many more groups exists. To force it to keep getting called to enumerate all groups, we have to set the `stop` variable to `false`. When all groups have been enumerated, the method gets called one last time, with the `assetGroup` variable set to `null`. So, we need to check this. To put all this in code:

```
if (null != assetGroup) {
  // Continue enumerating
  stop = false;
  // Determine what assets to enumerate
  assetGroup.SetAssetsFilter(ALAssetsFilter.AllPhotos);
  // Enumerate assets
  assetGroup.Enumerate(this.AssetEnumeration);
}
```

Calling the `SetAssetsFilter` method on the instance of `ALAssetGroup` class, we instruct it to filter what types of assets we want it to look for. After this, the process is similar to the groups enumeration. The `ALAssetGroup` class also contains an `Enumerate` method. It accepts a parameter of a delegate type, represented here by the `AssetsEnumeration` method. Its implementation is similar to the `GroupsEnumeration` method:

```
if (null != asset) {
  // Continue enumerating assets
  stop = false;
  // Output the asset url
  Console.WriteLine("Asset url: {0}",
    asset.DefaultRepresentation.Url.AbsoluteString);
```

The `ALAsset` class contains various information and properties. Most information is stored in its `DefaultRepresentation` property, which is of the type `ALAssetRepresentation`.

Multimedia Resources

There's more...

If the asset we are interested in is an image, we can get the actual image through the `DefaultRepresentation` property:

```
CGImage image = asset.DefaultRepresentation.GetImage();
```

Reading EXIF data

We can read a photo's **EXchangeable Image File format** (**EXIF**) metadata, through the `Metadata` property of `ALAssetRepresentation`, which is of the type `NSDictionary`, as follows:

```
NSDictionary metaData = asset.DefaultRepresentation.Metadata;
if (null != metaData){
  NSDictionary exifData = (NSDictionary)metaData[
    new NSString("{Exif}")];
}
```

Retrieving individual assets

We can also retrieve an individual asset if we know the asset's URL, through the `AssetForUrl` method of `ALAssetLibrary`.

See also

In this chapter:

- *Selecting images and videos*

8
Integrating iOS Features

In this chapter, we will cover:

- Starting phone calls
- Sending text messages and e-mails
- Using text messaging in our application
- Using e-mail messaging in our application
- Managing the address book
- Displaying contacts
- Managing the calendar

Introduction

Mobile devices offer a handful of features to the user. Creating an application that interacts with those features to provide a complete experience to users can surely be considered as an advantage.

In this chapter, we will discuss some of the most common features of iOS and how to integrate some or all of their functionality to our applications. We will see how to offer the user the ability to make telephone calls and send SMS and e-mails, either by using the native platform applications, or by integrating the native user interface in our projects. Also, we will discuss the following components:

- `MFMessageComposeViewController`: This controller is suitable for sending text (SMS) messages

Integrating iOS Features

- `MFMailComposeViewController`: This is the controller for sending e-mails with or without attachments
- `ABAddressBook`: This is the class that provides us access to the address book database
- `ABPersonViewController`: This is the controller that displays and/or edits contact information from the address book
- `EKEventStore`: This is the class that is responsible for managing calendar events

Furthermore, we will learn how to read and save contact information, how to display contact details, and interact with the device calendar.

Note that some of the examples in this chapter will require a device. For example, the simulator does not contain the messaging application. To deploy to a device, you will need to enroll as an iOS Developer through Apple's Developer Portal and obtain a commercial license of MonoTouch.

Starting phone calls

In this recipe, we will learn how to invoke the native phone application to allow the user to place a call.

Getting ready

Create a new project in MonoDevelop, and name it `PhoneCallApp`.

> The native phone application is not available on the simulator. It is only available on an iPhone device.

How to do it...

1. Add a button on the view of `MainController`, and override the `ViewDidLoad` method. Implement it with the following code. Replace the number with a real phone number, if you actually want the call to be placed:

   ```
   this.buttonCall.TouchUpInside += delegate {
     NSUrl url = new NSUrl("tel:+123456789012");
     if (UIApplication.SharedApplication.CanOpenUrl(url)){
       UIApplication.SharedApplication.OpenUrl(url);
     } else{
       Console.WriteLine("Cannot open url: {0}", url.AbsoluteString);
     }
   };
   ```

2. Compile and run the application on the device. Tap the **Call!** button to start the call. The following screenshot shows the phone application placing a call:

How it works...

Through the `UIApplication.SharedApplication` static property, we have access to the application's `UIApplication` object. We can use its `OpenUrl` method, which accepts an `NSUrl` variable to initiate a call:

```
UIApplication.SharedApplication.OpenUrl(url);
```

Since not all iOS devices support the native phone application, it would be useful to check for availability first:

```
if (UIApplication.SharedApplication.CanOpenUrl(url))
```

When the `OpenUrl` method is called, the native phone application will be executed, and it will start calling the number immediately. Note that the `tel:` prefix is needed to initiate the call.

There's more...

MonoTouch also supports the `CoreTelephony` framework, through the `MonoTouch.CoreTelephony` namespace. This is a simple framework that provides information on call state, connection, carrier info, and so on. Note that when a call starts, the native phone application enters into the foreground, causing the application to be suspended. The following is a simple usage of the `CoreTelephony` framework:

```
CTCallCenter callCenter = new CTCallCenter();
callCenter.CallEventHandler = delegate(CTCall call) {
  Console.WriteLine(call.CallState);
};
```

Integrating iOS Features

Note that the handler is assigned with an equals sign (=) instead of the common plus-equals (+=) combination. This is because `CallEventHandler` is a property and not an event. When the application enters into the background, events are not distributed to it. Only the last occured event will be distributed when the application returns to the foreground.

More info on OpenUrl

The `OpenUrl` method can be used to open various native and non-native applications. For example, to open a web page in Safari, just create an `NSUrl` object with the following link:

```
NSUrl url = new NSUrl("http://www.packtpub.com");
```

See also

In this chapter:

> - *Sending text messages and e-mails*

Sending text messages and e-mails

In this recipe, we will learn how to invoke the native mail and messaging applications within our own application.

Getting ready

Create a new project in MonoDevelop, and name it `SendTextApp`.

How to do it...

1. Add two buttons on the main view of `MainController`. Override the `ViewDidLoad` method of the `MainController` class, and implement it with the following code:

    ```
    this.buttonSendText.TouchUpInside += delegate {
      NSUrl textUrl = new NSUrl("sms:");
      if (UIApplication.SharedApplication.CanOpenUrl(textUrl)){
        UIApplication.SharedApplication.OpenUrl(textUrl);
      } else{
        Console.WriteLine("Cannot send text message!");
      }
    } ;
    this.buttonSendEmail.TouchUpInside += delegate {
      NSUrl emailUrl = new NSUrl("mailto:");
      if (UIApplication.SharedApplication.CanOpenUrl(emailUrl)){
        UIApplication.SharedApplication.OpenUrl(emailUrl);
      } else{
    ```

―― Chapter 8

```
        Console.WriteLine("Cannot send e-mail message!");
    }
} ;
```

2. Compile and run the application on the device. Tap on one of the buttons to open the corresponding application.

How it works...

Once again, using the `OpenUrl` method, we can send text or e-mail messages. In this example code, just using the `sms:` prefix will open the native text messaging application. Adding a cell phone number after the `sms:` prefix will open the native messaging application:

```
UIApplication.SharedApplication.OpenUrl(new
NSUrl("sms:+123456789012"));
```

> Apart from the recipient number, there is no other data that can be set before the native text message application is displayed.

195

Integrating iOS Features

For opening the native e-mail application, the process is similar. Passing the `mailto:` prefix opens the edit mail controller.

```
UIApplication.SharedApplication.OpenUrl(new NSUrl("mailto:"));
```

The `mailto:` url scheme supports various parameters for customizing an e-mail message. These parameters allows us to enter sender address, subject, and message:

```
UIApplication.SharedApplication.OpenUrl("mailto:recipient@example.
com?subject=Email%20with%20MonoTouch!&body=This%20is%20the%20
message%20body!");
```

There's more...

Although iOS provides access to opening the native messaging applications, pre-defining message content in the case of e-mails, this is where the control from inside the application stops. There is no way of actually sending the message through code. It is the user that will decide whether to send the message or not.

More info on opening external applications

The `OpenUrl` method provides an interface for opening the native messaging applications. Opening external applications has one drawback: the application that calls the `OpenUrl` method transitions to the background. Up to iOS version 3.*, this was the only way of providing messaging through an application. Since iOS version 4.0, Apple has provided the messaging controllers to the SDK. The following recipes discuss their usage.

See also

In this chapter:

- Starting phone calls
- Using text messaging in our application

Using text messaging in our application

In this recipe, we will learn how to provide text messaging functionality within our application using the native messaging user interface.

Getting ready

Create a new project in MonoDevelop, and name it `TextMessageApp`.

How to do it...

1. Add a button on the view of `MainController`. Enter the following using directive in the `MainController.cs` file:

    ```
    using MonoTouch.MessageUI;
    ```

2. Implement the `ViewDidLoad` method with the following code, changing the recipient number and/or the message body at your discretion:

    ```
    private MFMessageComposeViewController messageController;
    public override void ViewDidLoad (){
      base.ViewDidLoad ();
      this.buttonSendMessage.TouchUpInside += delegate {
        if (MFMessageComposeViewController.CanSendText){
          this.messageController = new
            MFMessageComposeViewController();
          this.messageController.Recipients = new
            string[] { "+123456789012" };
          this.messageController.Body = "Text from MonoTouch";
          this.messageController.MessageComposeDelegate =
            new MessageComposerDelegate();
          this.PresentModalViewController(
            this.messageController, true);
        } else{
          Console.WriteLine("Cannot send text message!");
        }
      } ;
    }
    ```

Integrating iOS Features

3. Add the following nested class:
   ```
   private class MessageComposerDelegate :
     MFMessageComposeViewControllerDelegate{
     public override void Finished (MFMessageComposeViewController
       controller, MessageComposeResult result){
       switch (result){
         case MessageComposeResult.Sent:
           Console.WriteLine("Message sent!");
         break;
         case MessageComposeResult.Cancelled:
           Console.WriteLine("Message cancelled!");
         break;
         default:
           Console.WriteLine("Message sending failed!");
         break;
       }
       controller.DismissModalViewControllerAnimated(true);
     }
   }
   ```

4. Compile and run the application on the device.
5. Tap the **Send message** button to open the message controller. Tap the **Send** button to send the message, or the **Cancel** button to return to the application.

How it works...

The `MonoTouch.MessageUI` namespace contains the necessary UI elements that allow us to implement messaging in an iOS application. For text messaging (SMS), we need the `MFMessageComposeViewController` class.

Only the iPhone is capable of sending text messages out of the box. With iOS 5, both the iPod and the iPad can send text messages, but the user might not have enabled this feature on the device. For this reason, checking for availability is the best practice. The `MFMessageComposeViewController` class contains a static method, named `CanSendText`, which returns a boolean value indicating whether we can use this functionality. The important thing in this case is that we should check if sending text messages is available prior to initializing the controller. This is because when you try to initialize the controller on a device that does not support text messaging, or the simulator, you will get the following message on the screen:

To determine when the user has taken action in the message UI, we implement a `Delegate` object and override the `Finished` method:

```
private class MessageComposerDelegate :
   MFMessageComposeViewControllerDelegate
```

Another option, provided by MonoTouch, is to subscribe to the `Finished` event of the `MFMessageComposeViewController` class.

Inside the `Finished` method, we can provide functionality according to the `MessageComposeResult` parameter. Its value can be one of the following three:

1. `Sent`: This value indicates that the message was sent successfully.
2. `Cancelled`: This value indicates that the user has tapped the **Cancel** button, and the message will not be sent.
3. `Failed`: This value indicates that message sending failed.

The last thing to do is to dismiss the message controller, which is done as follows:

```
controller.DismissModalViewControllerAnimated(true);
```

Integrating iOS Features

After initializing the controller, we can set the recipients and body message to the appropriate properties:

```
this.messageController.Recipients = new string[] { "+123456789012" };
this.messageController.Body = "Text from MonoTouch";
```

The `Recipients` property accepts a string array that allows for multiple recipient numbers.

You may have noticed that the `Delegate` object for the message controller is set to its `MessageComposeDelegate` property, instead of the common `Delegate`. This is because the `MFMessageComposeViewController` class directly inherits from the `UINavigationController` class, so the `Delegate` property accepts values of the type `UINavigationControllerDelegate`.

There's more...

The fact that the SDK provides the user interface to send text messages does not mean that it is customizable. Just like invoking the native messaging application, it is the user who will decide whether to send the message or discard it. In fact, after the controller is presented on the screen, any attempts to change the actual object or any of its properties will simply fail. Furthermore, the user can change or delete both the recipient and the message body. The real benefit though is that the messaging user interface is displayed within our application, instead of running separately.

SMS only

The `MFMessageComposeViewController` can only be used for sending **Short Message Service** (**SMS**) messages and not **Multimedia Messaging Service** (**MMS**).

Using e-mail messaging in our application

In this recipe, we will learn how to use the e-mail messaging interface within an application.

Getting ready

Create a new project in MonoDevelop, and name it `EmailMessageApp`.

How to do it...

1. Add a button on the view of `MainController` and the `MonoTouch.MessageUI` namespace in the `MainController.cs` file.
2. Enter the following code in the `ViewDidLoad` method:

```
this.buttonSendEmail.TouchUpInside += delegate {
    this.mailController = new MFMailComposeViewController();
```

```
     this.mailController.SetToRecipients(new string[]
       { "recipient@example.com" });
     this.mailController.SetSubject("Email from MonoTouch!");
     this.mailController.SetMessageBody("This is the message body!",
       false);
     this.mailController.Finished += this.MailController_Finished;
     if (MFMailComposeViewController.CanSendMail){
       this.PresentModalViewController(this.mailController, true);
     } else{
       Console.WriteLine("Cannot send email!");
     }
   };
```

3. Add the following method:

```
private void MailController_Finished (object sender,
  MFComposeResultEventArgs e){
  switch (e.Result){
    case MFMailComposeResult.Sent:
      Console.WriteLine("Email sent!");
    break;
    case MFMailComposeResult.Saved:
      Console.WriteLine("Email saved!");
    break;
    case MFMailComposeResult.Cancelled:
      Console.WriteLine("Email sending cancelled!");
    break;
    case MFMailComposeResult.Failed:
      Console.WriteLine("Email sending failed!");
      if (null != e.Error){
        Console.WriteLine("Error message: {0}",
          e.Error.LocalizedDescription);
      }
    break;
  }
  e.Controller.DismissModalViewControllerAnimated(true);
}
```

4. Compile and run the application either on the simulator or on the device.

5. Tap the **Send email** button to display the mail user interface. Send or cancel the message. The application will work on the simulator and behave just like the native mail application on devices, except for the fact that messages will not actually be sent or saved.

Integrating iOS Features

How it works...

The `MFMailComposeViewController` class provides the native mail composing interface. To determine whether the device is capable of sending e-mails, we first check its `CanSendMail` property.

Like the `MFMessageComposeViewController`, it contains a `Finished` event, which we use to respond to user actions, without having to implement a `Delegate` object. We do this inside the `MailController_Finished` method, based on the `MFComposeResultEventArgs.Result` property, which is of the type `MFMailComposeResult`. Its possible values will be one of the following:

- `Sent`: This value indicates that the e-mail message is queued for sending
- `Saved`: This value indicates that the user tapped the **Cancel** button, and the **Save Draft** option of the action sheet automatically appeared

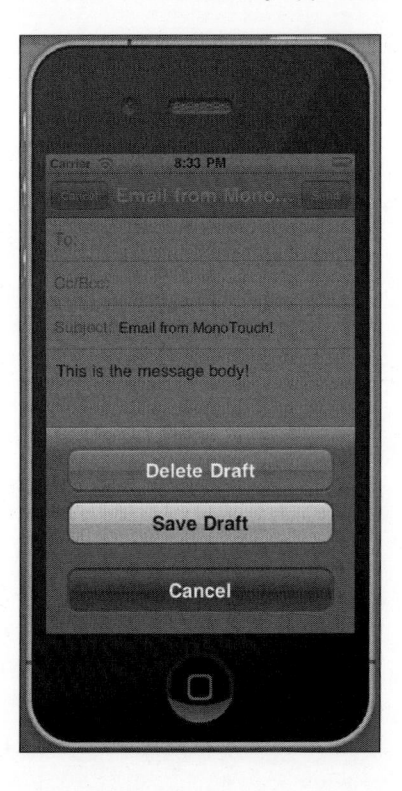

- `Cancelled`: This value indicates that the user tapped the **Cancel** button on the controller and selected the **Delete Draft** option on the action sheet
- `Failed`: This value indicates that e-mail message sending failed

After initializing the object, we can assign a recipient list, subject, and message body through the corresponding set of `Set` prefixed methods:

```
this.mailController.SetToRecipients(new string[] { "recipient@example.
com" });
this.mailController.SetSubject("Email from MonoTouch!");
this.mailController.SetMessageBody("This is the message body!",
false);
```

The second parameter of the `SetMessageBody` message, if set to `true`, informs the controller that the message should be treated as HTML.

There's more...

Apart from simple or HTML-formatted text, we can also send attachments. We can do this with the `AddAttachmentData` method:

```
this.mailController.AddAttachmentData(UIImage.FromFile("image.jpg").
   AsJPEG(), "image/jpg", "image.jpg");
```

The first parameter is of the type `NSData` and should contain the contents of the attachment. In this case, we attach an image through the `UIImage.AsJPEG()` method, which returns the image contents inside an `NSData` object. The second parameter represents the **Multipurpose Internet Mail Extensions** (**MIME**) type of the attachment, and the third parameter its file name. The project's source code contains a full and commented example.

Action sheet for drafts

The action sheet displayed when the user taps the **Cancel** button is automatically handled by the `MFMailComposeViewController`.

See also

In this chapter:

▶ *Using text messaging in our application*

Managing the address book

In this recipe, we will discuss how to access and manage the user's stored contacts in the device's address book.

Integrating iOS Features

Getting ready

Create a new project in MonoDevelop, and name it `AddressBookApp`.

How to do it...

1. Add a button on the view of `MainController`. Enter the following using directive in the `MainController.cs` file:

   ```
   using MonoTouch.AddressBook;
   ```

2. Override the `ViewDidLoad` method:

   ```
   public override void ViewDidLoad (){
     base.ViewDidLoad ();
     this.buttonGetContacts.TouchUpInside += delegate {
       ABAddressBook addressBook = new ABAddressBook();
       ABPerson[] contacts = addressBook.GetPeople();
       foreach (ABPerson eachPerson in contacts){
         Console.WriteLine(string.Format("{0} {1}",
           eachPerson.LastName, eachPerson.FirstName));
       }
     };
   }
   ```

3. Compile and run the application on the simulator.

4. Tap the **Get contacts** button, and watch the contact's names displayed in MonoDevelop's **Application Output** pad.

> After installation of the iOS SDK, the simulator does not contain any contacts. You can add contacts the same way you can do it on the device.

How it works...

The `MonoTouch.AddressBook` namespace contains all the classes that allow us to manage the device's address book. To access the data directly, we need an instance of the `ABAddressBook` class:

```
ABAddressBook addressBook = new ABAddressBook();
```

To get all the contacts stored in the address book, we call its `GetPeople()` method:

```
ABPerson[] contacts = addressBook.GetPeople();
```

This method returns an array of `ABPerson` objects, which contains all the information of individual contacts. To read the contacts' details, we iterate over the `ABPerson` array and get each contact's first and last names with the `FirstName` and `LastName` properties respectively:

```
Console.WriteLine(string.Format("{0} {1}", eachPerson.LastName,
eachPerson.FirstName));
```

There's more...

To get a contact's stored phone number(s), call the `GetPhones()` method:

```
ABMultiValue<string> phones = eachPerson.GetPhones();
Console.WriteLine(phones[0].Value);
```

It returns an object of type `ABMultiValue<string>`. `ABMultiValue<T>` is a generic collection, especially designed for multiple address book values.

Adding a phone number to a contact

To add a phone number to a contact, we can use the `ABPerson` class' `SetPhones` method. It accepts an `ABMultiValue<string>` object as its parameter, but we cannot add new values to `ABMultiValue` objects. We can, however, write values to an `ABMutableMultiValue<T>` object:

```
ABMutableMultiValue<string> newPhones = phones.ToMutableMultiValue();
```

This line of code creates a new instance of `ABMutableMultiValue<string>` object, which we then use to add the phone number(s) we want:

```
newPhones.Add("+120987654321", ABPersonPhoneLabel.iPhone);
eachPerson.SetPhones(newPhones);
addressBook.Save();
```

The second parameter of the `Add` method is the label the phone number will have when it is saved to the contact. It is important to call the `ABAddressBook.Save()` method, or else the changes will not be saved.

Displaying contacts

In this recipe, we will learn how to use the native address book user interface to display contact information.

Integrating iOS Features

Getting ready

Create a new project in MonoDevelop, and name it `DisplayContactApp`. Add a button on the view of `MainController`.

How to do it...

1. Create a field in the `AppDelegate` class for a `UINavigationController`:

   ```
   UINavigationController navController;
   ```

2. Instantiate the navigation controller, passing as its root controller an instance of the `MainController`:

   ```
   this.navController = new UINavigationController(new
     MainController());
   ```

3. Set the navigation controller as the window's root view controller:

   ```
   window.RootViewController = this.navController;
   ```

4. Add the namespaces `MonoTouch.AddressBook` and `MonoTouch.AddressBookUI` in the `MainController.cs` file.

5. Override the `ViewDidLoad` method of the `MainController` class, and implement it with the following code:

   ```
   ABAddressBook addressBook = new ABAddressBook();
   ABPerson[] contacts = addressBook.GetPeople();
   ABPersonViewController personController = new
     ABPersonViewController();
   personController.DisplayedPerson = contacts[0];
   this.buttonDisplayContact.TouchUpInside += delegate {
     this.NavigationController.PushViewController(
       personController, true);
   };
   ```

6. Compile and run the application on the simulator or the device.

7. Tap the **Display first contact** button to display the contact details.

How it works...

The `MonoTouch.AddressBookUI` namespace contains the controllers that the native `Contacts` application uses to allow the user to display and manage contacts. Each contact's details can be viewed with the `ABPersonViewController`. This controller must be presented through a `UINavigationController`, or else it will not display correctly.

After initializing it, we set the `ABPerson` object we want to be displayed to its `DisplayedPerson` property:

```
ABPersonViewController personController = new
  ABPersonViewController();
personController.DisplayedPerson = contacts[0];
```

Then, we push it to the navigation controller's stack:

```
this.NavigationController.PushViewController(personController, true);
```

There's more...

The `ABPersonViewController` can also be used for editing. To do this, set the `AllowsEditing` property to `true`:

```
personController.AllowsEditing = true;
```

The result will be exactly the same as the native `Contacts` application:

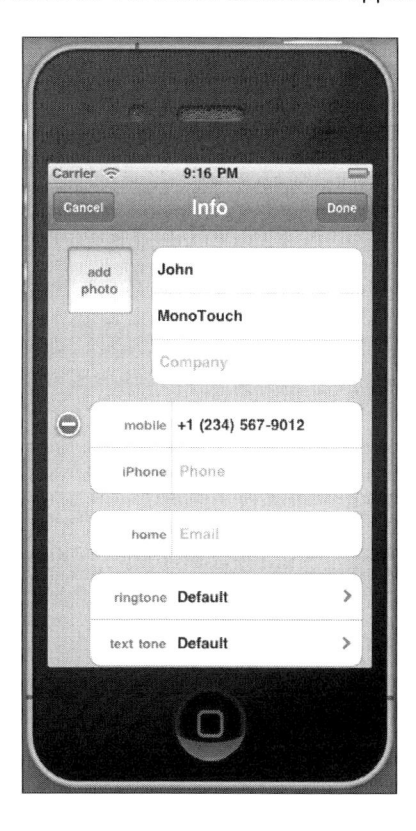

Note that changes are saved normally through the `ABPersonViewController`.

Integrating iOS Features

Other address book controllers

The `MonoTouch.AddressBookUI` namespace contains all the controllers we need to create our own custom contacts application:

- `ABPeoplePickerNavigationController`: This is a navigation controller that displays the saved contacts. The user can select a contact from the list.
- `ABPersonViewController` : This controller is described in the previous example.
- `ABNewPersonViewController`: This is the controller that creates a new contact.
- `ABUnknownPersonViewController`: This is the controller that is displayed with partial data for creating a new contact. This is similar to the controller that is displayed when we tap on an unknown number in the list of recent calls on the device.

See also

In this chapter:

- *Managing the address book*

Managing the calendar

In this recipe, we will learn how to create an event and save it to the device's calendar database.

Getting ready

Create a new project in MonoDevelop, and name it `CalendarEventsApp`.

> This project must be executed on a device. The native `Calendar` application is not installed on the simulator.

How to do it...

1. Add a button on the main view of the `MainController`. Add the namespace `MonoTouch.EventKit` in the `MainController.cs` file.
2. Finally, enter the following code in the `ViewDidLoad` method:

   ```
   this.buttonDisplayEvents.TouchUpInside += delegate {
     EKEventStore evStore = new EKEventStore();
     NSPredicate evPredicate = evStore.PredicateForEvents(
       DateTime.Now, DateTime.Now.AddDays(30), evStore.Calendars);
     evStore.EnumerateEvents(
   ```

Chapter 8

```
            evPredicate, delegate(EKEvent calEvent, ref bool stop) {
        if (null != calEvent){
          stop = false;
          Console.WriteLine("Event title: {0}\nEvent start date:
            {1}", calEvent.Title, calEvent.StartDate);
        }
      } );
    } ;
```

3. Compile and run the application on the device.
4. Tap the **Display events** button to output the calendar events of the next 30 days in the **Application Output** pad.

How it works...

The `MonoTouch.EventKit` namespace is responsible for managing the calendar events. To read the stored events, we first initialize an `EKEventStore` object:

```
EKEventStore evStore = new EKEventStore();
```

The `EKEventStore` class provides us access to the stored events. To retrieve the calendar events, we need a predicate of the type `NSPredicate`. We can create an instance through the `PredicateForEvents` method of the `EKEventStore` class:

```
NSPredicate evPredicate = evStore.PredicateForEvents(DateTime.Now,
    DateTime.Now.AddDays(30), evStore.Calendars);
```

The two first parameters are of the type `NSDate` (which can be implicitly converted to `DateTime`) and represent the start and end dates for which to search events. The third parameter is of the type `EKCalendar[]`, and it is an array of the calendars to search into. To search in all the available calendars, we pass the `EKEventStore.Calendars` property.

Finally, we call the `EnumerateEvents` method:

```
evStore.EnumerateEvents(evPredicate, delegate(EKEvent calEvent,
    ref bool stop) {
    //...
```

We pass the predicate we created earlier to the first parameter. The second parameter is a delegate of type `EKEventSearchCallback`. To read each event's data, we use its `EKEvent` object. Note that the process of enumerating calendar events is similar to the one that is used for enumerating assets from the assets library, as discussed in the previous chapter.

Integrating iOS Features

There's more...

As well as enumerating events, the `EKEventStore` allows us to create new ones. The following example creates and saves a new calendar event:

```
EKEvent newEvent = EKEvent.FromStore(evStore);
newEvent.StartDate = DateTime.Now.AddDays(1);
newEvent.EndDate = DateTime.Now.AddDays(1.1);
newEvent.Title = "MonoTouch event!";
newEvent.Calendar = evStore.DefaultCalendarForNewEvents;
NSError error = null;
evStore.SaveEvent(newEvent, EKSpan.ThisEvent, out error);
```

For creating a new `EKEvent` instance, we use the `EKEvent.FromStore` static method. We then set a start and end date, a title, and the calendar to which the event will be stored. Here, we use the default calendar that we can get with the `DefaultCalendarForNewEvents` property of `EKEventStore`. When we have everything set up, we call the `SaveEvent` method to save it.

Info on calendars

By default, the device has two calendars set up: `Home` and `Work`. Although we cannot create new calendars on the device, new calendars that are created on the computer that we use to synchronize the device are automatically added when syncing.

See also

In this book:

Chapter 7, Multimedia Resources:

> ▶ *Managing album items directly*

9
Interacting with Device Hardware

In this chapter, we will cover:

- Detecting device orientation
- Adjusting UI orientation
- Proximity sensor
- Retrieving battery information
- Handling motion events
- Handling touch events
- Recognizing gestures
- Custom gestures
- Using the accelerometer
- Using the gyroscope

Introduction

Today's mobile devices are equipped with very advanced hardware. Be it accelerometers to detect motion and orientation, proximity sensors, GPS modules, and among many other components, quite sophisticated multi-touch screens.

In this chapter, we will be focusing on how to use this hardware within our applications to provide the user with an experience that extends into the 3D world. Specifically, we will discuss how to adjust the user interface orientation according to the position of the device, how to use the proximity sensor, and read battery information. In a series of four tasks, we will learn how to capture user touches on the screen and recognize gestures.

Interacting with Device Hardware

Last but not least, we will create advanced applications that read the raw data from the accelerometer and gyroscope sensors to detect device motion and rotation, with detailed and simple guides.

Detecting device orientation

In this recipe, we will learn how to make an application that is aware of device orientation changes.

Getting ready

Create a new project in MonoDevelop, and name it `DeviceOrientationApp`.

How to do it...

1. Add a label on the view of `MainController`. Enter the following code in the `MainController` class:

   ```
   private NSObject orientationObserver;
   public override void ViewDidLoad (){
     base.ViewDidLoad ();
     UIDevice.CurrentDevice.
       BeginGeneratingDeviceOrientationNotifications();
     this.orientationObserver = NSNotificationCenter.DefaultCenter.
       AddObserver(UIDevice.OrientationDidChangeNotification,
       delegate {
       this.lblOrientation.Text =
         UIDevice.CurrentDevice.Orientation.ToString();
     } );
   }
   public override void ViewDidUnload (){
     base.ViewDidUnload ();
     NSNotificationCenter.DefaultCenter.
       RemoveObserver(this.orientationObserver);
     UIDevice.CurrentDevice.
       EndGeneratingDeviceOrientationNotifications();
   }
   ```

2. Compile and run the application on the simulator.
3. Rotate the simulator by holding the **Command** key on your Mac and pressing the left or right arrow keys.

Chapter 9

How it works...

Although the simulator lacks accelerometer hardware, it supports notifications for orientation changes.

The device orientation notification mechanism can be accessed through the `UIDevice.CurrentDevice` singleton object. To receive notifications, we first need to instruct the runtime to issue them. We do this with the following method:

```
UIDevice.CurrentDevice.
   BeginGeneratingDeviceOrientationNotifications();
```

This method turns the accelerometer on and starts generating orientation notifications. We then need to start observing for the notifications, in order to respond to changes:

```
this.orientationObserver = NSNotificationCenter.DefaultCenter.
   AddObserver(UIDevice.OrientationDidChangeNotification, delegate {
this.lblOrientation.Text =
   UIDevice.CurrentDevice.Orientation.ToString();
} );
```

Each time the device orientation changes, the observer triggers the anonymous method. In it, we output the orientation, which we get from the `Orientation` property, to the label.

Interacting with Device Hardware

The `ViewDidUnload` method is the method that is being called when the view controller unloads its view. Inside it, we make sure to remove the orientation observer, and we instruct the runtime to stop generating orientation notifications:

```
NSNotificationCenter.DefaultCenter.
  RemoveObserver(this.orientationObserver);
UIDevice.CurrentDevice.EndGeneratingDeviceOrientationNotifications();
```

There's more...

The `Orientation` property returns an enumeration of the type `UIDeviceOrientation`. Its values are the following:

- `Unknown`: This value specifies that the device orientation is unknown
- `Portrait`: This value specifies that the device is in its normal portrait orientation, with the **home** button on the bottom side
- `PortraitUpsideDown`: This value specifies that the device is in upside-down portrait orientation, with the **home** button on the top side
- `LandscapeLeft`: This value specifies that the device is in landscape orientation, with the **home** button on the left side
- `LandscapeRight`: This value specifies that the device is in landscape orientation, with the **home** button on the right side
- `FaceUp`: This value specifies that the device is parallel to the ground, with the screen facing up
- `FaceDown`: This value specifies that the device is parallel to the ground, with the screen facing down

`FaceUp` and `FaceDown` are two values that cannot be reproduced on the simulator.

Device orientation and user interface orientation

What can be clearly noticed in this example is that there is a difference between a device's orientation and that of the user interface. If the device is rotated, the label gets updated with the new orientation value, but the user interface does not respond to changes. In the next recipe, we will discuss how to rotate the user interface.

See also

In this chapter:

- *Adjusting UI orientation*
- *Using the accelerometer*

Chapter 9

Adjusting UI orientation

In this recipe, we will learn how to rotate the **User Interface** (**UI**)according to the screen orientation.

Getting ready

Create a new project in MonoDevelop, and name it `UIOrientationApp`.

How to do it...

1. Add a label on the view of `MainController`. Enter the following code in the `MainController` class:

    ```
    public override bool ShouldAutorotateToInterfaceOrientation (
      UIInterfaceOrientation toInterfaceOrientation){
      return true;
    }
    public override void DidRotate (
      UIInterfaceOrientation fromInterfaceOrientation){
      base.DidRotate (fromInterfaceOrientation);
      this.lblOutput.Text = this.InterfaceOrientation.ToString();
    }
    ```

2. Compile and run the application on the simulator.
3. Use *Command* + arrow keys to rotate the simulator. The **LandscapeRight** orientation is shown in the following image:

215

Interacting with Device Hardware

How it works...

To make our UI adjust to device orientations, all we need to do is override the view controller's `ShouldAutorotateToInterfaceOrientation` method:

```
public override bool ShouldAutorotateToInterfaceOrientation (
    UIInterfaceOrientation toInterfaceOrientation)
```

When the view controller loads, it checks the outcome of the method for each of the available orientations. The first time it receives `true` from it, it will automatically rotate the interface to that orientation. After loading, whenever the device rotates, the same process gets repeated.

The parameter of the method is an enumeration of the type `UIInterfaceOrientation`, and each time the method gets called, it contains the value of the orientation the interface checks for.

The `DidRotate` method is called after the interface orientation completes. We use the `UIViewController.InterfaceOrientation` property, which holds the information on the view controller's current orientation, to update the label:

```
this.lblOutput.Text = this.InterfaceOrientation.ToString();
```

There's more...

Returning `true` from the `ShouldAutorotateToInterfaceOrientation` method means that the interface will rotate on all device orientations. In most cases, this is not necessary and should even be avoided, depending on our application design. To make our interface rotate to landscape orientations only, the method should be implemented as follows:

```
public override bool ShouldAutorotateToInterfaceOrientation (
   UIInterfaceOrientation toInterfaceOrientation) {
   return toInterfaceOrientation ==
     UIInterfaceOrientation.LandscapeLeft || toInterfaceOrientation ==
     UIInterfaceOrientation.LandscapeRight;
}
```

Note that this implementation will force the UI to load at landscape mode.

User interface orientation on the simulator

If you implement the `ShouldAutorotateToInterfaceOrientation` method to only support landscape orientations, then the controller that loads the simulator "device" will also rotate at landscape orientation. However, this is for convenience only, since if you check the `UIDevice.CurrentDevice.Orientation` property, its value will be `UIDeviceOrientation.Portrait`.

Chapter 9

See also

In this chapter:

- *Detecting device orientation*
- *Using the accelerometer*

Proximity sensor

In this recipe, we will discuss using the proximity sensor to disable the device screen.

Getting ready

Create a new project in MonoDevelop, and name it `ProximitySensorApp`.

> The simulator does not support the proximity sensor.

How to do it...

For this task, no controls are needed, besides the `MainController` itself.

1. Declare an `NSObject` field that will hold the notification observer:

   ```
   private NSObject proximityObserver;
   ```

2. Enter the following code in the `ViewDidLoad` override:

   ```
   UIDevice.CurrentDevice.ProximityMonitoringEnabled = true;
   if (UIDevice.CurrentDevice.ProximityMonitoringEnabled){
     this.proximityObserver = NSNotificationCenter.DefaultCenter.
       AddObserver(UIDevice.ProximityStateDidChangeNotification,
       delegate(NSNotification ntf) {
       Console.WriteLine("Proximity state: {0}",
         UIDevice.CurrentDevice.ProximityState);
     } );
   }
   ```

3. Finally, enter the following code in the `ViewDidUnload` override:

   ```
   if (UIDevice.CurrentDevice.ProximityMonitoringEnabled){
     NSNotificationCenter.DefaultCenter.
       RemoveObserver(this.proximityObserver);
     UIDevice.CurrentDevice.ProximityMonitoringEnabled = false;
   }
   ```

Interacting with Device Hardware

4. Compile and run the application on the device.
5. Put your finger over the proximity sensor, or just hold it next to your ear as you would do when on a call. Watch the **Application Output** pad in MonoDevelop display the state of the sensor.

How it works...

Although the functionality of the proximity sensor is quite simple, it provides a very important feature. iOS devices have only one button on the front, which is the **home** button. Almost every user-device interaction is based on the touch-sensitive screen. This poses a problem on the iPhone: apart from its multiple features, it is also a phone. This means that it will most likely spend some time on the side of the user's face for making calls.

To avoid accidental virtual buttons being tapped, the proximity sensor gets activated when the phone application is running, to disable the screen when the device is near the user's ear, or whatever is over the sensor.

To enable the proximity sensor, set the property of the `UIDevice.CurrentDevice.ProximityMonitoringEnabled` to `true`:

```
UIDevice.CurrentDevice.ProximityMonitoringEnabled = true;
```

If the device does not support the proximity sensor, this property will return `false`, even after it has been set to `true`. So, after setting it to `true`, we can check it to see if the device supports the sensor:

```
if (UIDevice.CurrentDevice.ProximityMonitoringEnabled)
```

After checking, we can add an observer for getting notified of the sensor's state with the `UIDevice.ProximityStateDidChangeNotification` key:

```
this.proximityObserver = NSNotificationCenter.DefaultCenter.
  AddObserver(UIDevice.ProximityStateDidChangeNotification,
  delegate(NSNotification ntf) {
  Console.WriteLine("Proximity state: {0}",
    UIDevice.CurrentDevice.ProximityState);
} );
```

The `ProximityState` property returns `true` if the sensor has turned the screen off and `false` if it has turned it back on.

There's more...

The proximity sensor usage is not limited to phone call functionality. For example, if you are developing an application that could do some work while the device is in the user's pocket or purse, enabling the proximity sensor would make sure that no accidental controls are tapped. Or even save battery power, by just turning the screen off.

Chapter 9

Sensor support

Not all devices support a proximity sensor. If you are targeting various iOS devices, consider that the sensor will not be available on all of them.

See also

In this chapter:

- *Retrieving battery information*

Retrieving battery information

In this recipe, we will learn how to read the charging states of the device and its battery usage.

Getting ready

Create a new project in MonoDevelop, and name it `BatteryInfoApp`.

How to do it...

1. Add a label on the view of `MainController`. Enter the following code in the `MainController` class:

   ```
   private NSObject batteryStateChangeObserver;
   public override void ViewDidLoad (){
     base.ViewDidLoad ();
     UIDevice.CurrentDevice.BatteryMonitoringEnabled = true;
     this.batteryStateChangeObserver = NSNotificationCenter.
       DefaultCenter.AddObserver(UIDevice.
       BatteryStateDidChangeNotification, delegate
         (NSNotification ntf) {
         this.lblOutput.Text = string.Format("Battery state: {0}",
           UIDevice.CurrentDevice.BatteryState);
     } );
   }
   ```

2. Compile and run the application on the device.

3. After the application loads, disconnect and/or connect the USB cable of the device. Watch the battery state on the label.

219

Interacting with Device Hardware

How it works...

We can retrieve battery information through the `UIDevice` class. The first thing we have to do is to enable battery monitoring:

```
UIDevice.CurrentDevice.BatteryMonitoringEnabled = true;
```

On the simulator, which does not support battery monitoring, this property will return false, even after we have set it to true.

We can then add an observer for battery state change notifications through the `UIDevice.BatteryStateDidChangeNotification` key, as indicated in the highlighted code previously. The battery state can be retrieved through the `BatteryState` property:

```
this.lblOutput.Text = string.Format("Battery state: {0}",
    UIDevice.CurrentDevice.BatteryState);
```

Possible values of the `BatteryState` property are:

- `Unknown`: This value specifies that the battery state cannot be determined, or battery monitoring is disabled
- `Unplugged`: This value specifies that the device is running on battery power
- `Charging`: This value specifies that the device battery is charging, and the USB cable is connected
- `Full`: This value specifies that the device battery is full, and the USB cable is connected

There's more...

Apart from the battery state, we can get information on its power level. To do this, we need to add an observer for the `UIDevice.BatteryLevelDidChangeNotification` key:

```
private NSObject batterLevelChangeObserver;
//...
this.batterLevelChangeObserver = NSNotificationCenter.DefaultCenter
    .AddObserver(UIDevice.BatteryLevelDidChangeNotification,
    delegate(NSNotification ntf) {
    this.lblOutput.Text = string.Format("Battery level: {0}",
        UIDevice.CurrentDevice.BatteryLevel);
} );
```

The `BatteryLevel` property returns a float value in the range from `0.0` (battery empty) to `1.0` (battery full at 100 percent). If battery monitoring is disabled, it will return a value of `-1.0`.

Disabling battery monitoring

Always disable battery monitoring when not needed. The actual monitoring mechanism itself consumes battery power.

See also

In this chapter:

- *Proximity sensor*

Handling motion events

In this recipe, we will learn how to intercept and respond to shake gestures.

Getting ready

Create a new project in MonoDevelop, and name it `MotionEventsApp`.

How to do it...

1. Add a label on the view of `MainController`. Enter the following code in the `MainController` class:

    ```
    public override bool CanBecomeFirstResponder{
      get {  return true; }
    }
    public override void ViewDidAppear (bool animated){
      base.ViewDidAppear (animated);
      this.BecomeFirstResponder();
    }
    public override void MotionBegan (UIEventSubtype motion,
      UIEvent evt){
      base.MotionBegan (motion, evt);
      this.lblOutput.Text = "Motion started!";
    }
    public override void MotionEnded (UIEventSubtype motion,
      UIEvent evt){
      base.MotionEnded (motion, evt);
      this.lblOutput.Text = "Motion ended!";
    }
    public override void MotionCancelled (UIEventSubtype motion,
      UIEvent evt){
      base.MotionCancelled (motion, evt);
      this.lblOutput.Text = "Motion cancelled!";
    }
    ```

Interacting with Device Hardware

2. Compile and run the application on the device.
3. Shake the device and watch the output on the label. You can also test this application on the simulator.
4. After it loads, click on **Hardware | Shake Gesture** on the menu bar.

How it works...

By overriding the motion methods of the `UIViewController` class, we can intercept and respond to the motion events sent by the system. Just overriding these methods is not enough, though. For a controller to receive motion events, it needs to be the first responder. To make sure of this, we first override the `CanBecomeFirstResponder` property and return `true` from it:

```
public override bool CanBecomeFirstResponder{
   get { return true; }
}
```

Then, we make sure our controller becomes the first responder when its view has appeared by calling the `BecomeFirstResponder` method in the `ViewDidAppear` override:

```
public override void ViewDidAppear (bool animated){
  base.ViewDidAppear (animated);
  this.BecomeFirstResponder();
}
```

The `ViewDidAppear` method gets called after the view has appeared on the screen.

The system determines if a motion is a shake gesture and calls the appropriate methods. We can use the following three methods to override and capture shake gestures:

- `MotionBegan`: This method specifies that shaking motion started
- `MotionEnded`: This method specifies that shaking motion ended
- `MotionCancelled`: This method specifies that shaking motion cancelled

When the device starts moving, the `MotionBegan` method is called. If the motion lasts for about a second or less, the `MotionEnded` method is called. If it lasts longer, the system classifies it as not being a shake gesture and calls the `MotionCancelled` method. It is advisable to override all three methods and react accordingly when we want to implement shake gestures in an application.

There's more...

Motion events are only sent to objects inheriting the `UIResponder` class. This includes the `UIView` and `UIViewController` classes.

More info motion events

The motion event mechanism is fairly simple. It merely detects near-instant device shakes, without providing any information on their direction or rate. To handle motion events based on different characteristics, the accelerometer can be used in combination.

See also

In this chapter:

- *Using the accelerometer*

Handling touch events

In this recipe, we will learn how to intercept and respond to user touches.

Getting ready

Create a new project in MonoDevelop, and name it `TouchEventsApp`.

How to do it...

1. Add a label on the view of `MainController`, and enter the following code in the `MainController` class:

    ```
    public override void TouchesMoved (NSSet touches, UIEvent evt){
      base.TouchesMoved (touches, evt);
      UITouch touch = touches.AnyObject as UITouch;
      UIColor currentColor = this.View.BackgroundColor;
      float red, green, blue, alpha;
      currentColor.GetRGBA(out red, out green, out blue, out alpha);
      PointF previousLocation = touch.PreviousLocationInView(this.View);
      PointF touchLocation = touch.LocationInView(this.View);
      if (previousLocation.X != touchLocation.X){
        this.lblOutput.Text = "Changing background color...";
        float colorValue = touchLocation.X / this.View.Bounds.Width;
        this.View.BackgroundColor = UIColor.FromRGB(colorValue,
          colorValue, colorValue);
      }
    }
    ```

2. Compile and run the application on the simulator.

3. Click-and-drag sideways with the cursor on the simulator's screen, and watch the view's background color gradually change from white to black. Note that clicking with the cursor on the simulator screen is the equivalent of touching the device's screen with a finger.

Interacting with Device Hardware

How it works...

To respond to user touches, the object that acts as a touch receiver must have its `UserInteractionEnabled` property set to `true`. Almost every object is enabled for user interaction by default, except for those whose primary usage is not intended for direct user interaction, for example, the `UILabel` and the `UIImageView`. We need to set the `UserInteractionEnabled` to these objects explicitly. Apart from this, the objects that can handle touch events must inherit from the `UIResponder` class. Note that although the `UIViewController` class inherits from `UIResponder` and therefore can capture touch events, it does not have a `UserInteractionEnabled` property, and it is its main property of `UIView` that controls the delivery of touch events. What this means is that if you override the touch methods of a `UIViewController` but its view's `UserInteractionEnabled` property is set to `false`, these methods will not respond to user touches.

The methods responsible for handling the touch events are the following:

- `TouchesBegan`: This method is called when the user touches the screen
- `TouchesMoved`: This method is called when the user drags the finger on the screen
- `TouchesEnded`: This method is called when the user lifts the finger from the screen
- `TouchesCancelled`: This method is called when the touch event has been cancelled by a system event, for example, when a notification alert is displayed

The full project can be found in the downloaded source code. The `TouchesMoved` method implementation is explained here.

Every touch method has two parameters. The first parameter is of the type `NSSet` and contains the `UITouch` objects. The `NSSet` class represents a collection of objects, while the `UITouch` class holds the information for each user touch. The second parameter is of the type `UIEvent` and holds the information of the actual event.

We can retrieve the `UITouch` object related to the actual touch through the `NSSet.AnyObject` return value:

```
UITouch touch = touches.AnyObject as UITouch;
```

It returns an object of type `NSObject`, which we convert to a `UITouch`. We can get the previous and current locations of the touch through the following methods:

```
PointF previousLocation = touch.PreviousLocationInView(this.View);
PointF touchLocation = touch.LocationInView(this.View);
```

Both of them return a `PointF` struct containing the location of the touch in the receiver's coordinate system. After receiving the location of the touch, we adjust the background color accordingly.

There's more...

This example is based on single user touches. To enable a view to respond to multiple touches, we have to set its `MultipleTouchEnabled` property to `true`. We can then get all the `UITouch` objects in an array:

```
UITouch[] allTouches = touches.ToArray<UITouch>();
```

Getting the tap count

We can determine the number of consecutive user taps through the `UITouch.TapCount` property inside the `ToucheEnded` method.

See also

In this chapter:

- *MotionEvents*
- *Recognizing gestures*
- *Custom gestures*

Recognizing gestures

In this recipe, we will discuss how to recognize touch gestures and respond accordingly.

Getting ready

Create a new project in MonoDevelop, and name it `GestureApp`.

How to do it...

1. Add a label on the view of `MainController`. Enter the following `using` directive in the `MainController` class source file:

    ```
    using MonoTouch.ObjCRuntime;
    ```

2. Enter the following code in the `MainController` class:

    ```
    public override void ViewDidLoad (){
      base.ViewDidLoad ();
      UIPinchGestureRecognizer pinchGesture = new
        UIPinchGestureRecognizer(this, new Selector("PinchHandler:"));
      this.View.AddGestureRecognizer(pinchGesture);
    }
    [Export("PinchHandler:")]
    ```

Interacting with Device Hardware

```
        private void PinchHandler(UIGestureRecognizer gesture){
          UIPinchGestureRecognizer pinch = gesture as
            UIPinchGestureRecognizer;
          switch (pinch.State)
          {
            case UIGestureRecognizerState.Began:
              this.lblOutput.Text = "Pinch began!";
            break;
            case UIGestureRecognizerState.Changed:
              this.lblOutput.Text = "Pinch changed!";
            break;
            case UIGestureRecognizerState.Ended:
              this.lblOutput.Text = "Pinch ended!";
            break;
          }
        }
```

3. Compile and run the application on the simulator.
4. Hold down the **Option** key and click-drag with the mouse to perform the equivalent of a pinch on the simulator screen.

How it works...

Since the iOS 3.2 version was released along with the iPad, Apple introduced the `UIGestureRecognizer` class and its derivatives. The gesture recognizers make use of the multiple touch screens on iOS devices. **Gestures** are basically touch combinations, which can be performed for specific actions.

For example, pinching on a full-screen image in the native **Photos** application will zoom out. The action of pinching is the gesture the user performs, while the gesture recognizer is responsible for recognizing and delivering the gesture event to its receiver.

In this example, we create a `UIPinchGestureRecognizer`, which will recognize pinches performed on the screen. Its instance is created with the following code:

```
UIPinchGestureRecognizer pinchGesture = new
    UIPinchGestureRecognizer(this, new Selector("PinchHandler:"));
```

The constructor that initializes the instance takes two parameters. The first one is of type `NSObject`, and it is the target object that will receive the gesture. In this case, it is the `MainController` instance, which we pass with the `this` keyword. The second parameter is of the type `Selector`, contained in the `MonoTouch.ObjCRuntime` namespace that we added, and it represents the method that will be called when the recognizer receives a gesture. In simple words, a `Selector` in Objective-C is basically a method signature. The string we pass to its constructor represents the Objective-C method that will be called.

Since we are using C#, we can easily expose a method as an Objective-C `Selector`. We just create the method we want and decorate it with the `ExportAttribute`, making sure the string we pass to it is the same that we have passed to the `Selector` constructor:

```
[Export("PinchHandler:")]

private void PinchHandler(UIGestureRecognizer gesture)
```

Inside the method, we read the `State` property of the gesture recognizer object and respond accordingly.

There's more...

The state of each gesture recognizer is represented by an enumeration of the type `UIGestureRecognizerState`. Its values are:

- `Possible`: This value specifies that the gesture has not yet been recognized and is the default value
- `Began`: This value specifies that the gesture has started
- `Changed`: This value specifies that the gesture has changed
- `Ended`: This value specifies that the gesture has ended
- `Cancelled`: This value specifies that the gesture has been cancelled
- `Failed`: This value specifies that the gesture cannot be recognized
- `Recognized`: This value specifies that the gesture has been recognized

Advantage of gesture recognizers

The advantage of gesture recognizers is that they save developers the time to create their own gesture recognition mechanisms, through the touch events. Furthermore, they are based on the gestures that users are accustomed to using on iOS devices.

See also

In this chapter:

- *Touch events*
- *Custom gestures*

Interacting with Device Hardware

Custom gestures

In this recipe, we will learn how to create a custom gesture recognizer to create our own gesture.

Getting ready

Create a new project in MonoDevelop, and name it `CustomGestureApp`.

How to do it...

1. Add a label on the view of `MainController`. Create the following nested class in the `MainController` class:

    ```
    private class DragLowerLeftGesture : UIGestureRecognizer{
      public DragLowerLeftGesture(NSObject target, Selector action) :
        base(target, action){}
      private PointF startLocation;
      private RectangleF lowerLeftCornerRect;
      public override UIGestureRecognizerState State{
        get{
          return base.State;
        } set{
          base.State = value;
        }
      }
      public override void TouchesBegan (NSSet touches, UIEvent evt){
        base.TouchesBegan (touches, evt);
        UITouch touch = touches.AnyObject as UITouch;
        this.startLocation = touch.LocationInView(this.View);
        RectangleF viewBounds = this.View.Bounds;
        this.lowerLeftCornerRect = new RectangleF(0f,
          viewBounds.Height - 50f, 50f, 50f);
        if (this.lowerLeftCornerRect.Contains(this.startLocation)){
          this.State = UIGestureRecognizerState.Failed;
        } else{
          this.State = UIGestureRecognizerState.Began;
        }
      }
      public override void TouchesMoved (NSSet touches, UIEvent evt){
        base.TouchesMoved (touches, evt);
        this.State = UIGestureRecognizerState.Changed;
      }
    ```

```
            public override void TouchesEnded (NSSet touches, UIEvent evt){
              base.TouchesEnded (touches, evt);
              UITouch touch = touches.AnyObject as UITouch;
              PointF touchLocation = touch.LocationInView(this.View);
              if (this.lowerLeftCornerRect.Contains(touchLocation)){
                this.State = UIGestureRecognizerState.Ended;
              } else{
                this.State = UIGestureRecognizerState.Failed;
              }
            }
          }
```

2. Use the custom gesture recognizer as shown in the previous recipe.

How it works...

To create a gesture recognizer, declare a class that inherits from the `UIGestureRecognizer` class. In this example, we are creating a gesture that will be recognized by dragging the finger on the screen towards a `50x50` point rectangle in the lower-left corner.

```
        private class DragLowerLeftGesture : UIGestureRecognizer
```

The `UIGestureRecognizer` class contains the same touch methods that we use to intercept touches in views. We also have access to the view it was added to through its `View` property. Inside the `TouchesBegan` method, we determine the initial touch location. If it is outside the lower-left portion of the view, we set the `State` property to `Began`. If it is inside the lower-left portion, we set the `State` property to `Failed` so that the selector will not be called.

Inside the `TouchesEnded` method, we consider the gesture as `Ended` if the touch's location was inside the lower-left portion of the view. If it was not, the gesture recognition is considered as `Failed`.

The `TouchesMoved` method is where the `Changed` state will be set. For this simple gesture recognizer that we are creating, no other logic is needed in it.

There's more...

This is a simple gesture recognizer that depends on a single touch. With the information provided in the touch methods, we can create more complex gestures that will support multiple touches.

Interacting with Device Hardware

Another usage of custom gesture recognizers

There are some views that inherit from the `UIView` class, which according to Apple Developer Documentation should not be sub-classed. The `MKMapView` is one of these views, which is used to display maps. This poses a problem if we want to intercept the touch events from these views. Although we could use another view over it and intercept its touch events, it is a bit complex. A more simple approach is to create a simple custom gesture recognizer and add it to the view that we cannot sub-class. This way, we can intercept its touches without having to sub-class it.

See also

In this chapter:

- *Recognizing gestures*
- *Touch events*

Using the accelerometer

In this recipe, we will learn how to receive accelerometer events to create an application that is aware of device movement.

Getting ready

Create a new project in MonoDevelop, and name it `AccelerometerApp`.

> The simulator does not support the accelerometer hardware. The project in this example will work correctly on a device.

How to do it...

1. Add two buttons and a label on the view of `MainController`.
2. Override the `ViewDidLoad` method, and implement it with the following code:

   ```
   this.buttonStop.Enabled = false;
   UIAccelerometer.SharedAccelerometer.UpdateInterval = 1 / 10;
   this.buttonStart.TouchUpInside += delegate {
     this.buttonStart.Enabled = false;
     UIAccelerometer.SharedAccelerometer.Acceleration +=
       this.Acceleration_Received;
     this.buttonStop.Enabled = true;
   } ;
   this.buttonStop.TouchUpInside += delegate {
   ```

```
        this.buttonStop.Enabled = false;
        UIAccelerometer.SharedAccelerometer.Acceleration -=
           this.Acceleration_Received;
        this.buttonStart.Enabled = true;
    };
```

3. Add the following method in the class:

   ```
   private void Acceleration_Received (object sender,
       UIAccelerometerEventArgs e){
       this.lblOutput.Text = string.Format("X: {0}\nY: {1}\nZ: {2}",
          e.Acceleration.X, e.Acceleration.Y, e.Acceleration.Z);
   }
   ```

4. Compile and run the application on the device.
5. Tap the **Start accelerometer** button, and watch the values display on the label while moving or shaking the device.

How it works...

The `UIAccelerometer` class provides access to the accelerometer hardware through its `SharedAccelerometer` static property. To activate it, all we need to do is to assign a handler to its `Acceleration` event:

```
UIAccelerometer.SharedAccelerometer.Acceleration +=
   this.Acceleration_Received;
```

Inside the handler, we receive the accelerometer values through the `UIAccelerometerEventArgs.Acceleration` property. The property returns an object of the type `UIAcceleration`, which contains the accelerometer amount in three properties: `X`, `Y`, and `Z`.

These properties represent motion in the `X`, `Y`, and `Z` axes. Consider the following diagram:

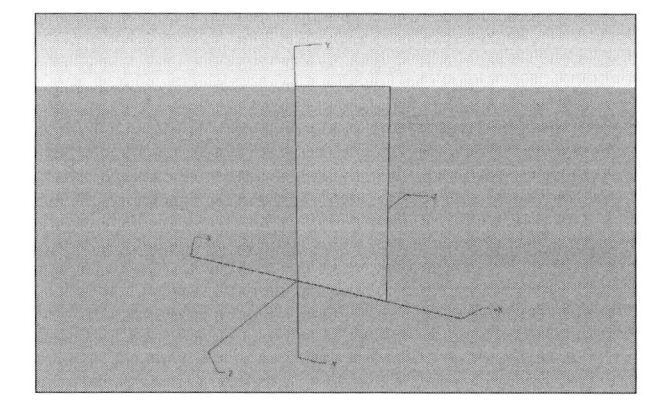

Each of these values measures the amount of gravitational force by which the device moved on each axis. For example, if X has a value of 1, then the device is moving on the X-axis to the right, with an acceleration of 1g. If X has a value of -1, then the device is moving on the X-axis to the left, with an acceleration of 1g. When the device is placed on a table with its back facing the floor and is not moving, the normal values of the acceleration should be close or equal to the following:

- X: 0
- Y: 0
- Z: -1

Although the device is not moving, Z will be -1, because the device measures the Earth's gravity.

We can set the interval by which the accelerometer will issue acceleration events by setting its UpdateInterval property:

```
UIAccelerometer.SharedAccelerometer.UpdateInterval = 1 / 10;
```

It accepts a double, which represents the interval by which the accelerometer will issue its acceleration events in seconds. Care must be taken when setting the update interval, because the more events the accelerometer has to issue for a specific period of time, the more battery power it consumes.

To stop using the accelerometer, all we need to do is to unhook the handler from the Acceleration event:

```
UIAccelerometer.SharedAccelerometer.Acceleration -= this.Acceleration_Received;
```

There's more...

The UIAcceleration class contains another useful property, named Time. It is a double representing the relative time on which the acceleration event occurred. It is relative to CPU time, and it is not suggested to use this value to calculate the exact timestamp of the event.

Consideration using the accelerometer

Although the iPhone's accelerometer is a very accurate and sensitive sensor, it should not be used for precise measurements. Also, the results it produces may vary among different iOS devices, even if those devices are of the same model.

See also

In this chapter:

- *Using the gyroscope*

Chapter 9

Using the gyroscope

In this recipe, we will learn how to use the built-in gyroscope.

Getting ready

Create a new project in MonoDevelop, and name it GyroscopeApp.

> The simulator does not support the gyroscope hardware. Also, only newer devices contain a gyroscope. If this application is executed on a device without a gyroscope, or on the simulator, no error will occur, but no data will be displayed.

How to do it...

1. Add two buttons and a label on the view of MainController. Add the namespace MonoTouch.CoreMotion in the MainController.cs file. Enter the following private field in the class:

   ```
   private CMMotionManager motionManager;
   ```

2. Override the ViewDidLoad method, and implement it with the following code:

   ```
   this.motionManager = new CMMotionManager();
   this.motionManager.GyroUpdateInterval = 1 / 10;
   this.buttonStart.TouchUpInside += delegate {
   this.motionManager.StartGyroUpdates(NSOperationQueue.MainQueue,
     this.GyroData_Received);
   };
   this.buttonStop.TouchUpInside += delegate {
     this.motionManager.StopGyroUpdates();
   };
   ```

3. Add the following method:

   ```
   private void GyroData_Received(CMGyroData gyroData,
     NSError error){
     Console.WriteLine("rotation rate x: {0}, y: {1}, z: {2}",
       gyroData.RotationRate.x, gyroData.RotationRate.y,
       gyroData.RotationRate.z);
   }
   ```

4. Compile and run the application on the device.

5. Tap the **Start gyroscope** button and rotate the device in all axes. Watch the values displayed in the **Application Output**.

Interacting with Device Hardware

How it works...

The gyroscope is a mechanism that measures orientation. Newer iOS devices support gyroscope hardware, along with the accelerometer, to give even more accurate measurements of device motion.

The `MonoTouch.CoreMotion` namespace wraps the objects contained in the native **CoreMotion Framework**. The process of using the gyroscope hardware in-code is similar to the one used for the accelerometer. The first difference is that there is no singleton object for the gyroscope in the `UIApplication` class. So, we need to create an instance of the `CMMotionManager` class:

```
private CMMotionManager motionManager;
//...
this.motionManager = new CMMotionManager();
```

Just like using the accelerometer, we can set the interval by which we will be receiving gyroscope events, in seconds:

```
this.motionManager.GyroUpdateInterval = 1 / 10;
```

To start receiving gyroscope events, we call the object's `StartGyroUpdates` method:

```
this.motionManager.StartGyroUpdates(NSOperationQueue.MainQueue,
    this.GyroData_Received);
```

This method is overloaded; the first overload is parameterless and when called, the values of gyroscopic measurements are set to the `GyroData` property. Using this overload is quite simple and easy, but there no events are triggered, and we have to provide a mechanism for reading the measurements from the property.

The second overload, which is used in this example, accepts two parameters. The first parameter is the `NSOperationQueue`, on which the updates will occur, and the second parameter is the handler that will be executed when an update occurs.

The `NSOperationQueue` class represents an iOS mechanism for managing `NSOperation` objects execution. We access the runtime's main operation queue through the static `NSOperationQueue.MainQueue` property. Basically, this way, we instruct the runtime to manage the delivery of the handler in a more effective manner.

The second parameter is a delegate of the type `CMGyroHandler`. Its signature, represented by the method we created, is like the following:

```
private void GyroData_Received(CMGyroData gyroData, NSError error)
```

The `CMGyroData` object contains the actual measurement values received from the gyroscope through its `RotationRate` property:

```
Console.WriteLine("rotation rate x: {0}, y: {1}, z: {2}",
   gyroData.RotationRate.x, gyroData.RotationRate.y,
   gyroData.RotationRate.z);
```

The rotation rate is reflected on the X, Y, and Z axes, represented by the corresponding X, Y, and Z properties. Each value is the amount of rotation-angle-per-second that occurred on that axis, in radians.

Although it might seem a bit complicated at first, it is actually simple. For example, a value of 0.5 in the Z-axis means that the device rotated with a rate of 0.5 radians/sec to the left. A value of -0.5 in the Z-axis means that the device rotated with a rate of 0.5 radians/sec to the right. The pattern for determining the rotation direction is based on the *right-hand rule*.

There's more...

If you want your application to be available only for devices that support the gyroscope, then add the key `UIRequiredDeviceCapabilities` in your project's `Info.plist` file, with the value `gyroscope`. If your application's functionality is based fully on the gyroscope, adding this key must be considered essential to avoid the application being downloaded by users with older devices, ending up with an application that does not work.

Determining gyroscope availability

To determine if the device the application is running on supports gyroscope hardware, check the value of the `GyroAvailable` property of the `CMMotionManager` instance.

Converting radians to degrees

A radian is an angle measurement unit. To convert an angle measurement from radians to degrees, consider the following method:

```
public static double RadiansToDegrees (double radians){
   return (radians * 180 / Math.PI);
}
```

See also

In this chapter:

- *Using the accelerometer*

10
Location Services and Maps

In this chapter, we will cover:

- Determining location
- Determining heading
- Using region monitoring
- Using significant-change location service
- Location services in the background
- Displaying maps
- Geocoding
- Adding map annotations
- Adding map overlays

Introduction

Today's smartphones and handheld devices are equipped with high-accuracy Global Positioning System (GPS) hardware. GPS hardware receives location information from a constellation of satellites. Apart from the satellites, iOS devices take advantage of the cellular and Wi-fi networks to provide location information to the user.

Location Services and Maps

In this chapter, we will discuss how to use the appropriate frameworks to take advantage of the location services of the device. Furthermore, we will learn how to display maps and annotate them. Specifically, we will focus on the following subjects:

- **Location services**: They provide the available services on a device for providing location information. These services are:
    - **Standard location service**: This is the location service that depends fully on the device's GPS module and provides the highest accuracy location data
    - **Region monitoring service**: This is the location service that monitors boundary crossings
    - **Significant-change location service**: This is the service that monitors for significant changes in location
- `CLLocationManager`: This is the class that allows us to use the location services
- `Compass`: This is the class that shows us how to use the built-in compass
- `MKMapView`: This is the view that is used to display maps
- `MKAnnotation`: This is the class that allows us to add annotations on maps
- `MKOverlay`: This is the class that allows us to add overlays on maps

Determining location

In this recipe, we will discuss how to receive the location information from the built-in GPS hardware.

Getting ready

Create a new project in MonoDevelop, and name it `LocationApp`. Add two buttons and a label on the view of `MainController`.

How to do it...

To retrieve location data from the built-in GPS hardware, we need to use the `CoreLocaction` framework. It is exposed through the `MonoTouch.CoreLocation` namespace:

```
using MonoTouch.CoreLocation;
```

1. Add the following code in the `MainController` class:

```
private CLLocationManager locationManager;
public override void ViewDidLoad (){
  base.ViewDidLoad ();
  this.locationManager = new CLLocationManager();
```

```
    this.locationManager.UpdatedLocation +=
      this.LocationManager_UpdatedLocation;
    this.locationManager.Failed += this.LocationManager_Failed;
    this.buttonStart.TouchUpInside += delegate {
      this.lblOutput.Text = "Determining location...";
      this.locationManager.StartUpdatingLocation();
    };
    this.buttonStop.TouchUpInside += delegate {
      this.locationManager.StopUpdatingLocation();
      this.lblOutput.Text = "Location update stopped.";
    };
  }
  private void LocationManager_Failed (object sender,
    NSErrorEventArgs e){
    this.lblOutput.Text = string.Format("Location update failed!
      Error message: {0}", e.Error.LocalizedDescription);
  }
  private void LocationManager_UpdatedLocation (object sender,
    CLLocationUpdatedEventArgs e){
    double latitude = Math.Round(e.NewLocation.Coordinate.
      Latitude, 4);
    double longitude = Math.Round(e.NewLocation.Coordinate.
      Longitude, 4);
    double accuracy = Math.Round(e.NewLocation.
      HorizontalAccuracy, 0);
    this.lblOutput.Text = string.Format("Latitude: {0}\nLongitude:
      {1},\nAccuracy: {2}m", latitude,   longitude, accuracy);
  }
```

2. Compile and run the application on the device.
3. Tap the start button to view your location coordinates on the screen.

> Projects using the `CoreLocation` framework to determine current position can work on the simulator. However, the coordinates will be fixed, with values of either Apple's headquarters in California, or the central coordinates for the country of the Mac computer of which the simulator is running on.

Location Services and Maps

How it works...

The location data the GPS module provides can be accessed through the `CLLocationManager` class. After initializing an instance of the class, we need to subscribe to its `UpdatedLocation` event:

```
this.locationManager = new CLLocationManager();
this.locationManager.UpdatedLocation +=
    this.LocationManager_UpdatedLocation;
```

Location data will become available as they are issued through this event. It is good practice to also subscribe to the `Failed` event:

```
this.locationManager.Failed += this.LocationManager_Failed;
```

When the location manager first requests for location updates, the user is informed through a system-specific alert, similar to the following screenshot:

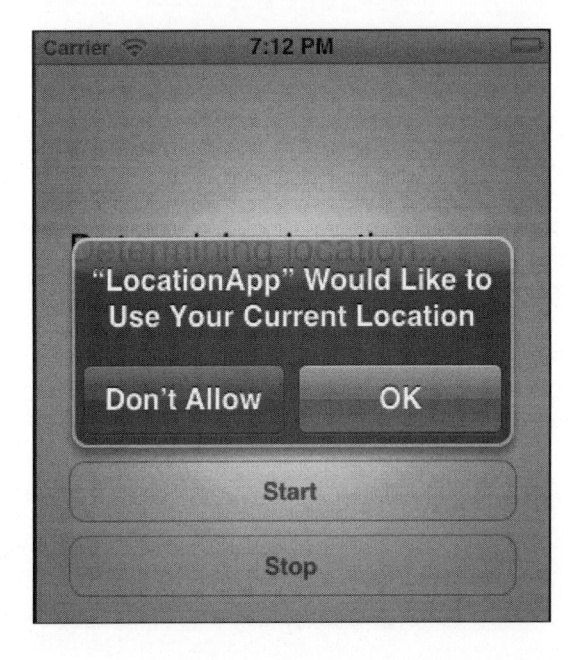

This alert basically asks for user permission to allow the application to retrieve location data. If the user denies this request, the `Failed` event will be triggered with the appropriate message. Future location requests will not trigger the permission alert, and the user will have to enable location services for the application through the device settings, so we need to handle this scenario accordingly.

After subscribing to the appropriate events, we request the delivery of location updates through the `StartUpdatingLocation` method:

```
this.locationManager.StartUpdatingLocation();
```

To stop receiving location updates, we call the `StopUpdatingLocation` method:

```
this.locationManager.StopUpdatingLocation();
```

There's more...

The `UpdatedLocation` event accepts delegates of the type `EventHandler<CLLocationUpdatedEventArgs>`. The `CLLocationUpdatedEventArgs` parameter contains two properties of the type `CLLocationCoordinate2D`. The `NewLocation` property contains the most recent location information, while the `OldLocation` property contains the previous location information. On the first location update, the `OldLocation` property will return `null`.

The coordinates are returned as values of the type `double` and represent the coordinates of the position in degrees:

```
double latitude = Math.Round(e.NewLocation.Coordinate.Latitude, 4);
double longitude = Math.Round(e.NewLocation.Coordinate.Longitude, 4);
double accuracy = Math.Round(e.NewLocation.HorizontalAccuracy, 0);
```

Negative `latitude` values indicate south coordinates, and positive values indicate north coordinates. Negative `longitude` values indicate west coordinates, while positive `longitude` values indicate east coordinates.

The `HorizontalAccuracy` property returns the accuracy in meters of the GPS fix. For example, a value of `17m` indicates that the location is determined within a circle of a diameter of 17m. Lower values indicate better accuracy.

GPS accuracy

The `UpdateLocation` event might be triggered without a new reading from the GPS. This is why we are provided with the previous location, so that we can compare the two values for determining whether we have a location change. Also, there is always a margin of error in the location data, which is independent of GPS hardware, and there are variable factors that define it, such as surrounding buildings, various obstacles, and so on. You will notice that the `HorizontalAccuracy` will return lower values when the device is outdoors, while higher values will be returned when we use the GPS indoors or on a city street with tall buildings.

Location services availability

Not all devices are equipped with location services hardware. Furthermore, even if a device is equipped with the appropriate hardware, location services could be disabled by the user.

Location Services and Maps

To determine if the location services are available or enabled on the device, we read the return value of the `CLLocationManager.LocationServicesEnabled` static property before initializing the location manager object:

```
if (CLLocationManager.LocationServicesEnabled) {
  // Initialize the location manager
  //...
}
```

Location services usage indicator

When any type of location service is used, the location services icon appears on the right side of the status bar, next to the battery indicator:

This indicator only appears on the device and not on the simulator.

See also

In this chapter:

- *Determining heading*
- *Location services in the background*

Determining heading

In this recipe, we will learn how to use the built-in compass to determine heading.

Getting ready

Create a new project in MonoDevelop, and name it `HeadingApp`. Just like in the previous task, add two buttons and a label on the view of `MainController`.

> The project in this task cannot be tested on the simulator. A device with compass hardware (magnetometer) is required.

Chapter 10

How to do it...

1. Heading information is once more retrieved through the `CLLocationManager` class. Create and initialize an instance in the `MainController` class.

2. Add the following code in the `ViewDidLoad` method:

   ```
   this.locationManager = new CLLocationManager();
   this.locationManager.UpdatedHeading +=
     this.LocationManager_UpdatedHeading;
   this.buttonStart.TouchUpInside += delegate {
      this.lblOutput.Text = "Starting updating heading...";
      this.locationManager.StartUpdatingHeading();
   };
   this.buttonStop.TouchUpInside += delegate {
      this.locationManager.StopUpdatingHeading();
      this.lblOutput.Text = "Stopped updating heading.";
   };
   ```

3. Add the following method:

   ```
   private void LocationManager_UpdatedHeading (object sender,
      CLHeadingUpdatedEventArgs e) {
      this.lblOutput.Text = string.Format("Magnetic heading: {0}",
         Math.Round(e.NewHeading.MagneticHeading, 1));
   }
   ```

4. Compile and run the application on the device.

5. Tap the start button and rotate the device to view the different heading values.

How it works...

To retrieve the heading information, we first need to subscribe to the location manager's `UpdatedHeading` event:

```
this.locationManager.UpdatedHeading +=
  this.LocationManager_UpdatedHeading;
```

To initiate the delivery of heading information, we call the `StartUpdatingHeading` method:

```
this.locationManager.StartUpdatingHeading();
```

Inside the `UpdatedHeading` event handler, we retrieve the heading information through the `MagneticHeading` property of the `CLHeading` object, exposed through the event arguments' `NewHeading` property:

```
this.lblOutput.Text = string.Format("Magnetic heading: {0}",
   Math.Round(e.NewHeading.MagneticHeading, 1));
```

Location Services and Maps

To stop retrieving heading updates, we call the `StopUpdatingHeading` method:

```
this.locationManager.StopUpdatingHeading();
```

There's more...

The heading is measured in degrees. The values for the four points of the horizon, as can be viewed on a simple compass, are the following:

- `0` or `360` **degrees**: North; the magnetometer will return values of up to `359.99` degrees, and then go to `0` when the device is heading north
- `90` **degrees**: East
- `180` **degrees**: South
- `270` **degrees**: West

Magnetic versus true heading

Magnetic heading is the heading that is based on what a normal compass will show as north. **True heading** is the true direction of north, based on the actual position of the Earth's north pole. There is a slight difference between the two, which varies with time, and it is usually about `2` degrees.

The `CLHeading` class provides both readings through the `MagneticHeading` and `TrueHeading` properties. This provides a significant help to developers, since calculating the difference between the two requires either expensive equipment, or very difficult calculations based on the time of year and other factors.

Compass availability

The magnetometer, a module that can determine the heading in degrees and provides compass functionality to devices, is not available on all devices. To check if a device can provide heading information, retrieve the value from the `CLLocationManager.HeadingAvailable` static property:

```
if (CLLocationManager.HeadingAvailable) {
  // Start updating heading
  //...
}
```

See also

In this chapter:

- *Determining location*
- *Location services in the background*

Using region monitoring

In this recipe, we will discuss how to use the GPS to respond to region-specific position changes.

Getting ready

Create a new project in MonoDevelop, and name it RegionApp. Add two buttons and a label on the view of MainController.

How to do it...

1. Create two fields in the MainController class:

   ```
   private CLLocationManager locationManager;
   private CLRegion region;
   ```

2. In the ViewDidLoad method, initialize it, and subscribe to the UpdatedLocation, RegionEntered, and RegionLeft events:

   ```
   this.locationManager.RegionEntered +=
     this.LocationManager_RegionEntered;
   this.locationManager.RegionLeft +=
     this.LocationManager_RegionLeft;
   this.locationManager.UpdatedLocation +=
     this.LocationManager_UpdatedLocation;
   ```

3. Enter the following event handlers in the class:

   ```
   private void LocationManager_UpdatedLocation (object sender,
     CLLocationUpdatedEventArgs e){
     if (e.NewLocation.HorizontalAccuracy < 100){
       this.region = new CLRegion(e.NewLocation.Coordinate, 100,
         "Home");
       this.locationManager.StartMonitoring(this.region, 65);
       this.locationManager.StopUpdatingLocation();
     }
   }
   private void LocationManager_RegionLeft (object sender,
     CLRegionEventArgs e){
     this.lblOutput.Text = string.Format("{0} region left.",
       e.Region.Identifier);
   }
   private void LocationManager_RegionEntered (object sender,
     CLRegionEventArgs e){
     this.lblOutput.Text = string.Format("{0} region entered.",
       e.Region.Identifier);
   }
   ```

Location Services and Maps

4. In the start button's `TouchUpInside` handler, call the `StartUpdatingLocation` method:

   ```
   this.locationManager.StartUpdatingLocation();
   ```

5. In the stop button's `TouchUpInside` handler, call the `StopMonitoring` method:

   ```
   this.locationManager.StopMonitoring(this.region);
   ```

This application needs to be tested on a device that supports region monitoring.

How it works...

Region monitoring is a feature that monitors for boundary crossings. When a boundary of a specific region is crossed, the `CLLocationManager` object issues the appropriate events:

```
this.locationManager.RegionEntered +=
  this.LocationManager_RegionEntered;
this.locationManager.RegionLeft += this.LocationManager_RegionLeft;
this.locationManager.UpdatedLocation +=
  this.LocationManager_UpdatedLocation;
```

In this example, we define the region based on the current location; hence, we also subscribe to the `UpdatedLocation` event.

When the application starts receiving location updates, it first checks for location accuracy:

```
if (e.NewLocation.HorizontalAccuracy < 100)
```

If the desired accuracy is achieved (<100m, modify at your discretion), we initialize the `CLRegion` object:

```
this.region = new CLRegion(e.NewLocation.Coordinate, 100, "Home");
```

The `CLRegion` class is used to define regions. Here, we create the region to be monitored based on our current location in the first parameter. The second parameter declares the radius around the coordinate, in meters, defining the region boundary. The third parameter is a string identifier for the region.

To start monitoring the region, we call the `StartMonitoring` method:

```
this.locationManager.StartMonitoring(this.region, 65);
```

The first parameter is the region to be monitored, while the second parameter defines the desired accuracy in meters for the boundary crossings. This value acts as an accuracy offset that prevents the system from triggering successive `enter` and `left` events when the user is traveling close to the region's boundary.

When region monitoring has started, the appropriate events will be triggered when the device enters or leaves the region based on the desired accuracy value.

There's more...

Region monitoring is a very useful feature. For example, an application could provide specific information to users based on their proximity to various areas. Furthermore, it can notify of boundary crossings while the application is in the background.

Region monitoring availability

To check if a device supports region monitoring, retrieve the value of the `RegionMonitoringAvailable` static property:

```
if (CLLocationManager.RegionMonitoringAvailable) {
  // Start monitoring a region
  //...
}
```

See also

In this chapter:

- *Using significant-change location service*
- *Location services in the background*

Using significant-change location service

In this recipe, we will learn how to use the significant-change location monitoring feature.

Getting ready

Create a new project in MonoDevelop, and name it `SLCApp`. Add a label and two buttons on the view of `MainController`.

How to do it...

1. Add the following code in the `ViewDidLoad` method:

    ```
    this.locationManager = new CLLocationManager();
    this.locationManager.UpdatedLocation +=
      this.LocationManager_UpdatedLocation;
    this.buttonStart.TouchUpInside += delegate {
      this.lblOutput.Text = "Starting monitoring significant location
        changes...";
      this.locationManager.
        StartMonitoringSignificantLocationChanges();
    ```

Location Services and Maps

```
    };
    this.buttonStop.TouchUpInside += delegate {
      this.locationManager.StopMonitoringSignificantLocationChanges();
      this.lblOutput.Text = "Stopped monitoring significant location
        changes.";
    };
```

2. Add the following method:

```
private void LocationManager_UpdatedLocation (object sender,
  CLLocationUpdatedEventArgs e) {
  double latitude = Math.Round(e.NewLocation.Coordinate.
    Latitude, 4);
  double longitude = Math.Round(e.NewLocation.Coordinate.
    Longitude, 4);
  double accuracy = Math.Round(e.NewLocation.
    HorizontalAccuracy, 0);
  this.lblOutput.Text = string.Format("Latitude: {0}\nLongitude:
    {1}\nAccuracy: {2}", latitude, longitude, accuracy);
}
```

3. Compile and run the application on the device.
4. Tap the **start** button to start monitoring for significant location changes.

How it works...

The significant-change location service monitors for significant location changes and provides location information when these changes occur. In terms of power consumption, it is the less demanding location service. It uses the device's cellular radio transceiver to determine the user's location. Only devices equipped with a cellular radio transceiver can use this service.

The code for using the significant-change location service is similar to the code of the standard location services. The only differences are the methods of starting and stopping the service. To start the service, we call the `StartMonitoringSignificantLocationChanges` method:

```
this.locationManager.StartMonitoringSignificantLocationChanges();
```

Location updates are issued through the `UpdatedLocation` event handler, which is the same event that we use for the standard location service:

```
this.locationManager.UpdatedLocation +=
  this.LocationManager_UpdatedLocation;
//...
private void LocationManager_UpdatedLocation (object sender,
  CLLocationUpdatedEventArgs e) {
  //...
}
```

Chapter 10

There's more...

The significant-change location service can report location changes while in the background, waking up the application.

Significant-change location service availability

To determine if a device is capable of using the significant-change location service, retrieve the value of the `SignificantLocationChangeMonitoringAvailable` static property:

```
if (CLLocationManager.SignificantLocationChangeMonitoringAvailable) {
  // Start monitoring for significant location changes.
  //...
}
```

See also

In this chapter:

- *Using region monitoring*
- *Location services in the background*

Location services in the background

In this recipe, we will discuss how to use location services while the application is in the background.

Getting ready

Create a new project in MonoDevelop, and name it `BackgroundLocationApp`. Just like in the previous tasks, add a label and two buttons on the view of `MainController`.

How to do it...

1. In the **Solution** pane, double-click on the **Info.plist** file to open it.
2. Under the **Advanced** tab, add a new key by clicking on the plus (**+**) sign or by right-clicking and selecting **New Key** from the context menu.
3. Select **Required background modes** from the drop-down list, or just type `UIBackgroundModes` in the field.
4. Expand the key and right-click on the empty item below it. Click **New Key** on the context menu. In its **Value** field, enter the word `location`.

249

Location Services and Maps

5. Save the document. When done, you should have something like in the following screenshot:

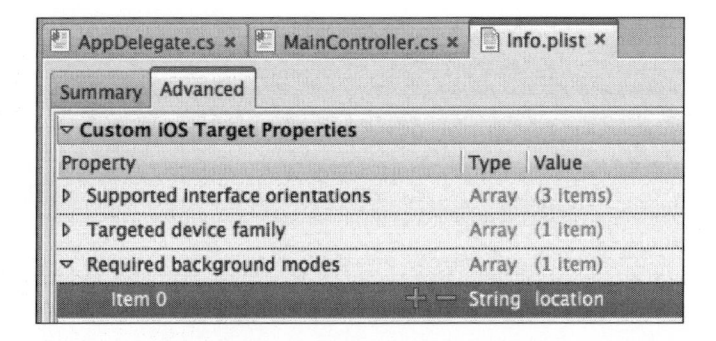

6. In the `MainController` class, enter the same code as the one used in the *Determining location* recipe in this chapter.

7. At the bottom of the `LocationManager_UpdatedLocation` method, add the following line:

   ```
   Console.WriteLine("{0}:\n\t{1} ", DateTime.Now,
     this.lblOutput.Text);
   ```

8. Compile and run the application on the device.

9. Tap the **Start** button to start receiving location updates. Press the **Home** button on the device to make the application move to the background. Watch MonoDevelop's **Application Output** pad displaying location updates.

How it works...

To receive location updates while the application is in the background, we need to set the location value to the `UIBackgroundModes` key in the **Info.plist** file. This basically makes sure that the application has the appropriate permission to receive location updates while it is in the background and that it will not get suspended.

To make sure that the application is receiving location updates, check the status bar. The location services icon should be displayed:

There's more...

Setting the `UIBackgroundModes` key for location services is only needed for the standard location service. By default both the region monitoring and significant-change location services support delivery of location updates while the application is in the background. While one of these location services has started updating for location data, the application can even be terminated. When a location update is received, the application is started or woken up from the suspended state and is given a limited amount of time to execute code.

To determine if an application has been started by one of these two location services, check the options parameter of the `FinishedLaunching` method in the `AppDelegate` class:

```
if (null != options){
  if (options.ContainsKey (UIApplication.LaunchOptionsLocationKey)){
    Console.WriteLine ("Woken from location service!");
    CLLocationManager locationManager = new CLLocationManager();
    locationManager.UpdatedLocation += this.LocationUpdatedHandler;
    locationManager.StartMonitoringSignificantLocationChanges();
  }
}
```

The options parameter is of the type `NSDictionary`. If this dictionary contains the `LaunchOptionsLocationKey`, then the application has been started or woken up from suspended state due to a location service. When that is the case, we need to call the `StartMonitoringSignificantLocationChanges` method on a `CLLocationManager` instance again to retrieve the location data.

The same applies to region monitoring location service. Note that if we use either of these two location services, but our application does not support the background delivery of location events, then we have to make sure to stop monitoring for location updates when they are no longer needed. If we do not, then the location services will continue to run, causing significant battery drain.

Restricting to supported hardware

If our application's features are fully dependent on location services and cannot operate correctly on devices that do not support them, we have to add the key `UIRequiredDeviceCapabilities` in the **Info.plist** file, with the value `location-services`.

Furthermore, when the application requires the use of the standard location service, which uses the GPS hardware, we need to add the value `gps` to this key. This way, we make sure the application will not be available through the application store to devices that are not equipped with the appropriate hardware.

Location Services and Maps

See also

In this chapter:

- *Determining location*

In this book:

Chapter 1, Development Tools:

- *Creating an iPhone project in MonoDevelop*

Displaying maps

In this recipe, we will learn how to display maps on the screen.

Getting ready

Create a new project in MonoDevelop, and name it `MapDisplayApp`.

How to do it...

1. Add an `MKMapView` on the view of `MainController`. Enter the following `using` directives:

    ```
    using MonoTouch.MapKit;
    using MonoTouch.CoreLocation;
    ```

2. Add the following code in the `MainController` class:

    ```
    public override void ViewDidLoad (){
      base.ViewDidLoad ();
      this.mapView.ShowsUserLocation = true;
      this.mapView.RegionChanged += this.MapView_RegionChanged;
    }
    private void MapView_RegionChanged (object sender,
      MKMapViewChangeEventArgs e){
      if (this.mapView.UserLocation.Location != null){
        CLLocationCoordinate2D mapCoordinate =
          this.mapView.UserLocation.Location.Coordinate;
        Console.WriteLine("Current coordinates: LAT: {0}, LON: {1}",
          mapCoordinate.Latitude, mapCoordinate.Longitude);
      }
    }
    ```

3. Compile and run the application either on the simulator or on the device. If the application is run on the simulator, the default location will be Apple's headquarters in **Cupertino**:

4. Zoom or pan the map to output the current location in the **Application Output**.

How it works...

The `MonoTouch.MapKit` namespace wraps all the objects contained in the `MapKit` framework. The `MapKit` framework uses Google maps to display maps.

The `MKMapView` is the default iOS view that displays maps. It is especially designed for this purpose, and it should not be sub-classed.

To display the user's location on the map, we set its `ShowsUserLocation` property to `true`:

```
this.mapView.ShowsUserLocation = true;
```

This activates the standard location service to start receiving location updates and handing them over to the `MKMapView` object internally.

Location Services and Maps

To determine when the user zooms or pans the map, we subscribe to the `RegionChanged` event:

```
this.mapView.RegionChanged += this.MapView_RegionChanged;
```

Inside the event handler, we retrieve the current location through the `UserLocation` property:

```
if (this.mapView.UserLocation.Location != null){
  CLLocationCoordinate2D mapCoordinate =
    this.mapView.UserLocation.Location.Coordinate;
  Console.WriteLine("Current coordinates: LAT: {0}, LON: {1}",
    mapCoordinate.Latitude, mapCoordinate.Longitude);
}
```

If the `ShowsUserLocation` property is set to `false`, the location services will not be activated, and the `UserLocation.Location` property will return `null`. It will also return `null` when the application runs for the first time, since it will ask the user for permission of using location services. However, a map will be displayed, as long as the device or simulator have an active Internet connection.

There's more...

We can set the center coordinate of the map to be displayed with the `SetCenterCoordinate` method:

```
CLLocationCoordinate2D mapCoordinates =
  new CLLocationCoordinate2D(0, 0);
this.mapView.SetCenterCoordinate(mapCoordinates, true);
```

The first parameter is the map coordinates that we want the map to be centered at, represented by an object of the type `CLLocationCoordinate2D`. The second parameter declares if we want the centering of the map to be animated or not.

Apart from centering the map, we can also set its zoom level. We do this through the `SetRegion` method:

```
this.mapView.SetRegion(MKCoordinateRegion.FromDistance(
  mapCoordinates, 1000, 1000), true);
```

The first parameter is of type `MKCoordinateRegion`. Here, its `FromDistance` static method is used to create an instance. Its first parameter is the coordinate of the region's center, while the next two parameters represent the horizontal and vertical span of the map to display, in meters. What this basically means is that the region represented by this `MKCoordinateRegion` instance will have `mapCoordinates` at the center, and the horizontal and vertical part of the map will each represent `1000` meters on the map.

Note that the `MKMapView` will set the actual region to an approximation to the values of `MKCoordinateRegion`. This is because the dimensions of `MKMapView` cannot always match the horizontal and vertical span values provided. For example, here we set a square region of `1000x1000` meters, but our `MKMapView` layout is not an absolute square, since it basically takes over all of the screen. We can retrieve the actual region of map the `MKMapView` is displaying through its `Region` property.

Things to have in mind when using MapKit

The `MapKit` framework uses the Google Maps and Google Earth APIs to display maps. Usage of this framework binds the developer with Google's terms of service, which can be viewed at `http://code.google.com/apis/maps/iphone/terms.html`.

One important term that can directly affect whether your application will be rejected or not on the Application Store is the usage of the Google logo over the maps. Care should be taken that the logo is always visible when displaying maps.

See also

In this chapter:

- *Geocoding*
- *Adding map annotations*
- *Adding map overlays*

Geocoding

In this recipe, we will learn how to provide address, city, or country information based on location coordinates.

Getting ready

Create a new project in MonoDevelop, and name it `GeocodingApp`.

How to do it...

1. Add an `MKMapView` on the top half of the view of `MainController` and a label and a button on the bottom half. Add the `MonoTouch.MapKit` and `MonoTouch.CoreLocation` namespaces.

Location Services and Maps

2. Enter the following `ViewDidLoad` override in the `MainController` class:

```
private MKReverseGeocoder reverseGeocoder;
public override void ViewDidLoad (){
  base.ViewDidLoad ();
  this.mapView.ShowsUserLocation = true;
  this.buttonGeocode.TouchUpInside += delegate {
    this.lblOutput.Text = "Reverse geocoding location...";
    this.buttonGeocode.Enabled = false;
    CLLocationCoordinate2D currentLocation =
      this.mapView.UserLocation.Location.Coordinate;
    this.mapView.SetRegion(MKCoordinateRegion.FromDistance(
      currentLocation, 1000, 1000), true);
    this.reverseGeocoder = new MKReverseGeocoder(currentLocation);
    this.reverseGeocoder.Delegate = new
      ReverseGeocoderDelegate(this);
    this.reverseGeocoder.Start();
  };
}
```

3. Create the following nested class:

```
private class ReverseGeocoderDelegate : MKReverseGeocoderDelegate{
  public ReverseGeocoderDelegate(MainController parentController){
    this.parentController = parentController;
  }
  private MainController parentController;
  public override void FoundWithPlacemark (MKReverseGeocoder
    geocoder, MKPlacemark placemark){
   this.parentController.lblOutput.Text = string.Format(
    "Locality: {0}\nAdministrative area: {1}\nCountry: {2}",
    placemark.Locality, placemark.AdministrativeArea,
    placemark.Country);
    geocoder.Dispose();
    this.parentController.buttonGeocode.Enabled = true;
  }
  public override void FailedWithError (MKReverseGeocoder
    geocoder, NSError error){
    this.parentController.lblOutput.Text = string.Format(
      "Reverse geocoding failed with error: {0}",
      error.LocalizedDescription);
    this.parentController.buttonGeocode.Enabled = true;
  }
}
```

Chapter 10

4. Compile and run the application either on the simulator or on the device. If run on the device, when you tap on the button, location information about the country and area you are in at the present time will be displayed on the label.

How it works...

Geocoding is the process of matching address information to geographic coordinates. **Reverse geocoding** is the process of matching geographic coordinates to address information. Only the latter is available on iOS. There are forward geocoding services available online that can be used, however.

To reverse geocode geographic coordinates, we use the `MKReverseGeocoder` class:

```
private MKReverseGeocoder reverseGeocoder;
```

This class needs a delegate object that will provide the information. The class we will create for the delegate object of `MKReverseGeocoder` must inherit the `MKReverseGeocoderDelegate` class:

```
private class ReverseGeocoderDelegate : MKReverseGeocoderDelegate
```

Inside the delegate object, we need to override two methods. The first one is `FoundWithPlacemark`:

```
public override void FoundWithPlacemark (MKReverseGeocoder geocoder,
    MKPlacemark placemark)
```

This is the method that will be triggered when the reverse geocoder retrieves the geocoding information. The information is contained in the `placemark` parameter, which is of the type `MKPlacemark`. As shown in the previous highlighted code, the information is available through various properties of the `MKPlacemark` class.

The second method we need to override is `FailedWithError`:

```
public override void FailedWithError (MKReverseGeocoder geocoder,
    NSError error)
```

This method is triggered when reverse geocoding fails for some reason. The information is contained in the `error` parameter.

To initialize the instance of the `MKReverseGeocoder` class, we pass the coordinates with an object of the type `CLLocationCoordinate2D` that we want geocoding information for, to its constructor:

```
this.reverseGeocoder = new MKReverseGeocoder(currentLocation);
```

Location Services and Maps

After assigning its delegate object, we call the `Start` method to reverse geocode the coordinates:

```
this.reverseGeocoder.Delegate = new ReverseGeocoderDelegate(this);
this.reverseGeocoder.Start();
```

There's more...

Detailed information on the location address can be retrieved through the `AddressDisctionary` property of the `MKPlacemark` class, which is of the type `NSDictionary`.

Things to have in mind when using the MKReverseGeocoder class

The `MKReverseGeocoder` class is part of the `MapKit` framework. Usage of this class binds the developer to Google's terms of service: http://code.google.com/apis/maps/iphone/terms.html.

One important term of using the reverse geocoding service is that it should always be used in combination with a Google map. Furthermore, to avoid abuse of the service, Apple recommends not to make more than one reverse geocoding call per minute.

See also

In this chapter:

- *Displaying maps*
- *Adding map annotations*
- *Adding map overlays*

Adding map annotations

In this recipe, we will discuss annotating a map to display various information.

Getting ready

Create a new project in MonoDevelop, and name it `MapAnnotateApp`.

How to do it...

1. Add an `MKMapView` on the view of `MainController`. Leave some room at the bottom, and add a button.

2. Add the namespaces `MonoTouch.MapKit` and `Monotouch.CoreLocation`, and enter the following code in the `ViewDidLoad` override:

   ```
   this.mapView.ShowsUserLocation = true;
   this.mapView.Delegate = new MapViewDelegate();
   this.buttonAddPin.TouchUpInside += delegate {
     CLLocationCoordinate2D mapCoordinate =
       this.mapView.UserLocation.Location.Coordinate;
     this.mapView.SetRegion(MKCoordinateRegion.FromDistance(
       mapCoordinate, 1000, 1000), true);
     MKPointAnnotation myAnnotation = new MKPointAnnotation();
     myAnnotation.Coordinate = mapCoordinate;
     myAnnotation.Title = "MyAnnotation";
     myAnnotation.Subtitle = "Standard annotation";
     this.mapView.AddAnnotation(myAnnotation);
   };
   ```

3. Create the following nested class:

   ```
   private class MapViewDelegate : MKMapViewDelegate{
     public override MKAnnotationView GetViewForAnnotation (MKMapView
       mapView, NSObject annotation){
       if (annotation is MKUserLocation){
         return null;
       } else{
         string reuseIdentifier = "MyAnnotation";
         MKPinAnnotationView pinView =
           mapView.DequeueReusableAnnotation(reuseIdentifier) as
           MKPinAnnotationView;
         if (null == pinView){
         pinView = new MKPinAnnotationView(annotation,
           reuseIdentifier);
         pinView.PinColor = MKPinAnnotationColor.Purple;
         pinView.AnimatesDrop = true;
         pinView.CanShowCallout = true;
       }
       return pinView;
       }
     }
   }
   ```

Location Services and Maps

4. Compile and run the application either on the simulator or on the device. If run on the simulator, when you tap on the button, the result should be similar to the following screenshot:

Tapping on **Add pin** displays the callout **bubble**, with the annotation title and subtitle.

How it works...

Annotating maps is very useful for providing various information along with map data. We can use the `MKPointAnnotation` class to create a simple annotation:

```
MKPointAnnotation myAnnotation = new MKPointAnnotation();
myAnnotation.Coordinate = mapCoordinate;
myAnnotation.Title = "MyAnnotation";
myAnnotation.Subtitle = "Standard annotation";
this.mapView.AddAnnotation(myAnnotation);
```

We assign the map coordinates the annotation will appear on and, optionally, a title and a subtitle. We then add the annotation to the map view with the `AddAnnotation` method.

Just adding an annotation object to a map view is not enough. The annotation needs a view that will display its information. This is accomplished by creating a delegate object for the map view and overriding its `GetViewForAnnotation` method:

```
public override MKAnnotationView GetViewForAnnotation (MKMapView
   mapView, NSObject annotation)
```

Since the map already displays the user location, an annotation already exists, and it is of the type `MKUserLocation`. Inside the `GetViewForAnnotation`, we have to make sure to provide a view for our own annotation by checking the type of annotation parameter:

```
if (annotation is MKUserLocation)
```

In this case, we just return `null`. If the annotation parameter is of the type `MKPointAnnotation`, then we first try to retrieve the view for it, in a similar fashion to the `UITableView` that creates the cells it contains:

```
MKPinAnnotationView pinView = mapView.DequeueReusableAnnotation(
    reuseIdentifier) as MKPinAnnotationView;
```

If the result of the `DequeueReusableAnnotation` method is `null`, then we initialize a new instance for our annotation view:

```
pinView = new MKPinAnnotationView(annotation, reuseIdentifier);
pinView.PinColor = MKPinAnnotationColor.Purple;
pinView.AnimatesDrop = true;
pinView.CanShowCallout = true;
```

The view we create for the annotation here is of the type `MKPinAnnotationView`. This is the standard view that is represented by a pin on the map. The properties that we set are pretty straightforward and define its appearance and behavior. The `PinColor` property defines the color of the pin, the `AnimatesDrop` property defines if the pin will be displayed on the map with an animation, and the `CanShowCallout` property defines if the annotation view will display the information of its underlying annotation in a callout "bubble".

After we have created the view for the annotation, we just return it from the method:

```
return pinView;
```

There's more...

We can also create custom annotations and annotation views. For annotations, we have to override the `MKAnnotation` class, while for annotation views we can override the `MKAnnotationView` class.

Annotation performance

Theoretically, we can add as many annotations as we want to a map view. Although the `MKMapView` can manage a large amount of annotations efficiently, it is strongly advised to take into account a performance degradation. A way to overcome this is to display annotations depending on the current map region, which basically manages the zoom level of the map. Another way is to make sure we use the same instances of annotation views for the annotations that do not need different annotation views.

Location Services and Maps

See also

In this chapter:

- *Displaying maps*
- *Adding map overlays*

In this book:

Chapter 5, Displaying Data:

- *Displaying data in a table*

Adding map overlays

In this recipe, we will discuss using overlays to draw on a map.

Getting ready

Create a new project in MonoDevelop, and name it `MapOverlayApp`.

How to do it...

1. Add an `MKMapView` on the view of `MainController`. Leave some room at the bottom, and add a button.

2. Add the namespaces `MonoTouch.MapKit` and `Monotouch.CoreLocation`, and enter the following code in the `ViewDidLoad` override:

   ```
   this.mapView.ShowsUserLocation = true;
   this.mapView.Delegate = new MapViewDelegate();
   this.buttonAddOverlay.TouchUpInside += delegate {
     CLLocationCoordinate2D mapCoordinate =
       this.mapView.UserLocation.Location.Coordinate;
     this.mapView.SetRegion(MKCoordinateRegion.FromDistance(
       mapCoordinate, 1000, 1000), true);
     MKCircle circleOverlay = MKCircle.Circle(mapCoordinate, 250);
     this.mapView.AddOverlay(circleOverlay);
   }
   ;
   ```

3. Add the following nested class:

   ```
   private class MapViewDelegate : MKMapViewDelegate{
     public override MKOverlayView GetViewForOverlay (MKMapView
       mapView, NSObject overlay){
       MKCircle circleOverlay = overlay as MKCircle;
   ```

```
            if (null != circleOverlay){
              MKCircleView circleView = new MKCircleView(circleOverlay);
              circleView.FillColor = UIColor.FromRGBA(
                1.0f, 0.5f, 0.5f, 0.5f);
              circleView.StrokeColor = UIColor.Red;
              circleView.LineWidth = 2f;
              return circleView;
            } else{
              return null;
            }
          }
        }
```

4. Compile and run the application either on the simulator or on the device. If run on the simulator, after tapping the button, the result should be similar to the following:

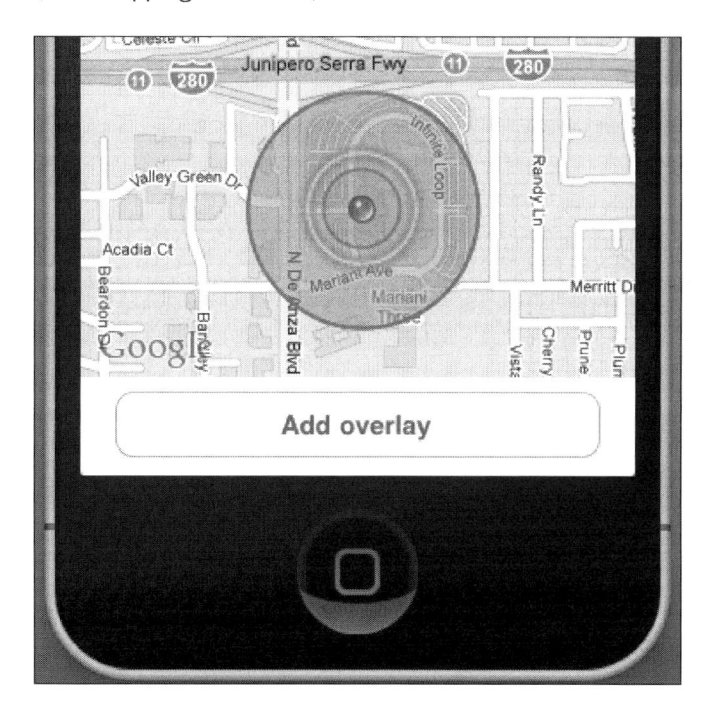

How it works...

While an MKAnnotation represents a point on a map, an MKOverlay object can represent an area on a map. In this example, we use the MKCircle class, which inherits from MKOverlay, to display a circle over an area on the map.

Location Services and Maps

We initialize an `MKCircle` instance with its `Circle` static method:

```
MKCircle circleOverlay = MKCircle.Circle(mapCoordinate, 250);
```

The first parameter represents the coordinates of the center of the circle, while the second parameter represents the radius of the circle, in meters. After initialization, we add the overlay to the map view with the `AddOverlay` method:

```
this.mapView.AddOverlay(circleOverlay);
```

Just like annotations, overlays require a view to display their information. To provide a view for our overlay, we override the `GetViewForOverlay` method in the map view's delegate object implementation:

```
public override MKOverlayView GetViewForOverlay (MKMapView mapView,
    NSObject overlay)
```

Inside this method, we first check if the overlay parameter is the type we want; in this case, an `MKCircle`:

```
MKCircle circleOverlay = overlay as MKCircle;
if (null != circleOverlay)
```

Then, we create an instance of the `MKCircleView` class and return it:

```
MKCircleView circleView = new MKCircleView(circleOverlay);
circleView.FillColor = UIColor.FromRGBA(1.0f, 0.5f, 0.5f, 0.5f);
circleView.StrokeColor = UIColor.Red;
circleView.LineWidth = 2f;
return circleView;
```

We set the appropriate properties that will define the appearance of our overlay. In this case, we set the `FillColor`, `StrokeColor`, and `LineWidth` properties.

There's more...

Overlays are handled efficiently by the map view. One important thing that the map view takes care for us is that when we scale the map, the overlay is automatically scaled to match each zoom level. This way, we do not need to scale the overlay manually in code.

Creating custom overlays

We can create our own custom overlays. To do this, we need to override the `MKOverlay` class for the overlay and the `MKOverlayView` class for the overlay view.

Standard overlay objects

Apart from the `MKCircle`, the other standard overlay objects are `MKPolygon` for creating polygon shapes and `MKPolyline` for creating polylines, like in a track-recording application.

See also

In this chapter:

- *Displaying maps*
- *Adding map annotations*

11
Graphics and Animation

In this chapter, we will cover:

- Animating views
- Transforming views
- Animation with images
- Animating layers
- Drawing lines and curves
- Drawing shapes
- Drawing text
- A simple drawing application
- Creating an image context

Introduction

In this chapter, we are going to discuss about custom drawing and animations. The iOS SDK contains two very useful frameworks for these tasks: Core Graphics and Core Animation.

These two frameworks simplify the process of animating UI elements and drawing 2D graphics on them. The effective usage of these two frameworks will make a difference between a dull and a stunning application. After all, these two frameworks play a very important role in making the iOS platform unique in its kind.

Graphics and Animation

We will learn how to provide simple or even more complicated animations for controls to provide a unique user experience. We will also see how to custom draw lines, curves, shapes, and text on the screen. Finally, with all the examples provided, we will create two drawing applications.

Animating Views

In this recipe, we will learn how to take advantage of `UIKit` animations to move a `UILabel` on the screen.

Getting ready

Create a new project in MonoDevelop, and name it `ViewAnimationApp`. Add a label and a button on the view of `MainController`.

How to do it...

1. Add the `MonoTouch.ObjCRuntime` namespace, and enter the following `ViewDidLoad` override:

   ```
   public override void ViewDidLoad (){
     base.ViewDidLoad ();
     this.lblOutput.BackgroundColor = UIColor.Green;
     this.buttonAnimate.TouchUpInside += delegate {
       RectangleF labelFrame = this.lblOutput.Frame;
       labelFrame.Y = 380f;
       UIView.BeginAnimations("LabelPositionAnimation");
       UIView.SetAnimationDuration(1);
       UIView.SetAnimationCurve(UIViewAnimationCurve.EaseInOut);
       UIView.SetAnimationDelegate(this);
       UIView.SetAnimationDidStopSelector(new
          Selector("LabelPositionAnimationStopped"));
       this.lblOutput.Frame = labelFrame;
       UIView.CommitAnimations();
     };
   }
   ```

2. Add the following method:

   ```
   [Export("LabelPositionAnimationStopped")]
   public void LabelAnimationStopped(){
     this.lblOutput.Text = "Animation ended!";
     this.lblOutput.BackgroundColor = UIColor.Red;
   }
   ```

3. Compile and run the application on the simulator.
4. Tap on the **Animate!** button, and watch the label move to the lower part of the view.

How it works...

The `UIView` class contains a number of various static methods that are targeted to animations. In this example, we simply change the position of a label with an animation.

To animate the change of position, we need to apply the changes after a call to the `BeginAnimations` method:

```
UIView.BeginAnimations("LabelPositionAnimation");
```

It accepts one string parameter, which declares the name of the animation. Changes we make to views after this call will be animated. But, we can also adjust various animation parameters:

```
UIView.SetAnimationDuration(1);
UIView.SetAnimationCurve(UIViewAnimationCurve.EaseInOut);
```

The `SetAnimationDuration` method defines the duration of the animation in seconds. The `SetAnimationCurve` method defines the default easing functions that will be applied to the animation at its start point and/or its end point.

We have the option of executing code when the animation completes. To do this, we first need to set the animation delegate object with the `SetAnimationDelegate` method:

```
UIView.SetAnimationDelegate(this);
```

In this example, we set our controller object, `MainController`, as the animation delegate object. After setting the delegate object, we need to set the selector that will be called when the animation completes:

```
UIView.SetAnimationDidStopSelector(new
   Selector("LabelPositionAnimationStopped"));
```

To create a `Selector` instance, we need to use the `MonoTouch.ObjCRuntime` namespace:

```
using MonoTouch.ObjCRuntime;
```

After making all the adjustments for our animation, we set the new value to the object that will be animated and call the `CommitAnimations` method:

```
this.lblOutput.Frame = labelFrame;
UIView.CommitAnimations();
```

Note that the code below the `BeginAnimations` call will be executed at the `CommitAnimations` line. Also, every animation started with the `BeginAnimations` method should have a corresponding call to the `CommitAnimations` method, or unexpected results will occur; for example, every change that is made to UI elements will be animated.

Graphics and Animation

There's more...

The `UIView` class also contains an overloaded `Animate` method. This method basically wraps all the methods we used here in one. The previous example, with the `Animate` method, is represented with the following code:

```
UIView.Animate(1, 0, UIViewAnimationOptions.CurveEaseInOut,
    delegate { this.lblOutput.Frame = labelFrame; },
    delegate { this.LabelAnimationStopped(); } );
```

The second parameter of this overload is the delay after which the animation will start.

UIKit animations and iOS versions

The `Animate` method was introduced on iOS version 4.0. When targeting an iOS version prior to 4, use the animation block, as defined by the `BeginAnimations` and `CommitAnimations` methods.

Animatable properties

`UIKit` animations support a specific set of `UIView` properties. These properties are called **animatable** properties. Following is a list of `UIView` properties that can be animated:

- Frame
- Bounds
- Center
- Transform
- Alpha
- BackgroundColor
- ContentStretch

Transforming views

In this recipe, we will rotate a `UILabel` by applying a transformation. Furthermore, the rotation will be animated.

Chapter 11

Getting ready

Create a new project in MonoDevelop, and name it `TransformViewApp`. Add a label and a button on the view of `MainController`.

How to do it...

1. Add the `MonoTouch.CoreGraphics` namespace:

   ```
   using MonoTouch.CoreGraphics;
   ```

2. Enter the following code in the `MainController` class:

   ```
   private double rotationAngle;
   public override void ViewDidLoad (){
     base.ViewDidLoad ();
     this.buttonRotate.TouchUpInside += delegate {
       this.rotationAngle += 90;
       CGAffineTransform transform = CGAffineTransform.MakeRotation(
         (float)this.DegreesToRadians(this.rotationAngle));
       UIView.BeginAnimations("RotateLabelAnimation");
       UIView.SetAnimationDuration(0.5f);
       this.lblOutput.Transform = transform;
       UIView.CommitAnimations();
       this.lblOutput.Text = string.Format("Rotated to {0} degrees.",
         this.rotationAngle);
       if (this.rotationAngle >= 360){
         this.rotationAngle = 0;
         this.lblOutput.Transform = CGAffineTransform.MakeIdentity();
       }
     };
   }
   public double DegreesToRadians (double degrees){
     return (degrees * Math.PI / 180);
   }
   ```

3. Compile and run the application on the simulator.

Graphics and Animation

4. Tap the button and watch the label rotate.

How it works...

The `MonoTouch.CoreGraphics` namespace is a wrapper around the `CoreGraphics` framework. This framework is the basic graphics framework of iOS.

To rotate a view, we need a transformation object that will be applied to the view through its `Transform` property:

```
CGAffineTransform transform = CGAffineTransform.MakeRotation(
    (float)this.DegreesToRadians(this.rotationAngle));
```

The transformation object is an instance of the class `CGAffineTransform` and is initialized through the `MakeRotation` static method. This method accepts a float value of the angle of rotation that we want to be applied, in radians. The `DegreesToRadians` method can be used to convert degrees to radians. After creating the transformation object, we assign it to the label's `Transform` property inside an animation block:

```
UIView.BeginAnimations("RotateLabelAnimation");
UIView.SetAnimationDuration(0.5f);
this.lblOutput.Transform = transform;
UIView.CommitAnimations();
```

Note that we need to increment the rotation angle each time the button is pressed, because the transformation we apply is not being auto-incremented. If we apply another rotation transformation object with the same angle, there will be no effect since it is basically the same transformation.

When the label has been rotated to a full circle (=360 degrees), we reset the `rotationAngle` value and the transformation object:

```
this.rotationAngle = 0;
this.lblOutput.Transform = CGAffineTransform.MakeIdentity();
```

The `MakeIdentity` static method creates an identity transformation object, which is the default transformation of all views, before applying transformation objects to them.

There's more...

The `CGAffineTransform` class contains various static methods for creating transformation objects. These are:

- `CGAffineTransformInvert`: This method inverts a current transformation and returns the result
- `MakeIdentity`: This method creates an identity transformation
- `MakeRotation`: This method creates a rotation transformation
- `MakeScale`: This method creates a scale transformation
- `MakeTranslation`: This method creates a translation transformation
- `Multiply`: This method multiplies two transformations and returns the result

Transformation and frame

After applying transformations on a view, its `Frame` property must not be taken into account. If there is a need for altering the view's size or position after a transformation has been applied, use the `Bounds` and `Center` properties, respectively.

See also

In this chapter:

- *Animating views*
- *Animating layers*

Graphics and Animation

Animation with images

In this recipe, we will create a simple slideshow of images using the built-in animation feature of `UIImageView`.

Getting ready

Create a new project in MonoDevelop, and name it `ImageAnimationApp`. Add a `UIImageView` and two buttons on the view of `MainController`. The sample project for this task contains three images. Add two or more images to the project, and set their **Build Action** to **Content**.

How to do it...

1. Enter the following `ViewDidLoad` override:

   ```
   public override void ViewDidLoad (){
     base.ViewDidLoad ();
     this.imageView.ContentMode = UIViewContentMode.ScaleAspectFit;
     this.imageView.AnimationImages = new UIImage[] {
       UIImage.FromFile("images/Kastoria.jpg"),
       UIImage.FromFile("images/Parga02.jpg"),
       UIImage.FromFile("images/Toroni.jpg")
     };
     this.imageView.AnimationDuration = 3;
     this.imageView.AnimationRepeatCount = 10;
     this.buttonAnimate.TouchUpInside += delegate {
       if (!this.imageView.IsAnimating){
         this.imageView.StartAnimating();
       }
     };
     this.buttonStop.TouchUpInside += delegate {
       if (this.imageView.IsAnimating){
         this.imageView.StopAnimating();
       }
     };
   }
   ```

2. Compile and run the application on the simulator.

3. Tap the **Animate images** button to start the animation.

How it works...

The `UIImageView` can accept an array of `UIImage` objects and automatically display them in a sequence.

To load the images that the view will animate, assign an array of the images to its `AnimationImages` property:

```
this.imageView.AnimationImages = new UIImage[] {
  UIImage.FromFile("images/Kastoria.jpg"),
  UIImage.FromFile("images/Parga02.jpg"),
  UIImage.FromFile("images/Toroni.jpg")
} ;
```

The sequence in which the images will be displayed is defined by their order in the array. After setting the images that will be animated, we set the duration of the animation in seconds and the number of times it will occur:

```
this.imageView.AnimationDuration = 3;
this.imageView.AnimationRepeatCount = 10;
```

To start or stop the animation, call the `StartAnimating` or `StopAnimating` methods, respectively.

There's more...

There is no relation between the `AnimationImages` and `Image` properties of the `UIImageView` class. Set an image to be displayed to the `Image` property before or after an animation, if one needs to be displayed when no animation takes place.

Checking for animation

To determine if an animation takes place, check the `IsAnimating` property of `UIImageView`.

See also

In this chapter:

- *Animating views*

In this book:

Chapter 2, User Interface: Views:

- *Displaying images*

Graphics and Animation

Animating layers

In this recipe, we will learn how to use the `Core Animation` framework to copy a `UILabel` on the screen, by animating its layer.

Getting ready

Create a new project in MonoDevelop, and name it `LayerAnimation`. Add two labels and a button on the view of `MainController`. Set text and background color for the first view and a different background color for the second view.

How to do it...

1. Add `MonoTouch.CoreAnimation` namespace:

    ```
    using MonoTouch.CoreAnimation;
    ```

2. Add a field of the type `CALayer` in the class:

    ```
    private CALayer copyLayer;
    ```

3. Add the following code in the `ViewDidLoad` override:

    ```
    this.buttonCopy.TouchUpInside += delegate {
       this.lblTarget.Text = string.Empty;
       this.lblTarget.BackgroundColor = UIColor.Blue;
       this.copyLayer = new CALayer();
       this.copyLayer.Frame = this.lblSource.Frame;
       this.copyLayer.Contents = this.lblSource.Layer.Contents;
       this.View.Layer.AddSublayer(this.copyLayer);
       CABasicAnimation positionAnimation =
         CABasicAnimation.FromKeyPath("position");
       positionAnimation.To = NSValue.FromPointF(this.lblTarget.Center);
       positionAnimation.Duration = 1;
       positionAnimation.RemovedOnCompletion = true;
       positionAnimation.TimingFunction = CAMediaTimingFunction.FromName(
           CAMediaTimingFunction.EaseInEaseOut);
       positionAnimation.AnimationStopped += delegate {
          this.lblTarget.BackgroundColor = this.lblSource.BackgroundColor;
          this.lblTarget.Text = this.lblSource.Text;
          this.lblTarget.TextColor = this.lblSource.TextColor;
          this.copyLayer.RemoveFromSuperLayer();
       };
    ```

```
    CABasicAnimation sizeAnimation =
      CABasicAnimation.FromKeyPath("bounds");
    sizeAnimation.To = NSValue.FromRectangleF(new RectangleF(0f, 0f,
      this.lblSource.Bounds.Width * 2f,
      this.lblSource.Bounds.Height * 2));
    sizeAnimation.Duration = positionAnimation.Duration / 2;
    sizeAnimation.RemovedOnCompletion = true;
    sizeAnimation.AutoReverses = true;
    this.copyLayer.AddAnimation(positionAnimation,
      "PositionAnimation");
    this.copyLayer.AddAnimation(sizeAnimation, "SizeAnimation");
};
```

4. Compile and run the application on the simulator.
5. Tap the **Copy** button to copy the contents of the first label to the second label with animation.

Graphics and Animation

How it works...

The `MonoTouch.CoreAnimation` namespace is a wrapper around the `Core Animation` framework.

Every view has a `Layer` property, which returns the view's `CALayer` object. In this task, we are creating an animation that graphically displays copying label contents from one label to another.

Instead of creating another label and moving it with `UIView` animation, we will create a layer and move that instead. We create the layer by setting its `Frame` and `Contents` property, the latter from the source label's layer. We then add the layer to the main view's layer with the `AddSublayer` method. After this point, the main view contains a layer, which displays the same contents and is on top of the source label.

```
this.copyLayer = new CALayer();
this.copyLayer.Frame = this.lblSource.Frame;
this.copyLayer.Contents = this.lblSource.Layer.Contents;
this.View.Layer.AddSublayer(this.copyLayer);
```

To animate the transition from the source label to the target label, we will use the `CABasicAnimation` class. The previous highlighted code shows how to initialize and set up the instances of the class. The `FromKeyPath` static method creates a new instance, accepting as a parameter the name of the layer's property that will be animated. The `To` property represents the value the property will be animated to. The `Duration` property represents the duration of the animation in seconds, while the `RemovedOnCompletion` property declares that the animation object should be removed from the layer when the animation finishes. The `TimingFunction` property sets the behavior of the animation. The `AnimationStopped` event is triggered when the animation finishes. Inside the handler we assign to it, we set the contents of the source label to the target label, thus completing the copy. The `AutoReverses` property states that when the value of the `To` property has been reached, the animation should be reversed. It is this property that gives the effect of the label getting bigger and subsequently smaller when it reaches its final position.

The animations start when they are added to the layer:

```
this.copyLayer.AddAnimation(positionAnimation, "PositionAnimation");
this.copyLayer.AddAnimation(sizeAnimation, "SizeAnimation");
```

There's more...

A list of strings that the `FromKeyPath` method accepts can be found in the following link: http://developer.apple.com/library/ios/#documentation/Cocoa/Conceptual/CoreAnimation_guide/Articles/KVCAdditions.html#//apple_ref/doc/uid/TP40005299.

Apart from the `To` property, the `CABasicAnimation` class has two more properties for defining the animation: `From` and `By`. They are all of the type `NSObject`, but the actual values that should be assigned to them should be of the type `NSValue`. The `NSValue` class contains various static methods for creating instances of it.

Layers

Layers are very powerful and efficient objects that can be used for both drawing and animations. Using layers to perform animations on views, instead of the actual views themselves, is strongly suggested.

See also

In this chapter

- *Animating Views*

Drawing lines and curves

In this recipe, we will implement custom drawing to draw two lines on a `UIView`.

Getting ready

Create a new project in MonoDevelop, and name it `DrawLineApp`.

How to do it...

1. Add a new class to the project, and name it `DrawingView`. Derive it from `UIView`:

    ```
    public class DrawingView : UIView
    ```

2. Add the following `using` directive in the `DrawingView.cs` file:

    ```
    using MonoTouch.CoreGraphics;
    ```

3. Override the `Draw` method of `UIView`, and implement it with the following code:

    ```
    public override void Draw (RectangleF rect){
      base.Draw (rect);
      Console.WriteLine("DrawingView draw!");
      using (CGContext context = UIGraphics.GetCurrentContext()){
        context.SetLineWidth(5f);
        context.SetStrokeColorWithColor(UIColor.Green.CGColor);
        context.AddLines(new PointF[] {
          new PointF(0f, this.Bounds.Height),
          new PointF(this.Bounds.Width, 0f)
    ```

Graphics and Animation

```
        } );
        context.StrokePath();
        context.SetStrokeColorWithColor(UIColor.Red.CGColor);
    context.MoveTo(0, this.Bounds.Height);
    context.AddCurveToPoint(0f, this.Bounds.Height, 50f,
      this.Bounds.Height / 2f, this.Bounds.Width, 0f);
        context.StrokePath();
    }
}
```

4. In the `ViewDidLoad` override of the `MainController`, initialize and add the view:

   ```
   DrawingView drawingView = new DrawingView(this.View.Bounds);
   drawingView.BackgroundColor = UIColor.Gray;
   this.View.AddSubview(this.drawingView);
   ```

5. Compile and run the application on the simulator. The result should be similar to the following:

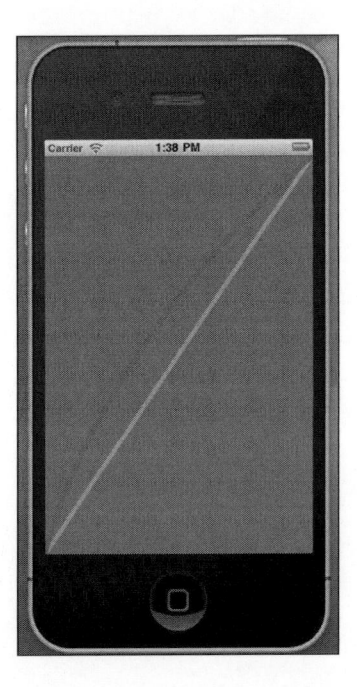

How it works...

The `MonoTouch.CoreGraphics` namespace is a wrapper around the native `Core Graphics` framework. The `Core Graphics` framework contains the necessary objects for custom drawing on views.

To draw on a view, we have to override its `Draw(RectangleF)` method:

```
public override void Draw (RectangleF rect)
```

Inside the `Draw` method, we need an instance of the current graphics context:

```
using (CGContext context = UIGraphics.GetCurrentContext())
```

A graphics context is represented by the `CGContext` class. The `UIGraphics.GetCurrentContext` static method returns an instance of the current context.

The `CGContext` class contains various methods that allows us to draw on the view. We need to set the line width, the color, and then add the type of drawing:

```
context.SetLineWidth(5f);
context.SetStrokeColorWithColor(UIColor.Green.CGColor);
context.AddLines(new PointF[] {
  new PointF(0f, this.Bounds.Height),
  new PointF(this.Bounds.Width, 0f)
} );
```

To add a line, we use the `AddLines` method that accepts an array of `PointF` structs containing the start and end points of each line. Just adding the lines to the context is not enough. To present the drawing on the view, we call the `StrokePath` method:

```
context.StrokePath();
```

To add another item to the drawing, we repeat the steps accordingly. The `MoveTo` method moves the current point so that the additional item will have a starting point for the curve.

There's more...

The `Draw` method is being called by the runtime when it needs to draw the contents of a view. We can only get the instance of the current graphics context inside the `Draw` method. We should not call it directly, since the `UIGraphics.GetCurrentContext` method will return `null` if we do. If we need to force the runtime to call the `Draw` method, we need to call `SetNeedsDisplay()`. Care should be taken when calling it, since drawing operations are expensive in terms of CPU usage.

When there is no need for causing the entire view area to be redrawn, we can call the `SetNeedsDisplayInRect` method, passing the `RectangleF` in the view's coordinate system of the area that we want to be updated.

Graphics and Animation

Graphics context on a UIImageView

The current graphics context of a `UIImageView` is reserved for drawing the contents of the image. Calling `SetNeedsDisplay` on a custom view deriving from `UIImageView` has the same effect as calling the `Draw` method directly. If we need to draw on a custom image view, we have to either add another view on top of it and draw on that, or draw on a custom layer and add it to the view's main layer.

See also

In this chapter:

- *Drawing text*

In this book:

Chapter 2, User Interface: Views:

- *Creating a custom view*

Drawing shapes

Following the example in the previous recipe, we will draw a circle and a square on the screen.

Getting ready

Create a new project in MonoDevelop, and name it `DrawShapeApp`. Add a custom view like in the previous task, and name it `DrawingView`.

How to do it...

1. Add the following code in the `Draw` method override:

   ```
   using (CGContext context = UIGraphics.GetCurrentContext()){
     context.SetFillColorWithColor(UIColor.Blue.CGColor);
     context.SetShadow(new SizeF(10f, 10f), 5f);
     context.AddEllipseInRect(new RectangleF(100f, 100f,
       100f, 100f));
     context.FillPath();
     context.SetFillColorWithColor(UIColor.Red.CGColor);
     context.AddRect(new RectangleF(150f, 150f, 100f, 100f));
     context.FillPath();
   }
   ```

2. Compile and run the application on the simulator. The result on the screen should be similar to the following:

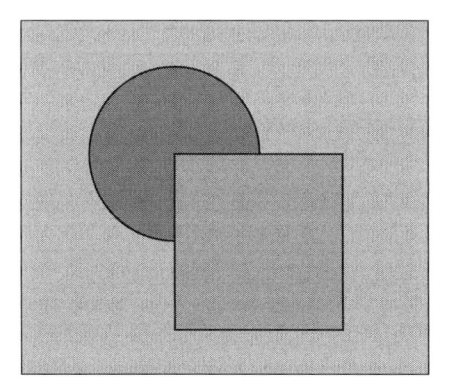

How it works...

To draw shapes on a view, we need to call the appropriate method. We first set the fill color of the `CGContext` instance:

```
context.SetFillColorWithColor(UIColor.Blue.CGColor);
```

To draw a circle, we call the `AddEllipseInRect` method, passing a `RectangleF` object containing the bounding rectangle of the circle:

```
context.AddEllipseInRect(new RectangleF(100f, 100f, 100f, 100f));
```

Whether the shape will be an ellipse or an absolute circle is defined through the bounding rectangle's size. We then call the `FillPath` method:

```
context.FillPath();
```

The shadow effect is defined by the `SetShadow` method:

```
context.SetShadow(new SizeF(10f, 10f), 5f);
```

The first parameter, which is of the type `SizeF`, defines the offset of the shadow, while the second parameter defines the amount of blur.

There's more...

When the `SetShadow` method is called, all objects that are added to the context are displayed with a shadow. To remove the shadow, call the `SetShadowWithColor` method, passing either a fully transparent color or `null` for the color parameter.

Graphics and Animation

Transparent colors

To fill a shape with a transparent color, create a `CGColor` instance with the appropriate values:

```
context.SetFillColorWithColor(new CGColor(1f, 0f, 0f, 0.5f));
```

This will create a red color with its alpha set to 50 percent.

See also

In this chapter:

- *Drawing lines and curves*

Drawing text

In this recipe, we will learn how to draw styled text with an outline.

Getting ready

Create a new project in MonoDevelop, and name it `DrawTextApp`. Add the `DrawingView` class that we created in the previous tasks to the project.

How to do it...

1. Implement the following `Draw` method override in the `DrawingView` class:

   ```
   using (CGContext context = UIGraphics.GetCurrentContext()){
     context.SetFillColorWithColor(UIColor.Yellow.CGColor);
     context.SetTextDrawingMode(CGTextDrawingMode.FillStroke);
     NSString drawText = new NSString("This text is drawn!");
     drawText.DrawString(new PointF(10f, 100f),
       UIFont.FromName("Verdana-Bold", 28f));
   }
   ```

2. Compile and run the application on the simulator. The text will be displayed on the screen. The result should be similar to the following:

How it works...

The `NSString` class contains the very useful method `DrawString`, which draws the text it contains to the current context. To provide the outline effect, we call the `SetTextDrawingMode` method:

```
context.SetTextDrawingMode(CGTextDrawingMode.FillStroke);
```

We pass the `CGTextDrawingMode.FillStroke` value. Since we have not set a stroke color to the context, it defaults to black.

Finally, the `DrawString` method is called:

```
drawText.DrawString(new PointF(10f, 100f), UIFont.FromName(
   "Verdana-Bold", 28f));
```

This method is overloaded. The overload we use here accepts a `PointF` struct, which represents the location of the string in the view's coordinate system, and a `UIFont` instance that represents the font by which the text will be rendered on the screen.

There's more...

The `CGContext` class contains the method for drawing text. We first need to call `SelectFont` method to assign the font:

```
context.SelectFont("Verdana-Bold", 28f, CGTextEncoding.MacRoman);
```

We then call the `ShowTextAtPoint` method to draw the text:

```
context.ShowTextAtPoint(10, 100, drawText.ToString());
```

This will give the following result:

The text will be displayed at the correct position, but reversed. To correct this, we need to set a transformation matrix to the `TextMatrix` property:

```
context.TextMatrix = new CGAffineTransform(1, 0, 0, -1, 0, 0);
```

Graphics and Animation

The biggest advantage in using the `CGContext` class' methods is that we can easily transform the text appearance. For example, by applying a slightly different transformation matrix, we can easily display skewed text:

```
context.TextMatrix = new CGAffineTransform(1, 1, 0, -1, 0, 0);
```

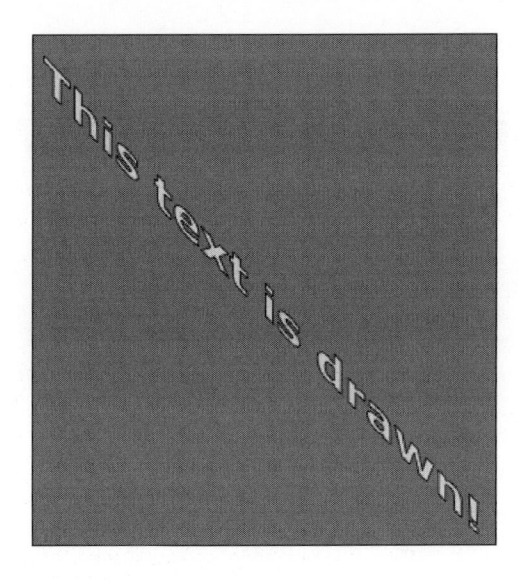

Size of drawn text

The `DrawString` method of the `NSString` class returns the size of the bounding rectangle of the text. We can, however, get the size of the text before drawing through the `StringSize` method:

```
Console.WriteLine("Text size: {0}",
    drawText.StringSize(UIFont.FromName("Verdana-Bold", 28f)));
```

See also

In this chapter:

- *Drawing lines and curves*
- *Drawing shapes*

A simple drawing application

In this recipe, we will use the techniques that we learned to create a drawing application.

Chapter 11

Getting ready

Create a new project in MonoDevelop, and name it `FingerDrawingApp`. Once again, we will need a custom view. Add a class deriving from `UIView`, and name it `CanvasView`.

How to do it...

1. Implement the `CanvasView` class with the following code:

```
public class CanvasView : UIView{
  public CanvasView (RectangleF frame) : base(frame){
    this.drawPath = new CGPath();
  }
  private PointF touchLocation;
  private PointF previousTouchLocation;
  private CGPath drawPath;
  private bool fingerDraw;
  public override void TouchesBegan (NSSet touches, UIEvent evt){
    base.TouchesBegan (touches, evt);
    UITouch touch = touches.AnyObject as UITouch;
    this.fingerDraw = true;
    this.touchLocation = touch.LocationInView(this);
    this.previousTouchLocation =
      touch.PreviousLocationInView(this);
    this.SetNeedsDisplay();
  }
  public override void TouchesMoved (NSSet touches, UIEvent evt){
    base.TouchesMoved (touches, evt);
    UITouch touch = touches.AnyObject as UITouch;
    this.touchLocation = touch.LocationInView(this);
    this.previousTouchLocation =
      touch.PreviousLocationInView(this);
    this.SetNeedsDisplay();
  }
  public override void Draw (RectangleF rect){
    base.Draw (rect);
    if (this.fingerDraw){
      using (CGContext context = UIGraphics.GetCurrentContext()){
        context.SetStrokeColorWithColor(UIColor.Blue.CGColor);
        context.SetLineWidth(5f);
      context.SetLineJoin(CGLineJoin.Round);
      context.SetLineCap(CGLineCap.Round);
        this.drawPath.MoveToPoint(this.previousTouchLocation);
```

Graphics and Animation

```
            this.drawPath.AddLineToPoint(this.touchLocation);
            context.AddPath(this.drawPath);
            context.DrawPath(CGPathDrawingMode.Stroke);
        }
      }
    }
}
```

2. Compile and run the application on the simulator or on the device.
3. Touch and drag your finger (or click-and-drag with the cursor) and start drawing!

How it works...

In this task, we are combining touch events and custom drawing to create a simple drawing application. When the user touches and moves the finger on the screen, we keep the touch location points information and use them in the `Draw` method to draw lines.

After setting the touch locations to the class fields, we call `SetNeedsDisplay` to force the `Draw` method to be called. The `fingerDraw` field is used to determine if the `Draw` method was called by a touch on the screen and not by the runtime when the view is first loaded.

Every time we call a method to draw something to a graphics context, the previous drawings in that context are cleared. To avoid this behavior, we use a `CGPath` object. We can add various drawing objects in a `CGPath` and display these objects on the screen by adding them to the graphics context. So, every time the user moves the finger on the screen, the new lines defined by the touch location points are added to the path, and the path is drawn on the current context.

Chapter 11

Note that we need to hold information of both the current touch location and the previous one. This is because the `AddLineToPoint` method accepts one point, which defines the end point of the line, assuming there already is a point in the path. The starting point of each line is defined by calling `MoveToPoint`, passing the previous touch location point.

The path that is drawn on the screen by sliding the finger on it is basically comprised of a series of consecutive straight lines. The result, however, is a smooth path that follows the finger movement, because the `TouchesMoved` method is triggered every time there is a single movement of the finger on the screen.

After adding the line to the path, we add it to the context and draw it:

```
context.AddPath(this.drawPath);
context.DrawPath(CGPathDrawingMode.Stroke);
```

There's more...

Two new `CGContext` methods are introduced in this task: `SetLineJoin` and `SetLineCap`. The `SetLineJoin` method sets how each line will be joined to the previous one, while the `SetLineCap` sets the appearance of the endpoint of a line.

The values they accept are explained as follows:

- `SetLineJoin`
    - `CGLineJoin.Miter`: Joins two lines with an angled corner
    - `CGLineJoin.Round`: Joins two lines with a rounded end
    - `CGLineJoin.Bevel`: Joins two lines with a squared end
- `SetLineCap`
    - `CGLineCap.Butt`: The line will end with a squared edge on the endpoint
    - `CGLineCap.Round`: The line will end with a rounded edge that expands beyond the endpoint
    - `CGLineCap.Square`: The line will end with a squared edge that expands beyond the endpoint

Clear the drawing

To clear the drawing, we simply have to set the `fingerDraw` variable to `false` and call `SetNeedsDisplay`. This way, the `Draw` method will be called without our custom drawing code, clearing the current context.

Graphics and Animation

See also

In this chapter:

- *Drawing lines and curves*
- *Drawing shapes*
- *Drawing text*

Creating an image context

In this recipe, we will expand the finger drawing application that we created previously by providing the user with the feature of saving the created drawings.

Getting ready

Create a new project in MonoDevelop, and name it `ImageContextApp`. Add the `CanvasView` class that we created in the previous task to the project.

How to do it...

1. Add two buttons on the view of `MainController`. One will be used for saving the image and the other for clearing the current drawing.

2. Add the following methods in the `CanvasView` class:

   ```
   public UIImage GetDrawingImage(){
     UIImage toReturn = null;
     UIGraphics.BeginImageContext(this.Bounds.Size);
     using (CGContext context = UIGraphics.GetCurrentContext()){
       context.SetStrokeColorWithColor(UIColor.Blue.CGColor);
       context.SetLineWidth(10f);
       context.SetLineJoin(CGLineJoin.Round);
       context.SetLineCap(CGLineCap.Round);
       context.AddPath(this.drawPath);
       context.DrawPath(CGPathDrawingMode.Stroke);
       toReturn = UIGraphics.GetImageFromCurrentImageContext();
     }
     UIGraphics.EndImageContext();
     return toReturn;
   }
   public void ClearDrawing(){
     this.fingerDraw = false;
     this.drawPath.Dispose();
     this.drawPath = new CGPath();
     this.SetNeedsDisplay();
   }
   ```

3. Add the following code in the `MainController` class:

   ```
   private CanvasView canvasView;
   public override void ViewDidLoad (){
     base.ViewDidLoad ();
     this.canvasView = new CanvasView(new RectangleF(
       this.View.Bounds.Location, new SizeF(this.View.Bounds.Width,
       this.buttonClear.Frame.Top - 10f)));
     this.canvasView.BackgroundColor = UIColor.Gray;
     this.View.AddSubview(this.canvasView);
     this.buttonSave.TouchUpInside += delegate {
       UIImage drawingImage = this.canvasView.GetDrawingImage();
       drawingImage.SaveToPhotosAlbum(delegate(
         UIImage image, NSError error) {
         if (error != null){
           Console.WriteLine("Error saving image! {0}",
             error.LocalizedDescription);
         }
       } );
     } ;
     this.buttonClear.TouchUpInside += delegate {
       this.canvasView.ClearDrawing();
     } ;
   }
   ```

4. Compile and run the application on the simulator.
5. Draw something on the canvas, and tap the **Save drawing** button to save your drawing.
6. Tap on the **Clear** drawing button to clear the canvas. You can then check the simulator's photo albums for your drawing.

How it works...

Using the `UIGraphics` class, we can create an image context through which we can retrieve our drawing in a `UIImage` object.

To create an image context, inside the `GetDrawingImage` method we call the `BeginImageContext` static method, passing the size we want the image context to have:

```
UIGraphics.BeginImageContext(this.Bounds.Size);
```

The current context is now the image context that we created with the `BeginImageContext` call. We then repeat the code we have in the `Draw` method, only this time there is no need to add new lines to the path. We simply add the path we already have to the context and draw it.

Graphics and Animation

After adding the path, we get the context image by calling the `GetImageFromCurrentContext` method:

```
toReturn = UIGraphics.GetImageFromCurrentImageContext();
```

Finally, we have to end the image context block and return the `UIImage` object:

```
UIGraphics.EndImageContext();
return toReturn;
```

To clear the drawing from the screen, we simply have to set the `fingerDraw` variable to `false` and dispose and prepare our `CGPath` object for re-use, inside the `ClearDrawing` method:

```
this.fingerDraw = false;
this.drawPath.Dispose();
this.drawPath = new CGPath();
```

To reflect the clearing on the screen immediately, we call the `SetNeedsDisplay` method:

```
this.SetNeedsDisplay();
```

There's more...

We cannot create an image context inside the `Draw` method. That is because when we call the `BeginImageContext` method, a context is actually created, but the view's default context remains as the current context. Hence, the `GetImageFromCurrentImageContext` method would return `null`.

Drawing on UIImageView

The technique discussed here can be used to draw on custom `UIImageViews`. To display the drawing when the finger slides on the screen, we would simply have to set its `Image` property to the image we get from the image context.

Background on saved drawings

You will notice that although we are setting the `CanvasView` background to gray, the saved drawings are with a white background. This is because the view's background color is not included in the drawing. To include it, we would just have to draw a rectangle with the same color as the background color to the graphics context.

See also

In this chapter:

- Drawing lines and curves
- Drawing shapes
- Drawing text
- A simple drawing application

12
Multitasking

In this chapter, we will cover:

- Detecting application states
- Receiving notifications for application states
- Running code in the background
- Playing audio in the background
- Network connectivity maintenance

Introduction

When the iOS platform was introduced in 2007, bringing lots of exciting new features to users, it drastically changed the concept of mobile devices.

Despite its huge success, it lacked some features at the time that were considered as "basic". One of these features was multitasking; that is, support for running multiple processes at the same time. The platform actually did support multitasking to system processes internally, but it was not available to developers. Starting with iOS 4, Apple provided support for multitasking, although it is still quite different to what most developers are accustomed to.

In this chapter, we will discuss how to make use of the platform's multitasking features. We will see under what circumstances we can use these features and what functionality we can provide through multitasking to the users of our applications. Specifically, we will learn about an application's states and its runtime lifecycle. Through a series of detailed example projects, we will be able to execute code while an application is in the background, support audio playback, and VoIP connection maintenance.

Multitasking

Detecting application states

In this recipe, we will discuss how to detect and respond accordingly when an application transitions from the active to the inactive state, and vice versa.

Getting ready

Create a new project in MonoDevelop, and name it `AppStateApp`. There is no need for a view controller in this example.

How to do it...

1. Add the following method overrides in the `AppDelegate` class:

   ```
   public override void OnActivated (UIApplication application){
     Console.WriteLine("Activated, application state: {0}",
       application.ApplicationState);
   }
   public override void OnResignActivation (UIApplication
     application){
     Console.WriteLine("Resign activation, application state: {0}",
       application.ApplicationState);
   }
   public override void DidEnterBackground (UIApplication
     application){
     Console.WriteLine("Entered background, application state: {0}",
       application.ApplicationState);
   }
   public override void WillEnterForeground (UIApplication
     application){
     Console.WriteLine("Will enter foreground, application state:
       {0}", application.ApplicationState);
   }
   ```

2. Compile and run the application either on the simulator or on the device.
3. Press the **home** button to suspend the application, and watch the **Application Output** pad in MonoDevelop.

How it works...

The `UIApplicationDelegate` class contains methods that are triggered at specific notifications issued by the runtime. These methods are:

- `OnActivated`: This method is called when the application is made active, for example, when unlocking the screen, or when the application starts.

- `OnResignActivation`: This method is called when the application is about to become inactive, for example, when the screen is locked or when the multitasking bar is presented.
- `DidEnterBackground`: This method is called when the application has entered the background, for example, when pressing the **home** button. The application is suspended.
- `WillEnterForeground`: This method is called when the application is about to return to the foreground.

Note that when the application is moved to the background, both the `OnResignActivation` and `DidEnterBackground` methods are called. Similarly, when the application is moved to the foreground, both the `WillEnterForeground` and `OnActivated` methods are called.

All these methods contain one parameter, which contains the `UIApplication` instance of the application. The `UIApplication` class contains the property `ApplicationState`, which returns the state of the application in values of the `UIApplicationState` property. These values are:

- `Active`: This value indicates that the application is active
- `Inactive`: This value indicates that the application is inactive, for example, when a notification alert is displayed
- `Background`: This value indicates that the application is in the background

There's more...

Multitasking is a feature of iOS 4+, and not all devices support multitasking, even if they are running on iOS 4+. For versions prior to 4, when the **home** button is pressed, the `WillTerminate` method is called:

```
public override void WillTerminate (UIApplication application){
   Console.WriteLine("App will terminate!");
}
```

There are cases, however, in which iOS will kill your application; for example, when a memory warning is issued and your application does not free up resources. The `WillTerminate` method will also be called in these cases.

Support for multitasking

To check if the device supports multitasking, check the `UIDevice.CurrentDevice.IsMultitaskingSupported` property.

Multitasking

Proper usage

These methods are very useful because they allow us to save the current data that is presented to the user when the application changes state. When the application transitions to an inactive or background state, each method is given a limited amount of time to execute, so we should make sure they do not perform long-running operations, or iOS will kill the application.

Receiving notifications for application states

In this recipe, we will discuss getting notified to application state changes outside the scope of the `UIApplicationDelegate` implementation.

Getting ready

Create a new project in MonoDevelop, and name it `NotifyStatesApp`. Add a view with controller to the project, and name it `MainController`.

How to do it...

1. Enter the following fields in the `MainController` class:

   ```
   private NSObject didEnterBgdObserver;
   private NSObject willEnterFgdObserver;
   ```

2. Create the following methods:

   ```
   private void AddAppStateObservers(){
     this.didEnterBgdObserver = NSNotificationCenter.DefaultCenter.
       AddObserver(UIApplication.DidEnterBackgroundNotification,
       delegate(NSNotification obj) {
         Console.WriteLine("App entered background, app state: {0}",
           UIApplication.SharedApplication.ApplicationState);
     } );
     this.willEnterFgdObserver = NSNotificationCenter.DefaultCenter.
       AddObserver(UIApplication.WillEnterForegroundNotification,
       delegate(NSNotification obj) {
         Console.WriteLine("App will enter foreground, app state: {0}",
           UIApplication.SharedApplication.ApplicationState);
     } );
   }
   private void RemoveAppStateObservers(){
     NSNotificationCenter.DefaultCenter.RemoveObservers(new
       NSObject[] { this.didEnterBgdObserver,
       this.willEnterFgdObserver });
   }
   ```

Chapter 12

3. In the `ViewDidLoad` override, call the `AddAppStateObservers` method:

    ```
    this.AddAppStateObservers();
    ```

4. Compile and run the application on the simulator.

5. Press the **home** button, and watch the output in the **Application Output** pad. It should be similar to the following screenshot:

```
Application Output
Launching application
Application launched. PID = 14254
Loaded assembly: /Developer/MonoTouch/usr/lib/mono/2.1/monotouch.dll
Loaded assembly: /Developer/MonoTouch/usr/lib/mono/2.1/System.Core.dll
Loaded assembly: /Developer/MonoTouch/usr/lib/mono/2.1/System.dll
Loaded assembly: /Users/mrmojo/Projects/forBook_iOS5/CH12_code/NotifyStatesApp/NotifyStatesApp/bin/iPhoneSimulator/Debug/NotifyStatesApp.exe
Loaded assembly: /Developer/MonoTouch/usr/lib/mono/2.1/Mono.Security.dll
Loaded assembly: /Developer/MonoTouch/usr/lib/mono/2.1/System.Xml.dll
App entered background, app state: Background
```

How it works...

Apart from calling the methods of the `UIApplicationDelegate` object for application states, iOS issues notifications that we can receive. This is very useful, because in most cases we need to be notified for application state changes outside of the scope of the `AppDelegate` class.

To accomplish this, we use the `NSNotificationCenter`:

```
this.didEnterBgdObserver = NSNotificationCenter.DefaultCenter.
  AddObserver(UIApplication.DidEnterBackgroundNotification,
  delegate(NSNotification obj) {
  Console.WriteLine("App entered background, app state: {0}",
    UIApplication.SharedApplication.ApplicationState);
} );
```

The notification keys we are interested in are exposed through the `UIApplication` static properties. This example only adds notification observers for transition between background and foreground.

The result is similar to the example of the previous recipe, but only after the `MainController` is loaded.

There's more...

To add notification observers for when the application is activated or resigns activation, we use the `UIApplication.DidBecomeActiveNotification` and `UIApplication.WillResignActiveNotification` keys, respectively.

299

Multitasking

Removing notification observers

To remove the notification observers when they are no longer needed, call the `RemoveAppStateObservers` method inside the `ViewDidUnload` override:

```
this.RemoveAppStateObservers();
```

See also

In this chapter:

- *Detecting application states*

Running code in the background

In this recipe, we will learn how to execute code in the background, taking full advantage of iOS' multitasking feature.

Getting ready

Create a new project in MonoDevelop, and name it `BackgroundCodeApp`. There is no need for a view controller in this example.

How to do it...

1. Enter the following code in the `AppDelegate` class:

    ```
    private int taskID;
    public override void DidEnterBackground (UIApplication
      application){
      if (UIDevice.CurrentDevice.IsMultitaskingSupported &&
        this.taskID == 0){
        this.taskID = application.BeginBackgroundTask(delegate {
          application.EndBackgroundTask(taskID);
          this.taskID = 0;
        } );
        ThreadPool.QueueUserWorkItem(delegate {
          for (int i = 0; i < 60; i++){
            Console.WriteLine("Task: {0} - Current Time: {1}",
              this.taskID, DateTime.Now);
            Thread.Sleep(1000);
          }
          application.EndBackgroundTask(this.taskID);
          this.taskID = 0;
        } );
    ```

```
      }
    }
    public override void WillEnterForeground (UIApplication
      application){
      if (this.taskID != 0){
        Console.WriteLine("Background task is running!");
      } else{
        Console.WriteLine("Background task completed!");
      }
    }
```

2. Compile and run the application on the simulator.
3. Press the **home** button to make the application enter the background, and watch the **Application Output**.
4. Before the background task completes (one minute), bring the application to the foreground by either tapping on its icon in the multitasking bar, or on its icon on the **home** screen.

How it works...

In the previous tasks, we learned how to get informed of an application's transitions from the foreground to the background, and vice versa.

Multitasking on iOS is not quite what we are used to on other platforms. The iOS platform makes sure that the foreground application will have all the available resources at its disposal (and the user's). To accomplish this, when the application enters the background, it is being suspended by the operating system. When it is suspended, it does not execute any code whatsoever.

If we want to prevent the application from being suspended when the user presses the **home** button, we can ask for background time. The time we ask for is limited to 600 seconds (10 minutes), which is more than enough for the majority of tasks we are likely to perform in the background (for example, save UI state, complete a file download/upload, close any open connections, and so on).

To ask for background time, we call the `BeginBackgroundTask` method of our `UIApplication` instance:

```
    this.taskID = application.BeginBackgroundTask(delegate {
      application.EndBackgroundTask(taskID);
      this.taskID = 0;
    } );
```

Multitasking

The method accepts one parameter of the type `NSAction` and returns an integer, which corresponds to the task ID. The `NSAction` parameter represents the block of code that will be executed just before the background time elapses. Inside that block of code, we have to call the `EndBackgroundTask` method, passing the ID of the task that was started, which will inform the runtime that we no longer need background time. Each call of `BeginBackgroundTask` should be followed by a call to `EndBackgroundTask`. If we do not call this method and the background time elapses, the application will be terminated.

After calling the `BeginBackgroundTask` method, we can execute the code we want. To allow the `DidEnterBackground` method to complete and to avoid blocking the main thread, we just enclose our code to either an asynchronous call, or in a separate thread. In this example, we use a thread from the `ThreadPool`. Since this specific task will be completed before the time we have elapses, we call the `EndBackgroundTask` method to let the system know that the job is done. The block of code we passed to the `BeginBackgroundTask` method will not be executed, since we ended the task.

There are cases, however, where the user might bring the application to the foreground while a background task is still running. To cover this scenario, we need to override the `WillEnterForeground` method and handle it in an appropriate manner. We can either stop the background task (by calling `EndBackgroundTask`), or provide some sort of feedback to the user that a task is still running. Making an asynchronous call to our code in this scenario is best practice. If the code of our background task is synchronous, when the user brings the application to the foreground and the task is still running, the application will be frozen until the task completes.

There's more...

To know how much time is left to perform background tasks, we can check the value of the `BackgroundTimeRemaining` property:

```
Console.WriteLine("Remaining time: {0}",
   application.BackgroundTimeRemaining);
```

Important considerations for background code

- **Do not update the UI while the application is in the background**: doing so may cause your application to be terminated or crash. Any updates to UI elements that take place while the application is in the background are queued to be performed when it returns to the foreground. This will surely make the application unresponsive.

- **Do not inform the user to bring your application to the foreground, just to give more time to the task**: doing so will surely get your application rejected from the application store approval process. If a background task is in progress and the user brings the application to the foreground, moving the application back to the background again basically resets the background time.

- Perform lightweight operations in the background to avoid the runtime from killing your application.
- Avoid using external resources (for example, resources retrieved through the assets library).

See also

In this chapter:

- *Detecting application states*

Playing audio in the background

In this recipe, we will learn how to prevent the application from being suspended, in order to allow audio playback.

Getting ready

Create a new project in MonoDevelop, and name it `BackgroundAudioApp`. Add a button on the view of `MainController`.

How to do it...

1. Open the `Info.plist` file, and add the key `UIBackgroundModes`.
2. Add the item audio under it. Add the `MonoTouch.AVFoundation` namespace.
3. Enter the following code in the `MainController` class:

```
private AVAudioPlayer audioPlayer;
public override void ViewDidLoad (){
  base.ViewDidLoad ();
  NSError error = null;
  AVAudioSession.SharedInstance ().SetCategory
    (AVAudioSession.CategoryPlayback, out error);
  if (error != null){
    Console.WriteLine("Error setting audio session category: {0}",
      error.LocalizedDescription);
  }
  this.audioPlayer = AVAudioPlayer.FromUrl(NSUrl.FromFilename
    ("audio/sound.m4a"));
  this.buttonStart.TouchUpInside += delegate {
    this.audioPlayer.Play();
  } ;
}
```

Multitasking

4. Add a sound file to the project, and set its **Build Action** to **Content**. This example uses a 20 second-long sound file named `sound.m4a`.
5. Compile and run the application on the device.
6. Tap the **Start playing** button, and press the **home** button to make the application enter the background. Notice that the sound continues playing.

How it works...

To make sure our application will be able to play audio while it is in the background, we have to set the audio item in the `UIBackgroundModes` key in the `Info.plist` file.

In this example, we use the `AVAudioPlayer` class to play a sound file. Just creating an instance of the class and calling its `Play` method is not enough though. We have to set a specific type for the audio session category:

```
NSError error = null;
AVAudioSession.SharedInstance ().SetCategory
   (AVAudioSession.CategoryPlayback, out error);
```

The static method `AVAudioSession.SharedInstance` returns the current audio session object. The audio session category is set to `AVAudioSession.CategoryPlayback`, which allows the `AVAudioPlayer` to play sounds while the application is in the background. This requirement is specific to objects in the `MonoTouch.AVFoundation` namespace.

There's more...

The available audio session categories are the following:

- `CategoryAmbient`: In this category, sounds are silenced when the device screen locks or when the device sound silence switch is on. Sounds from external resources (such as the iPod application) are mixed with this category.
- `CategorySoloAmbient`: This is the default category. Sounds from external resources are silenced with this category. Sounds are silenced when the screen is locked or when the device silent switch is on.
- `CategoryPlayback`: In this category, sounds are not silenced when the screen is locked or when the silent switch is on. Sounds from external resources are silenced, but can be mixed if the `MonoTouch.AudioToolbox.AudioSession.OverrideCategoryMixWithOthers` property is set to `true`.
- `CategoryRecord`: This category is for recording audio. All audio playback is silenced. Recording continues even when the screen is locked.

- `CategoryPlayAndRecord`: This category is for applications that need to record and play audio. Sounds from external resources are silenced, but can be mixed if the `MonoTouch.AudioToolbox.AudioSession.OverrideCategoryMixWithOthers` property is set to `true`. Sounds continue playing when the screen is locked or the silent switch is on.
- `CategoryAudioProcessing`: This category is specific for processing audio. Sound playback and recording is disabled.

Background state for audio

Even when the application is configured through the `Info.plist` file to support background audio playback, when the playback completes, the application will be suspended.

See also

In this chapter:

- *Network connectivity maintenance*

In this book:

Chapter 10, Location Services and Maps:

- *Location services in the background*

Network connectivity maintenance

In this recipe, we will learn how to periodically wake the application to perform network connectivity checks.

Getting ready

Create a new project in MonoDevelop, and name it `NetCheckApp`. There is no need for a view controller in this example.

Multitasking

How to do it...

1. Add the following `DidEnterBackground` override in the `AppDelegate` class:

   ```
   public override void DidEnterBackground (UIApplication
     application){
     application.SetKeepAliveTimeout(610, delegate {
       Console.WriteLine("App woken up for network connection
         maintenance!");
     } );
   }
   ```

2. Add the `UIBackgroundModes` key in the `Info.plist` file with the item `voip`.

How it works...

Apple provides this multitasking feature to allow applications utilizing **Voice over Internet Protocol** (**VoIP**) communication to perform periodic network connectivity checks with the appropriate servers. To allow the application to be woken for this functionality, call the `SetKeepAliveTimeout` method of the `UIApplication` class:

```
application.SetKeepAliveTimeout(610, delegate {
  Console.WriteLine("App woken up for network connection
    maintenance!");
} );
```

The first parameter is the interval in seconds at which the application will be woken. The minimum interval that is allowed is 600 seconds (10 minutes). Setting an interval below the minimum value will cause the method to fail, and the application will be suspended. The second parameter is the handler that will be executed just before the interval elapses. This handler has only 30 seconds to execute. If it takes more than 30 seconds, the application will be terminated.

There's more...

The objects that can be used for network connectivity in the keep alive handler are `NSInputStream`, `NSOutputStream`, and `NSUrlRequest`.

Combining items for the UIBackgroundModes key

An application can use any combination or all of the available items for the `UIBackgroundModes` key. However, avoid adding a background mode for implementing different functionality than what it is intended for. In this case, your application will probably be rejected from the application store.

See also

In this chapter:

- *Playing audio in the background*

In this book:

Chapter 10, Location Services and Maps:

- *Location services in the background*

13 Localization

In this chapter, we will cover:

- Creating an application for different languages
- Localizable resources
- Regional formatting

Introduction

With the release of the iOS platform and the global software marketplace in the form of the application store, Apple has made it easier for developers to distribute applications worldwide.

But, users worldwide will not even bother to download and use an application that is released in a language they do not understand. To broaden the user base for their applications, developers have to localize it. Localization is the process of translating text into multiple languages, providing resources specific to multiple regions, thus creating an application that will target audiences of different cultures.

In this chapter, we will discuss the best practices to provide translated text that will be displayed according to each user's locale preferences. We will also see how to provide resources (images, videos) based on these preferences. Finally, we will use common .NET practices for formatting dates, currencies, and numbers.

Creating an application for different languages

In this recipe, we will create an application that will support two different languages.

Localization

Getting ready

Create a new project in MonoDevelop, and name it `MultipleLanguageApp`.

How to do it...

1. Add two labels on the view of `MainController`.
2. Add two folders to the project. Name them `en.lproj` and `es.lproj` respectively.
3. Create two text files with a text editor application. Enter the following text in the first file:

   ```
   // Localized output on MainController
   "Have a nice day!" = "Have a nice day!";
   ```

   Save it as `Localizable.strings` inside the `en.lproj` folder.

4. Enter the following text in the second file:

   ```
   // Localized output on MainController
   "Have a nice day!" = "Tenga un buen día!";
   ```

   Save it with the same name, `Localizable.strings`, inside the `es.lproj` folder this time. Set both files' **Build Action** to **Content**.

   > The `Localizable.strings` files must be saved in either `UTF8` or `UTF16` encodings.

5. Enter the following code in the `MainController` class:

   ```
   public override void ViewWillAppear (bool animated){
   base.ViewWillAppear (animated);
   this.lblLocale.Text = string.Format("Locale: {0} - Language: {1}",
     NSLocale.CurrentLocale.LocaleIdentifier,
     NSLocale.PreferredLanguages[0]);
   string resourcePath = NSBundle.MainBundle.PathForResource(
     NSLocale.PreferredLanguages[0], "lproj");
   NSBundle localeBundle = NSBundle.FromPath(resourcePath);
   this.lblLocalizedOutput.Text = localeBundle.LocalizedString("Have
     a nice day!", "Localized output on MainController");
   }
   ```

6. Through the **settings** application on the simulator, set the language to **English** (if it is not set already), and run the application. The message will be displayed in English. Try setting the language of the simulator to **Spanish,** and run the application again. The message will be displayed in Spanish.

How it works...

To make it easy for developers to provide support for multiple languages in applications, iOS reads text in different languages from the corresponding language folder. In this application, we support both English and Spanish. Their corresponding folders are `en.lproj` and `es.lproj`, respectively. When we call the `LocalizedString` method, it looks for and parses the file `Localizable.strings` to return the appropriate text.

The contents of the strings files are defined by a set of quoted key/value pairs, in a C style syntax, ending each set with a semicolon:

```
// Localized output on MainController
"Have a nice day!" = "Have a nice day!";
```

As you can see, we can also provide comments to assist the job of the person that will translate the text, even if we do it ourselves.

The `NSLocale.PreferredLanguages` static property returns a string array of the user's preferred language identifiers. The first item in this array is the currently selected language. If the selected language is **English**, it will return `en`; if it is **Spanish**, it will return `es`, and so on.

The `NSBundle.PathForResource` method returns the path of the application bundle for the parameters we pass to it. We use this path to get the appropriate `NSBundle` instance, according to the selected language:

```
string resourcePath = NSBundle.MainBundle.PathForResource(
    NSLocale.PreferredLanguages[0], "lproj");
NSBundle localeBundle = NSBundle.FromPath(resourcePath);
```

We then call the `LocalizedString` method to display the appropriate text:

```
this.lblLocalizedOutput.Text = localeBundle.LocalizedString("Have a
    nice day!", "Localized output on MainController");
```

The first parameter's purpose is dual. It is not only the key to look for to return the translated text, but also the text that will be displayed in case the specified localization path is not found. The second parameter is the comment, or any instruction we want to give to the translator. It is not displayed and basically not used. We can pass `null` to this parameter and no error will occur. It is wise, however, to always include a comment or instruction, since it will help avoid confusion when translating multiple strings.

There's more...

It is advisable to always provide keys that can act as the fallback text to be displayed in **English**, in case the language the user has selected is not included in our application.

Localization

However, the `LocalizedString` method is overloaded. The second overload accepts three parameters. Consider the following example:

```
this.lblLocalizedOutput.Text = localeBundle.LocalizedString("Have a
    nice day!", "Have a nice day!", "Localizable");
```

The first parameter is the key to look for. The second parameter is the fallback value, in case the specified localization path is not found. The third parameter is the name of the file containing the strings, without the `.strings` extension. This overload is more helpful, and we can use different keys for our strings that will help us identify where that particular string is used in the code. For example, in this case, we could set the key in the strings file to `MainController.lblLocalizedOutput`:

```
// Localized output on MainController
"MainController.lblLocalizedOutput" = "Have a nice day!";
```

And use it in our code as follows:

```
this.lblLocalizedOutput.Text = localeBundle.LocalizedString(
    "MainController.lblLocalizedOutput", "Have a nice day!",
    "Localizable");
```

This overload also helps us separate our strings into multiple `.strings` files, passing the corresponding file name as parameter #3.

The last overload contains four parameters. The first three are the same as the second overload. The fourth parameter is simply the comment we want the particular string to have.

Localization in real-world application scenarios

In this example, we use the `PathForResource` method to get an instance of the current locale bundle. This is because the values returned from the `LocalizedString` method are cached. In real-world application scenarios, where the application would be downloaded in a specific language and the user would most likely never change the language of the device to use it, just calling `NSBundle.MainBundle.LocalizedString` would be enough.

Localizable resources

A localizable resource is content, such as images, sound files, and so on, which is specific to a locale. In this recipe, we will learn how to load and display resources, based on the user's localization preferences.

Getting ready

Create a new project in MonoDevelop, and name it `LocalizableResourcesApp`.
Add a label and a `UIImageView` on the view of `MainController`.

Chapter 13

How to do it...

1. Add two folders for **English** and **Spanish** locales to the project. Add one image in each folder, with the same filename. Set their **Build Action** to **Content**.

2. Enter the following code in the `MainController` class:
   ```
   public override void ViewWillAppear (bool animated){
     base.ViewWillAppear (animated);
     this.lblLanguage.Text = NSLocale.PreferredLanguages[0];
     this.imageView.Image = UIImage.FromFile(NSBundle.
       MainBundle.PathForResource("flag", "jpg"));
   }
   ```

3. Compile and run the application on the simulator with **English** language selected in the **settings** application. The result should be similar to the following screenshot:

Localization

4. Now, set the simulator's language to **Spanish,** and run the application again. The Spanish flag should be displayed instead:

How it works...

The `PathForResource` method automatically searches for the appropriate language folder and loads the resource specified through its arguments. In this example, we pass the method's result to the `UIImage.FromFile` method to load the image and assign it to the image view's `Image` property.

There's more...

Apart from images, we can use the `PathForResource` method to load videos, PDF files, and any other localizable resource we need.

More info on localizable resources

We need to make sure that the resource for the specific language folder exists. If it does not, an exception will occur. A way to avoid this is to add one universal image file in the project and use a `Localizable.strings` file inside each language folder containing the paths to the resources:

```
// US flag image
"flag_path"="en.lproj/flag.jpg";
```

To load the appropriate flag, we load the image with the `LocalizedString` method:

```
this.Image = UIImage.FromFile(NSBundle.MainBundle.LocalizedString(
   "flag_path", "path/to/universal/image.jpg", "Localizable"));
```

This way, the image `image.jpg` is loaded if the corresponding language folder is not found.

See also

In this chapter:

- *Creating an application for different languages*

Regional formatting

Regional formatting is how various information, such as currency, date and time, and so on, is displayed according to different regions of the world. In this recipe, we will discuss how to display formatted numbers and dates according to the user's regional formatting settings.

Getting ready

Create a new project in MonoDevelop and name it `RegionalFormattingApp`.

How to do it...

1. Add five labels on the view of `MainController`. Enter the following code in the `MainController` class:

```
public override void ViewDidAppear (bool animated){
   base.ViewDidAppear (animated);
   this.lblLocale.Text = string.Format("Locale: {0}",
      NSLocale.CurrentLocale.LocaleIdentifier);
   this.lblDate.Text = string.Format("Date: {0}",
      DateTime.Now.ToLongDateString());
   this.lblTime.Text = string.Format("Time: {0}",
      DateTime.Now.ToLongTimeString());
```

Localization

```
       this.lblCurrency.Text = string.Format("Currency: {0:c}", 250);
       this.lblNumber.Text = string.Format("Number: {0:n}", 1350);
}
```

2. Compile and run the application on the simulator with regional formatting set to **United States and Spanish | Spain** under **Settings | General | International | Region Format**. The output with the two different regional formats will be something like in the following screenshots:

> Locale: en_US
> Date: Sunday, July 24, 2011
> Time: 8:16:10 PM
> Currency: $250.00
> Number: 1,350.00

> Locale: es_ES
> Date: domingo, 24 de julio de 2011
> Time: 20:17:17
> Currency: 250,00 €
> Number: 1.350,00

How it works...

To format dates, currencies, and numbers, we use standard .NET code. For date and time, the `DateTime.ToLongDateString` and `DateTime.ToLongTimeString` methods return the values according to the locale, respectively.

For currency and numbers, we use C# numerical strings:

```
this.lblCurrency.Text = string.Format("Currency: {0:c}", 250);
this.lblNumber.Text = string.Format("Number: {0:n}", 1350);
```

There's more…

The `System.Globalization` namespace is supported in MonoTouch. To display the current locale, consider the following line of code:

```
Console.WriteLine(CultureInfo.CurrentCulture.Name);
```

Note that there is one difference between this code and the `NSLocale.CurrentLocale.LocaleIdentifier`. The former uses a dash (-), while the latter uses an underscore (_) in the locale name.

14
Deploying

In this chapter, we will cover:

- Creating profiles
- Creating an ad-hoc distribution bundle
- Preparing an app for the App Store
- Submitting to the App Store

Introduction

The process of deploying apps to devices or the App Store is considered quite complicated. This, of course, is for the benefit of developers also, since various certificates and profiles are required to get the application bundle from the development Mac to a device.

In this chapter, we will walk through all the required steps for preparing and installing the appropriate certificates on the development computer. We will also learn how to create the provisioning profiles that will allow us to deploy the application to a device, whether it is our own, or to send it to beta testers for installation on theirs.

Finally, we will see how to prepare the application for App Store submission and the process for the final release to the App Store.

Creating profiles

In this recipe, we will go through a step-by-step guide to creating and installing the appropriate certificates and provisioning profiles that are required for deploying an application to the device.

Deploying

How to do it...

The following steps will guide you through creating your developer certificate and appropriate provisioning profiles for an application.

We will start with the developer certificate.

1. Log in to the iOS Developer website: http://developer.apple.com/ios.
2. Go to the iOS Provisioning Portal.
3. Go to **Certificates** from the menu on the left.
4. If this is the first time you are working with developer certificates on your Mac, download and install the **WWDR intermediate certificate**. You will find the link under the **Development** tab.
5. Under the **How To** tab, you will find the instructions for creating a Certificate Sign in Request, which is a requirement for issuing your developer certificate and how to download and install it.
6. If the developer certificate has been installed correctly, you will be able to select it in your project's options in MonoDevelop, under the **iPhone Bundle Signing** node in the **Identity** drop-down list:

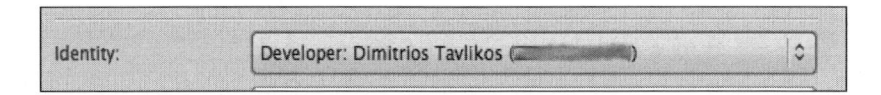

> Identity: Developer: Dimitrios Tavlikos ( )

You can view your developer certificate under the **Development** tab in the **Certificates** option on the **iOS Provisioning Portal**.

Now that we have issued and installed our developer certificate, we need to register the devices that we will be using for debugging.

1. Click on the **Devices** option on the menu on the left.
2. Under the **Manage** tab, click on the **Add Devices** button.
3. In the **Device Name** field, enter a name that will allow you to identify the particular device (for example, My iPhone).
4. In the **Device ID** field, enter the device's **Unique Device Identifier** (**UDID**). You can find the device's UDID by connecting the device to your Mac and opening **iTunes**. Under the device's **Summary** tab, clicking on the serial number will switch to the UDID. Press *Command + C* to copy the UDID to the clipboard.
5. Click on the plus (**+**) button and then **Submit**. Repeat all the steps for all the devices you want to add.

Chapter 14

Next, we need an **App ID**.

1. Click on the **App IDs** option on the menu on the left.
2. Under the **Manage** tab, enter a description/name for your application. Do not use special characters and spaces.
3. Leave the **Bundle Seed ID (App ID Prefix)** option to **Generate New**.
4. Enter a **Bundle Identifier**. The best practice for bundle identifier is to follow the example and recommendation given just above the field. The **Bundle Identifier** is important, as you will need it in at least one more step in the deployment process.
5. Click on the **Submit** button to create the App ID.

Almost there. Time for the provisioning profile.

1. Click on the **Provisioning** option on the menu on the left.
2. Under the **Development** tab, click the **New Profile** button.
3. Enter a profile name. You can enter any character you want in this field.
4. In the **Certificate** option, select the developer certificate for the profile. If you have successfully created your developer certificate, your name (or the name of whom the iOS Developer account belongs to) will be displayed with a checkbox next to it. Tick the checkbox.
5. In the **App ID** option, select the **App ID** for the provisioning profile you are creating.
6. In the **Devices** option, check on the device(s) that will be included in the provisioning profile. Your application can only be installed on the devices you select here.
7. Click on the **Submit** button to complete the creation of the profile.
8. If the provisioning profile status is **Pending** in the list, just refresh the page.
9. Click the Download button on the row of your profile to download it. A file with a .mobileprovision extension will be downloaded.
10. Connect your device to your Mac. Close **iTunes** if it is open.

Deploying

11. Double-click on the `.mobileprovision` file you downloaded in *step 9*. Xcode will open and install the provisioning profile on your device. You can check this by viewing the profile status in Xcode's **Organizer** window. To display the **Organizer** window, press *Shift + Command + 2*, or select **Window | Organizer** from the menu. You can view the provisioning profiles for each device by selecting the **Provisioning** option on the left:

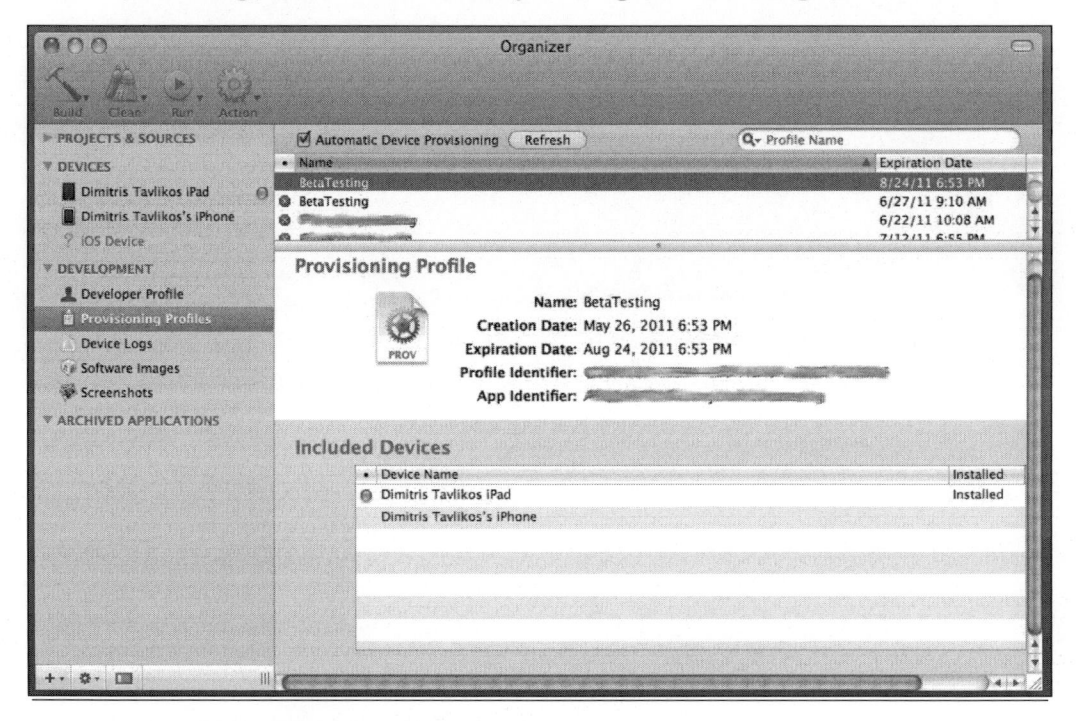

Provisioning profiles marked with the red **X** indicate that they are expired.

How it works...

The process described in this recipe will allow you to deploy and debug your application on a device connected to your Mac. It will not allow you to distribute your application to beta testers or to the App Store.

The Developer certificate is the certificate that allows the compilation of applications that will be deployed to devices. It is only meant for development, and one developer certificate corresponds to one iOS Developer Program enrollment. After creating and installing it on the development machine, you cannot issue a new one. An existing development certificate, however, can be transferred to other Macs.

Each provisioning profile holds information on what devices it can be installed on. An Apple Developer enrolled to the iOS Developer Program can add up to 100 devices and include them in a provisioning profile.

Chapter 14

The App ID is the identifier of your application. Create one App ID for each of your applications.

The provisioning profile is the electronic signature that allows your application to be deployed on the device. Each provisioning profile corresponds to one application and holds all the appropriate permissions that will allow the application to execute on the device(s) included in it and the App ID information. It is also what distinguishes an application for development or distribution. Provisioning profiles are issued with an expiration time. At the time of writing, it is about one year.

There's more...

To compile and debug an application on the device, select the developer certificate and provisioning profile in MonoDevelop, under the **iPhone Bundle Signing** node in **Project Options**:

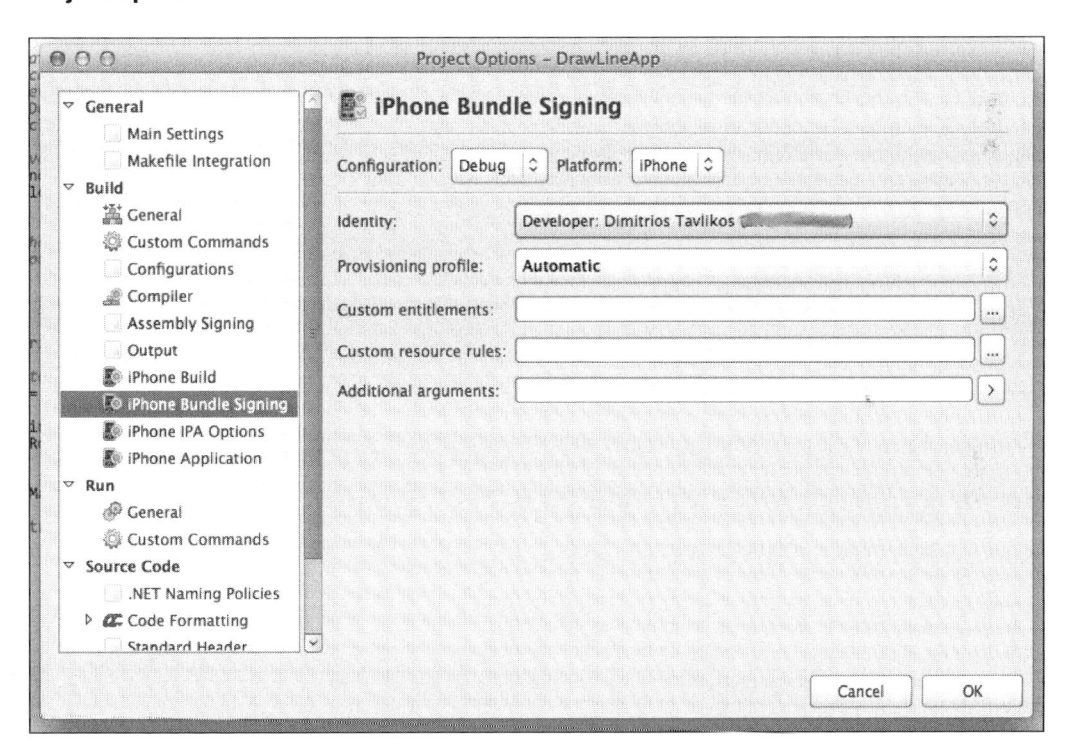

This has to be done for each build configuration (**Debug**, **Release**, and so on).

Deploying

Under the **iPhone Application** node, set the **Display name**, **Bundle Identifier**, and **Bundle version** fields for your application. If you leave them blank, MonoDevelop will set their values to default. Specifically, the **Bundle Identifier** will be set to the one that is included in the App ID. However, if you set the **Bundle Identifier** to something other than what is declared in the App ID, an error on compilation will occur.

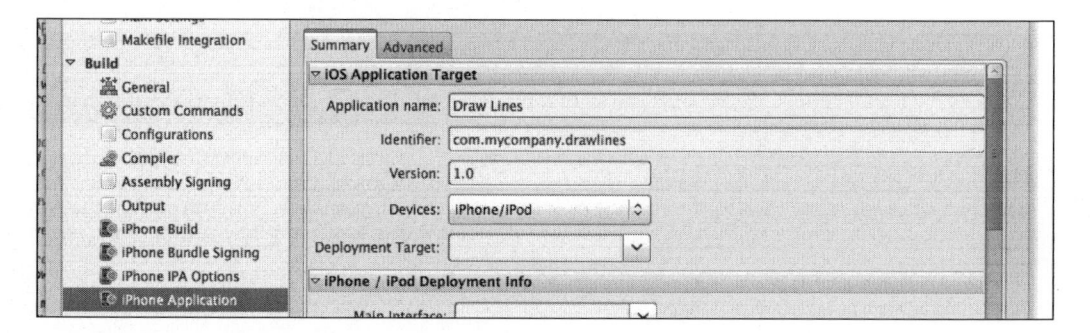

Provisioning profiles expiration

When a provisioning profile expires, the application will no longer work on the device. You can either renew the existing profile or create a new one and install it on the device again.

See also

In this chapter:

- Creating an ad-hoc distribution bundle

In this book:

Chapter 1, Development Tools:

- Compiling

Creating an ad-hoc distribution bundle

In this recipe, we will learn how to create a bundle of our application, which we will be able to send to beta testers for them to test on their devices.

Getting ready

To create an ad-hoc distribution bundle, make sure you have created an App ID on the iOS Provisioning Portal for your application.

How to do it...

The process of creating ad-hoc provisioning profiles is similar to the process of creating development distribution profiles. The following steps will guide you through the process.

1. **Distribution certificate**: For distributing applications to various devices that are not connected to your Mac, but also for submitting to the application store, you need a distribution certificate to be installed. Follow the same steps described in the previous task for creating a developer certificate. This time, though, you will have to work under the **Distribution** tab in the **Certificates** menu option in the **iOS Provisioning Portal**.

2. **Ad-hoc distribution provisioning profile**:
    - In the **iOS Provisioning Portal**, go to **Provisioning | Distribution**.
    - In the **Distribution Method** field, select **Ad Hoc**.
    - Enter a **Profile Name** for the profile. It would be good to add the word `AdHoc` to the name for future reference, for example, `MyAppAdHoc`.
    - The **Distribution Certificate** is automatically selected.
    - Select the **App ID**.
    - Select the devices for the profile.
    - Click on **Submit** to create the profile.
    - Download the profile from the displayed list. Once more, you will get a `.mobileprovision` file. Double-click on it to allow Xcode to install it. A device does not need to be connected at this point. Do not delete the file; we will need it later.

3. **Create an ad-hoc build**:
    - With your project loaded in MonoDevelop, go to **Project | Solution Options**.
    - Under **Build | Configurations**, create a new configuration by clicking on **Add**.
    - Enter a name for the configuration. The name used here is `MyAppDistribution`.

Deploying

- Select **iPhone** in the **Platform** option. The following screenshot shows how the **New Configuration** dialog should look:

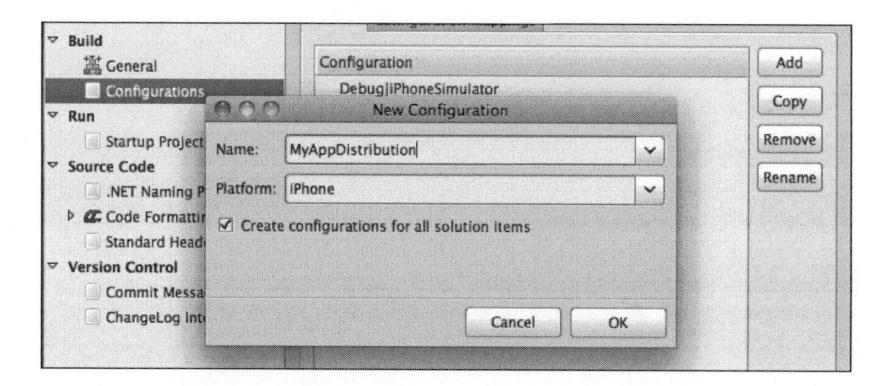

Make sure the **Create configurations for all solution items** option is checked.

- Click on the **OK** button.
- Add a new **Property List** file to the project, and name it Entitlements.

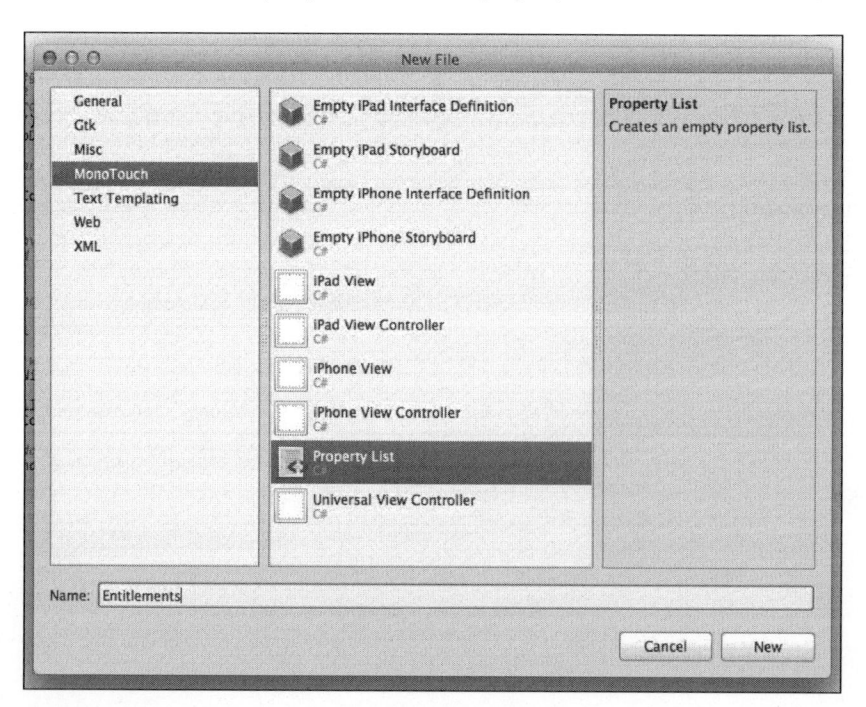

- MonoDevelop will automatically load the `Entitlements.plist` file with the **Property List Editor**. Add the key `get-task-allow`, and set its **type** to **Boolean**. Set its value to **No**.
- Under the **iPhone Bundle Signing** node of the project options, select the configuration we created earlier (`MyAppDistribution`). Set the **Custom entitlements** field to the `Entitlements.plist` file, which was created in the previous steps. It can easily be found by clicking on the **browse (...)** button next to the field.
- Set the Distribution profile and the appropriate provisioning profile for ad-hoc distribution in the same window.
- Set the project's current configuration to the distribution configuration created earlier (`MyAppDistribution`).
- Build the project.

The application is now ready for ad-hoc distribution!

4. **Distributing to beta testers**:
   - Open **Finder,** and navigate to the `bin` folder of your project.
   - Open the `iPhone/MyAppDistribution` folder. Compress the application bundle with OS X's default compression tool by right-clicking and selecting **Compress "MyApp"** (or whatever the name of your application is). The application bundle is a folder displayed with the following icon:

   - Send the zipped application bundle along with the `.mobileprovision` file to your beta testers.
   - To install the application, your application's beta testers have to extract the application bundle from the zip archive.
   - After extracting it, dragging-and-dropping it in **iTunes** in the **Apps** section, along with the `.mobileprovision` file, imports it in **iTunes Library**. Note that the application will be displayed in **iTunes** with a default icon. This is normal for ad-hoc distribution if you haven't set any icons for the application.
   - Synchronize the device in **iTunes**.
   - If the beta testers are working with **iTunes** on a Windows machine, instruct them not to use the default decompression utility, but a third-party application.

Deploying

How it works...

For distributing applications, we need a distribution certificate. Just like the developer certificate, the distribution certificate is created once, but can be transferred to another Mac if needed.

The creation process of the ad-hoc distribution provisioning profile is the same as the process for creating development provisioning profiles. The only difference is that we have the option of the type of distribution, which is either *App Store* or *Ad Hoc*.

The configuration we created is not a requirement, but it helps us organize the build process better. It also saves us from having to set the different provisioning profiles and settings for each build.

The `Entitlements.plist` file, along with the `get-task-allow` key, is for preventing the application from trying to find a debugger to connect to upon startup.

There's more...

MonoDevelop provides an option for directly creating and zipping the application bundle. **Select Project | Zip App bundle...** on the menu, and after selecting a location and filename for the output, it will compile and zip the application bundle.

Syncing ad-hoc app bundles with iTunes

Different users have different settings set up in their iTunes application. In case a user syncs the device and cannot find the application on the device, make sure the application is selected for syncing, under the **Apps** tab of the selected device in **iTunes**.

See also

In this chapter:

- *Creating profiles*

Preparing an application for the App Store

In this recipe, we will discuss the important steps we need to take for preparing an application for the App Store.

Getting ready

Follow the steps in the previous recipes to create an App Store distribution profile for your application.

How to do it...

One very important step in the preparation for the App Store regards the images that should be included in your application.

- **App Icon**: This is the icon that will represent your application on the users' devices. For iPhone and iPod Touch, prepare an icon with dimensions of `57x57` pixels for the lower-resolution screens and an icon with dimensions of `114x114` pixels for the higher-resolution screens (for example, iPhone 4 and newer). For the iPad, the icon size should be `72x72` pixels.

  Save the icon files with the `PNG` format. You can name them whatever you want, but it is a good practice to keep a consistent naming scheme, for example, `Icon-57.png`, `Icon-114.png`, and so on.

  Add the image files to the project. Open the project options dialog and go to the **iPhone Icons** section of the **iPhone Application** node, under the **Summary** tab, as shown in the following screenshot:

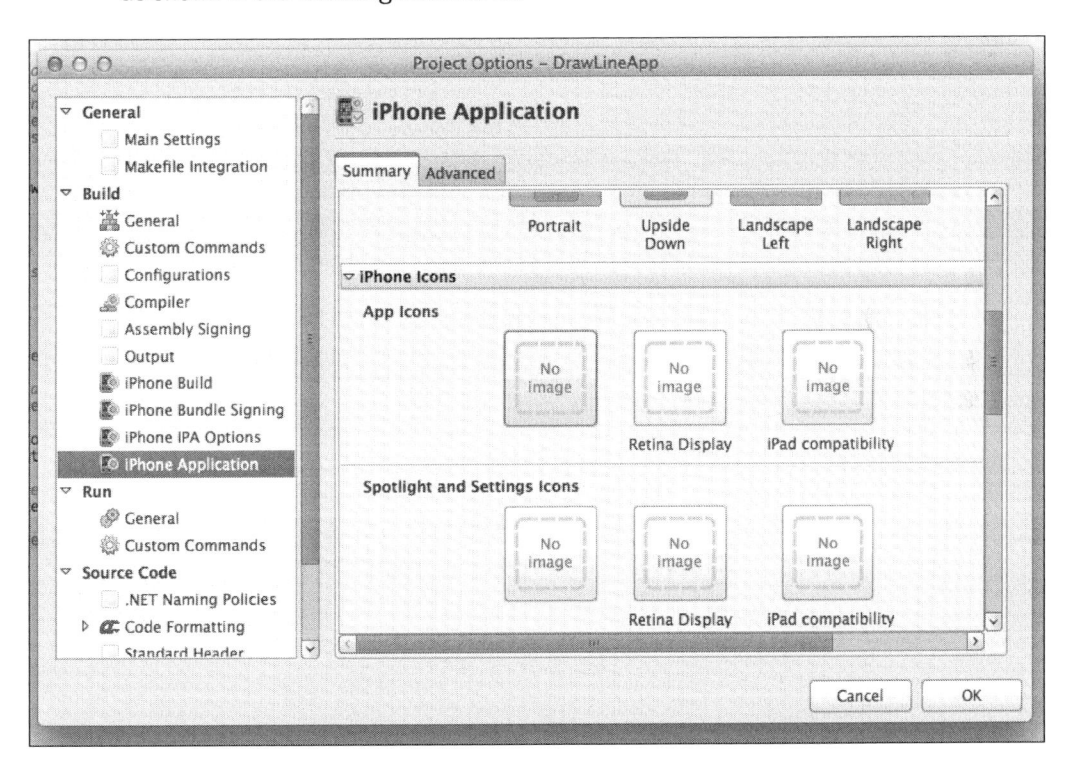

Click on the appropriate button to find the icon file and assign it. Note that the image selection dialog that will open only looks in files included in your project. So, make sure to add your images to the project first. There is no need to set their **Build Action** to **Content**. Click on the **OK** button to save the changes to the project.

Deploying

- **Launch image**: The launch image is the first thing that is displayed when an application starts. Prepare a launch image in at least two dimensions for iPhone and iPod Touch applications: `320x480` pixels for the lower version and `640x960` pixels for the higher version. Name the files `Default.png` and `Default@2x.png` respectively, and add them to the project. Set their **Build Action** to **Content**.

   If your application is universal and, therefore, downloadable by iPad users, or it is an iPad-only application, then you should provide launch images for each of the application's supported orientations. The sizes should be `768x1004` pixels for the portrait versions and `1024x748` for the landscape versions. For an application that supports portrait and landscape-right orientations, the filenames should be `Default-Portrait.png` and `Default-LandscapeRight.png`, respectively.

- **Final Settings**: Last but not least, fill the appropriate application information in the **Summary** tab of the **iPhone Application** node in the **project** options, as described in the *Creating Profiles* recipe in the beginning of this chapter. Build the project and compress the application bundle. Your application is ready for submission!

How it works...

The applications icons are very important. It is what the user will see on the device screen and tap to start your application. Although all application icons appear as buttons with rounded corners and a lighting effect, you should not include these graphical features in your icons. These graphical features are automatically rendered upon application submission to the application store. The icons should be perfect squares. Also, always provide a background for the icons. Do not use transparencies, because any transparencies on the icon will be displayed with the black color, potentially destroying your intended icon appearance.

The launch image is displayed first when the application starts. When a screen goes blank at startup, it means that there is no launch image. According to Apple's *iOS Human Interface Guidelines* (`http://developer.apple.com/library/ios/#documentation/UserExperience/Conceptual/MobileHIG/Introduction/Introduction.html`), this image should be the first screen that is loaded when the application completes the launch process and is ready to accept input. It should only contain the static content of the first screen and not content that is likely to change, such as localized text. For example, the following screenshot illustrates the launch image of the g-force measurement app, GBox.

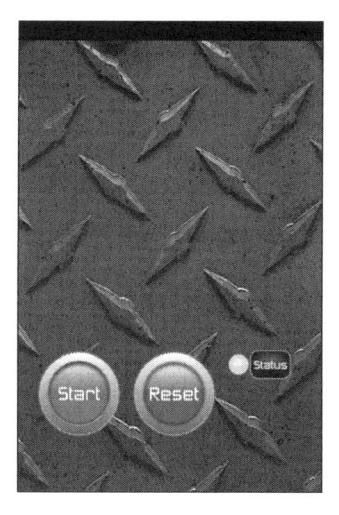

The following screenshot shows the application after it is fully loaded.

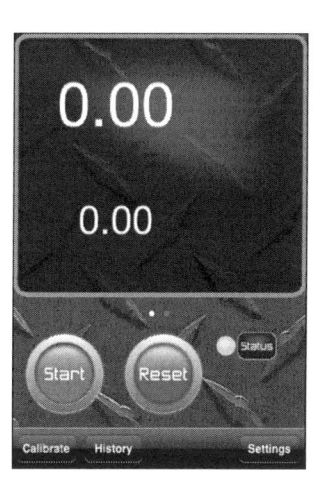

There's more...

The launch image is there to provide a sense of responsiveness to the user while the application loads, avoiding blank screens. Although the *iOS Human Interface Guidelines* are what the name suggests, guidelines, it is a good practice to follow them. Apple suggests avoiding the usage of the launch image for splash screens, "about" information and branding.

Deploying

Lighting effect on icons

If we would like to provide our own lighting effect for the icon, or even not allow the default iOS one to be displayed, we can add the `UIPrerenderedIcon` key to the `Info.plist` file with its **type** set to **Boolean** and enable it. This setting prevents the shine effect from being created when the application icon is displayed on the device's home screen.

See also

In this chapter:

- *Creating profiles*

Submitting to the App Store

In this recipe, we will go through the required steps to submit an application to the App Store.

Getting ready

For this task, you will have to have your zipped distribution application bundle ready.

How to do it...

Follow the steps below for submitting your application to the App Store.

1. **Screenshots**: Prepare screenshots that display various aspects of your application. For iPhone/iPod Touch apps, the dimensions should be `320x480` for portrait and `480x320` for landscape. For iPad applications the dimensions of the screenshots should be `768x1024` for portrait and `1024x768` for landscape. If the application does not hide the status bar, it would be better if it was included in the screenshots. For each application, we can have up to five screenshots on the App Store.

2. **App Store icon**: Prepare the icon that will represent the application on the App Store. Its dimensions must be `512x512` pixels, and it must be the same as the application icon.

3. **Description and keywords**: Prepare the text that describes your application. Try to include the most significant features. Remember, the description is what users will read before downloading the application, so the more appealing it is, the better.

    Prepare keywords that will help your application climb on top of the search results.

    Both application description and keywords are required.

4. **Log in to iTunes Connect**: iTunes Connect is the developer portal for managing and submitting applications (among other App Store related stuff). Log in to iTunes Connect (`http://itunesconnect.apple.com`) with your Apple Developer ID. Click on the link **Manage your Applications**. Then, click on the **Add New App** button on the top-left. Follow the steps to complete the application preparation on the portal. When you finish, make sure the application status is **Waiting for Upload**.

5. **Uploading**: After you have created a new application on the portal, you can upload the zipped application bundle with the **Application Loader**. It is installed by default with Xcode, and it can be found under the path `/Developer/Application/Utilities`, or by searching through the **Spotlight**.

   When you start **Application Loader**, it will ask you to log in with your **Apple Developer ID**. After logging in, you will be presented with the following window:

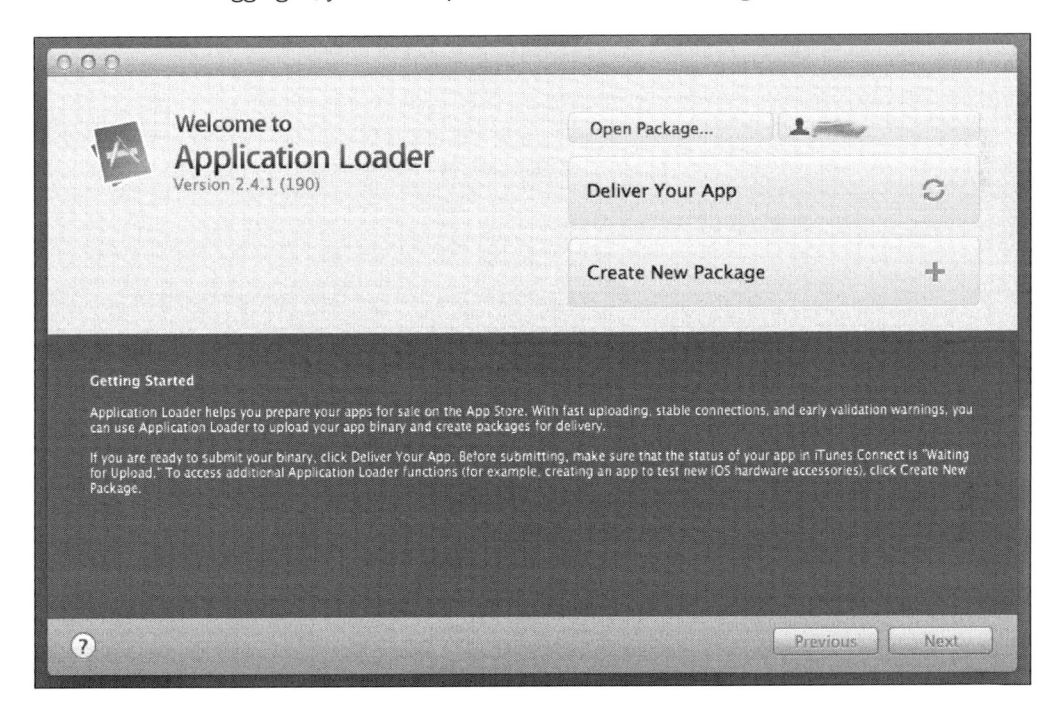

Deploying

6. Click on the **Deliver Your App** button, and it will connect to **iTunes Connect**, and find the applications you have in the **Waiting for Upload** status, and load them in the list box:

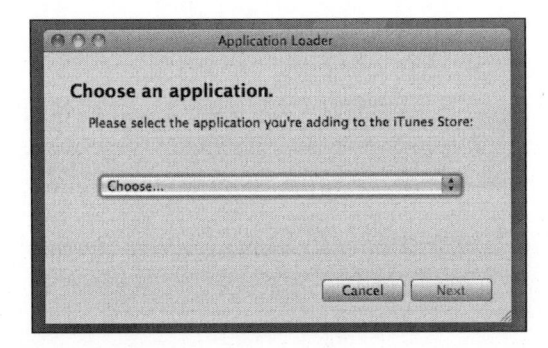

You will then be presented with a summary view of your application:

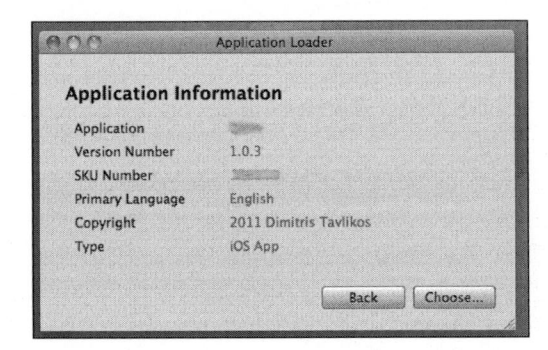

7. Click the **Choose...** button, and a dialog will appear that will allow you to select the zipped application bundle. After selecting it, proceed with the upload. You are all set! If all steps have been completed correctly, the application will be uploaded, and it will be under review for release on the App Store.

How it works...

Application screenshots and the App Store icon are very important. They can be in any of the JPG, TIF, or PNG formats, in RGB color, and at a resolution of at least 72 DPI.

But the images are important only when users are already viewing your application in the App Store. The keywords and the description are the parameters that will allow your application to come up higher on search results and make the user decide whether the application is worth the download. Especially regarding the keywords, choose them wisely. Do not include as many as you can; fewer keywords that reflect the key aspects of the application are always better.

iTunes Connect is the developer portal for managing applications, reviewing financial data, application downloads, and includes the contracts and agreements a developer needs to sign. Make sure you read and accept the contracts, or else you will not be able to proceed with the application preparation process. During that process, you are required to provide the necessary information for your application that is described previously and also the price range if it is a paid application, the countries in which it will be available, as well as the release date for it, if you do not want it to be released automatically as soon as it has passed through the App Store review process.

When everything is set up correctly and the application's status is **Waiting for Upload**, you can then run the **Application Loader** to upload it. Periodically and with each release of iOS and iOS SDK versions, various components or procedures change. Always make sure your iOS SDK version is up-to-date.

There's more...

At some point in the application preparation process, you will be required to enter a **Stock Keeping Unit** (**SKU**) number. This number is a unique identifier for each product or service. It can be any number you want, but keep a specific pattern to keep track of the identifiers, for example, when you develop additional applications.

See also

In this chapter:

- *Preparing an app for the App Store*

15
iOS 5 Features

In this chapter, we will cover:

- Reproducing the page curl effect
- Styling views
- Twitter integration
- Working with the split keyboard

Introduction

The fifth major release of iOS brought over 200 new features. In this chapter, we will work on only a few of them, which mostly have to do with enhanced user experience.

Specifically, we will create a project that displays content separated into pages, which the user can navigate through like in a normal book, with the help of the newly introduced UIPageViewController class.

We will then discuss the UIAppearance class, which allows us to style controls included in our application in a more flexible and easy manner. Social sharing could also not be absent in today's devices, so we will create a project that allows the user to use Twitter, using the TWTweetComposeViewController.

In the last recipe of this chapter, we will work with the new split keyboard feature for the iPad, to learn how we can adjust content according to the position of the virtual keyboard on the screen.

iOS 5 Features

Reproducing the page curl effect

In this recipe, we will create an app that displays content like a book, with the help of the `UIPageViewController` class.

Getting ready

Create a new iPhone project in MonoDevelop, and name it `BookApp`. Apart from the `MainController`, add another controller, and name it `Page`. Configure the appearance of the `Page` controller however you like. In the source code for this recipe, it contains a `UIImageView` and a `UILabel`.

How to do it...

1. Enter the following code in the `MainController` class:

```
private UIPageViewController pageViewController;
private int pageCount = 3;
public override void ViewDidLoad (){
  base.ViewDidLoad ();
  Page firstPage = new Page(0);
  this.pageViewController = new UIPageViewController(
    UIPageViewControllerTransitionStyle.PageCurl,
    UIPageViewControllerNavigationOrientation.Horizontal,
    UIPageViewControllerSpineLocation.Min);
  this.pageViewController.SetViewControllers(new
    UIViewController[] { firstPage },
    UIPageViewControllerNavigationDirection.Forward,
    false, s => { });
  this.pageViewController.GetNextViewController =
    this.GetNextViewController;
  this.pageViewController.GetPreviousViewController =
    this.GetPreviousViewController;
  this.pageViewController.View.Frame = this.View.Bounds;
  this.View.AddSubview(this.pageViewController.View);
}

private UIViewController GetNextViewController(
  UIPageViewController pageController, UIViewController
  referenceViewController){
  Page currentPageController = referenceViewController as Page;
  if (currentPageController.PageIndex >= (this.pageCount - 1)){
    return null;
  } else{
    int nextPageIndex = currentPageController.PageIndex + 1;
```

```
        return new Page(nextPageIndex);
      }
    }
    private UIViewController GetPreviousViewController(
      UIPageViewController pageController, UIViewController
      referenceViewController){
      Page currentPageController = referenceViewController as Page;
      if (currentPageController.PageIndex <= 0){
        return null;
      } else{
        int previousPageIndex = currentPageController.PageIndex - 1;
        return new Page(previousPageIndex);
      }
    }
```

2. Add a property to the `Page` class, and change its constructor, as shown in the following code:

```
public Page (int pageIndex) : base ("Page", null){
  this.PageIndex = pageIndex;
}
public int PageIndex{
  get;
  private set;
}
```

3. Finally, configure the content that will be displayed in the `Page`, in the `ViewDidLoad` method:

```
this.imageView.Image = UIImage.FromFile(string.Format(
  "images/{0}.jpg", this.PageIndex + 1));
this.lblPageNum.Text = string.Format("Page {0}",
  this.PageIndex + 1);
```

4. Compile and run the application on the simulator.

iOS 5 Features

5. Click-and-drag on the simulator's screen area to change page. The result should look similar to the following screenshot:

How it works...

The `UIPageViewController` class introduced with iOS 5 was a desired component by many developers. It allows us to navigate through content with the effect of a real book, like in Apple's iBooks application.

We initialize it with the following line:

```
this.pageViewController = new UIPageViewController(
  UIPageViewControllerTransitionStyle.PageCurl,
  UIPageViewControllerNavigationOrientation.Horizontal,
  UIPageViewControllerSpineLocation.Min);
```

The first parameter of the constructor determines the type of the effect. The only available value right now is `PageCurl`. The second parameter determines the orientation of the effect. `Horizontal` is the value for the effect similar to a book, while `Vertical` is the value for the effect similar to a notebook, where the pages are bound at the top. The third parameter determines the position of the bind of the book. `Min` declares that the bind is on one edge of the screen; in this case, on the left side.

After initializing the page controller, we need to set its first page by calling its `SetViewControllers` method:

```
this.pageViewController.SetViewControllers(new UIViewController[] {
firstPage }, UIPageViewControllerNavigationDirection.Forward,
   false, s => { });
```

Its first parameter is an array of `UIViewController` objects. We can set either one or two controllers for this parameter, depending on the device orientation. For example, if the application supported landscape orientation, we might want to show two pages at the same time. The second parameter basically determines the navigation direction of the included pages. `Forward` means that the next page will be loaded if we swipe from right to left on the screen, while `Reverse` means that the previous page will be loaded for the same swipe. The last parameter is of the delegate type `UICompletionHandler` and represents the handler to be executed after the controllers have been added. In this example, we do not need it, so we just pass an empty lambda.

Next, we need to provide the data source for the rest of the pages of our "book". Once again, MonoTouch simplifies things for us by providing two very helpful properties for us to use: `GetNextViewController` and `GetPreviousViewController`. These properties merely represent the callback methods we would have to override if we were creating a `Delegate` object for the page controller. Apart from their names, the signatures of these two methods are identical:

```
UIViewController GetNextViewController(UIPageViewController
   pageController, UIViewController referenceViewController);
UIViewController GetPreviousViewController(UIPageViewController
   pageController, UIViewController referenceViewController);
```

The first parameter gives us the page controller, while the second parameter gives us the controller that is currently displayed on screen when the method is called.

In the implementation of these methods, we simply have to return the controller that should be loaded next, or before the current one. If we do not want the effect to be activated, we just return `null`.

Last but not least, we set the size of the page controller's view and add it to a superview, so that it will be displayed:

```
this.pageViewController.View.Frame = this.View.Bounds;
this.View.AddSubview(this.pageViewController.View);
```

iOS 5 Features

There's more...

If we would like our application to support landscape orientation, we would first have to implement the `ShouldAutoRotateToInterfaceOrientation` method in the `MainController` class, returning `true` from it for the orientation we wish to support. Secondly, we would have to provide two view controllers to the `SetViewControllers` method of the `UIPageViewController` class.

Double sided pages

As you might have noticed in the screenshot of this recipe, when we turn a page, its content is displayed in reverse on the page's back, like when we see through a page in real books. We have the option of creating double-sided pages by setting the `UIPageViewController.DoubleSided` property to `true`.

Styling views

In this recipe, we will discover how we can easily style buttons across our application.

Getting ready

Create a new project in MonoDevelop, and name it `StyleButtonsApp`. Add the `MainController` and another controller with the name `ModalController`.

How to do it...

1. Add one button on each of the controllers. In the `MainController` class, implement the `ViewDidLoad` method with the following code:

   ```
   public override void ViewDidLoad (){
     base.ViewDidLoad ();
     UIButton.Appearance.BackgroundColor = UIColor.Gray;
     UIButton.Appearance.SetTitleColor(UIColor.White,
       UIControlState.Normal);
     this.buttonPresent.TouchUpInside += delegate(object sender,
       EventArgs e) {
         this.PresentModalViewController(new ModalController(), true);
     };
   }
   ```

2. Implement the `ViewDidLoad` method of the `ModalController` class, to dismiss it when the button is tapped:

   ```
   this.buttonDismiss.TouchUpInside += delegate(object sender,
     EventArgs e) {
       this.DismissModalViewControllerAnimated(true);
   };
   ```

3. Compile and run the application on the simulator.
4. Tap on the **Present** button to display the modal controller. Note that the buttons of both the `MainController` and `ModalController` have the same background color and text color.

How it works...

To make all the buttons in our application look the same, we use the `Appearance` static property of the `UIButton` class. This property returns the object that inherits the `UIAppearance` class, which is the class that reflects the Objective-C `UIAppearance` protocol to MonoTouch.

This way, we have an `Appearance` static property for all views that support it, strongly-typed according to the view we want to style. For the `UIButton`, the `Appearance` property returns a `UIButtonAppearance` object. After we set the values we want in this object, all instances of `UIButton` in the application will share the same styling.

So, in this example, as shown in the highlighted code, we set the background color and text color we want all of our buttons to have, and the runtime takes care of the rest for us.

There's more...

Styling our controls globally in our application is a very nice feature, but one might agree that it is a bit limiting. What if we wanted to style specific `UIButtons` in our application, instead of all? Consider the following code:

```
UIButton.UIButtonAppearance buttonStyle =
   UIButton.AppearanceWhenContainedIn(typeof(ModalController));
buttonStyle.BackgroundColor = UIColor.Red;
```

The `AppearanceWhenContainedIn` method returns the corresponding `UIAppearance` object, in this case `UIButtonAppearance`, and accepts a variable number of parameters of the type `System.Type (params Type[] containers)`. This code will style only instances of `UIButton` that are contained in `ModalController` objects only.

Although the number of parameters of the method is variable, the sequence of `Type` objects that we pass determines its behavior. For example, the following call would apply the styles we set to instances of `UIButton` contained in `ModalController`, only when `ModalController` is contained in `MainController`.

```
UIButton.AppearanceWhenContainedIn(typeof(MainController),
   typeof(ModalController));
```

iOS 5 Features

Specific properties

Every class that inherits from `UIView` inherits the `UIAppearance` class. However, not all properties of each class support it. For example, through the `UIButtonAppearance` object, we can set the background color of every `UIButton` in our application, but we cannot set the title.

Twitter integration

In this recipe, we will create an application that implements Twitter sharing, to allow the user to send tweets.

Getting ready

Create a new project in MonoDevelop, and name it `TweetApp`. Add the `MainController` to the project.

How to do it...

1. Add a button on the view of `MainController` and the `MonoTouch.Twitter` namespace in the class. Next, enter the following code:

   ```
   private TWTweetComposeViewController tweetController;
   public override void ViewDidLoad (){
     base.ViewDidLoad ();
     this.buttonTweet.TouchUpInside += delegate(object sender,
       EventArgs e) {
       if (TWTweetComposeViewController.CanSendTweet){
         this.tweetController = new TWTweetComposeViewController();
         this.tweetController.SetInitialText("Tweet from
           MonoTouch!");
         this.tweetController.AddUrl(NSUrl.FromString(
           "http://software.tavlikos.com"));
         this.tweetController.SetCompletionHandler(delegate(
           TWTweetComposeViewControllerResult tweetResult) {
           if (tweetResult ==
             TWTweetComposeViewControllerResult.Cancelled){
             Console.WriteLine("Tweet cancelled!");
           } else{
             Console.WriteLine("Tweet sent!");
           }
           this.DismissModalViewControllerAnimated(true);
         } );
         this.PresentModalViewController(this.tweetController, true);
       } else{
         Console.WriteLine("Cannot use Twitter on this device!");
   ```

Chapter 15

```
        }
    } ;
}
```

2. Compile and run the application on the simulator. If a Twitter account has not been set on the simulator, it can easily be configured through the `Settings` application.
3. Tap the button to present the Twitter controller. The result should be similar to the following screenshot:

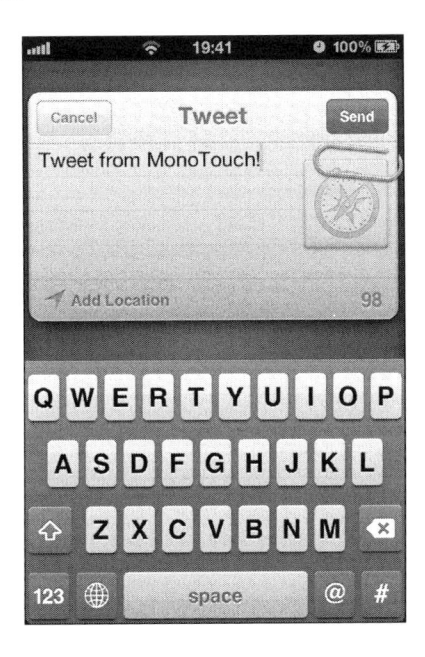

How it works...

iOS provides the `TWTweetComposeViewController` class that provides the sharing functionality. This controller's is the same as the native interface that is used to share a photo from the device album. Just like similar native controllers, we can only set its content before it is presented. We cannot make modifications to it after it has been displayed to the user, and the user is responsible whether to send it or discard it.

We can determine if the user has configured a Twitter account on the device by reading the `CanSendTweet` static property:

```
if (TWTweetComposeViewController.CanSendTweet)
```

If we present the controller without an account set on the device, a native alert will be presented, giving the user the option to configure an account before proceeding.

iOS 5 Features

We then initialize the controller and set the text to be filled, if we wish, with the `SetInitialText` method:

```
this.tweetController = new TWTweetComposeViewController();
this.tweetController.SetInitialText("Tweet from MonoTouch!");
```

We also have the option of adding URLs or images in the tweet, with the `AddUrl` and `AddImage` methods, respectively.

In order to get feedback of whether the user has sent or cancelled the tweet, we call the `SetCompletionHandler` method, passing the callback to be called:

```
this.tweetController.SetCompletionHandler(delegate(TWTweetComposeView
   ControllerResult tweetResult) {
```

This callback accepts one parameter of the enumeration type `TWTweetComposeViewControllerResult`, and it can contain either of the two values `Done` or `Cancelled`.

Last but not least, we should dismiss the controller in the callback.

> Manually dismissing the `TWTweetComposeViewController` is not a requirement. If we do not dismiss it manually, however, it has been noticed that although the controller is dismissed when the user tapped on **Send**, it takes two taps on the **Cancel** button to dismiss it.

There's more...

Apart from sending tweets, the `MonoTouch.Twitter` namespace also wraps the `TWRequest` class that allows us to read Twitter information, such as the user's timeline, through Twitter API URLs. Data received this way are in the form of JSON objects, and it is our responsibility of reading them properly.

Supporting landscape orientation

The `TWTweetComposeViewController` supports landscape orientation. To enable it, we just have to override the `ShouldAutoRotateToInterfaceOrientation` method in the controller that presents it.

Working with the split keyboard

In this recipe, we will create an iPad application that is aware of the changes to the positioning of the virtual keyboard, to adjust our content accordingly.

Chapter 15

Getting ready

Create a new iPad project in MonoDevelop, and name it `SplitKeyboardApp`. Add the `MainController` to the project.

How to do it...

1. Add a `UITextField`, and position it at the center of `MainController`. Resize the text field so that its width expands across the screen. Add the following code in the `MainController` class:

   ```
   private NSObject kbdFrameChangedObserver;
   public override void ViewDidLoad (){
     base.ViewDidLoad ();
     this.kbdFrameChangedObserver = NSNotificationCenter.
       DefaultCenter.AddObserver(new NSString("
       UIKeyboardDidChangeFrameNotification"),
       this.KeyboardFrameChanged);
   }
   private void KeyboardFrameChanged(NSNotification ntf){
     Console.WriteLine("Keyboard frame changed!");
     if (ntf.UserInfo != null){
       NSObject frameEndObj = null;
       if (ntf.UserInfo.TryGetValue(UIKeyboard.FrameEndUserInfoKey,
         out frameEndObj)){
         RectangleF keyboardFrame = (frameEndObj as
           NSValue).RectangleFValue;
         RectangleF textFieldFrame = this.txtInput.Frame;
         if (textFieldFrame.IntersectsWith(keyboardFrame)){
           textFieldFrame.Y = keyboardFrame.Y -
             (textFieldFrame.Height + 40f);
           UIView.BeginAnimations("");
           this.txtInput.Frame = textFieldFrame;
           UIView.CommitAnimations();
         }
       }
     }
   }
   ```

2. Compile and run the application on the simulator.

3. Tap on the text field to show the keyboard. If the keyboard on the iPad simulator has not been previously used, it will default to its normal state, which is at the bottom and merged.

iOS 5 Features

4. Tap-and-drag the **hide keyboard** key at the bottom-right corner to move the keyboard, so that it splits, and leave it over the text field.

Hide keyboard button

Watch the text field animate right above the keyboard. The result should be similar to the following screenshot:

How it works...

To detect the position of the split keyboard, we first need to add an observer for the `UIKeyboardDidChangeFrameNotification` key:

```
this.kbdFrameChangedObserver = NSNotificationCenter.
    DefaultCenter.AddObserver(new NSString(
    "UIKeyboardDidChangeFrameNotification"),
    this.KeyboardFrameChanged);
```

Inside the `KeyboardFrameChanged` callback, we get the value of the `FrameEndUserInfoKey` key from the `UserInfo` dictionary. This value, returned as an `NSObject`, is actually an `NSValue` object that contains the frame of the keyboard. We read the `RectangleFValue` property from it to get the `RectangleF` object that holds the frame values of the keyboard:

```
if (ntf.UserInfo.TryGetValue(UIKeyboard.FrameEndUserInfoKey, out
  frameEndObj)){
  RectangleF keyboardFrame = (frameEndObj as
  NSValue).RectangleFValue;
}
```

The rest of the code moves the text field above the keyboard. Change it as you please!

There's more...

The `UserInfo` property of the `NSNotification` class returns an `NSDictionary` object, which contains various information about the keyboard. To enumerate the keys it contains, a simple `foreach` will do:

```
foreach (NSString eachItem in ntf.UserInfo.Keys){
  Console.WriteLine("Key: {0}", eachItem);
}
```

Problems moving the keyboard?

The hide keyboard key presents a small "context menu" when we tap and hold on it. This menu gives us the option of docking and merging (or the opposite) the keyboard. To move the keyboard in the position we want, we have to start dragging as soon as we tap on the key.

Index

Symbols

57x57 pixels 329
72x72 pixels 329
114x114 pixels 329
8080 port 163
.mobileprovision file 322
.NET Framework 11
.NET languages 11
.NET serialization
   used, for storing data 123-125
.plist files 22

A

ABAddressBook class 192, 204
ABAddressBook.Save() method 205
ABNewPersonViewController 208
ABPeoplePickerNavigationController 208
ABPerson array 205
ABPerson object 205, 207
ABPersonViewController 192, 206-208
ABUnknownPersonViewController 208
Acceleration event 231
accelerometer
   using 230-232
accelerometer events
   receiving, for application creation 230-232
Accessory property 141
AccessoryView property 141
ActionAttribute 36
actions
   about 8
   adding, to interface objects 35
   working 36
AddAnnotation method 260
AddAppStateObservers method 299
AddAttachmentData method 203
AddEllipseInRect method 283
AddImage method 346
AddImagesToAlbum method 176
AddLines method 281
AddLineToPoint method 289
Add method 205
AddObserver() method 67
AddOverlay method 264
address book
   managing 203, 205
   phone number, adding to contact 205
AddressBookApp
   creating 204
address book controllers
   ABNewPersonViewController 208
   ABPeoplePickerNavigationController 208
   ABPersonViewController 208
   ABUnknownPersonViewController 208
AddressDisctionary property 258
AddSublayer method 278
AddSubview() method 47
AddUrl method 346
ad-hoc build
   creating 325
ad-hoc distribution bundle
   ad-hoc build, creating 325
   beta testers, distributing 327
   creating 324-327
   distribution certificate 325
   provisioning profile 325
   syncing, with iTunes 328
   working 328
AdjustsFontSizeToFitWidth property 56, 57

AfterMainController class 104
ALAsset class 189
ALAssetLibrary 190
ALAssetRepresentation 189
ALAssetsLibrary class 174, 188
AllowsAirPlay property 182
AllowsEditing property 207
Alpha property 270
AlwaysBounceHorizontal property 74
AlwaysBounceVertical property 74
animatable properties 270
Animate method 270
animation
  determining 275
AnimationImages property 275
AnimationStopped event 278
annotation performance 261
anonymous() method 67
AnyObject parameter 83
AppDelegate class 20, 49, 89, 206, 251, 296
    299, 300
AppDelegate.cs 18, 19
Appearance property 343
AppearanceWhenContainedIn method 343
App Icon 329
App ID
  about 323
  creating 321
Apple Developer
  URL 9
Apple developer tools
  URL 12
Apple iOS developer portal
  URL 12
Apple's Developer portal
  URL 8
application
  compiling 323
  debugging 323
  notification observers, adding 299
  preparing, for App Store 328-330
application control state 51
application, for different languages
  creating 309-312
Application Loader 335
ApplicationState property 297

application states
  detecting 296, 297
  notifications, receiving for 298, 299
application submission steps
  App Store icon, preparing 332
  description, preparing 332
  iTunes Connect, logging to 333
  keywords, preparing 332
  screenshots, preparing 332
  uploading 333
  working 334
App Store
  application, final settings 330
  application, preparing 328-330
  application, submitting to 332, 334
ASMX web service 168
AssetForUrl method 190
assetGroup parameter 189
AssetsEnumeration method 189
Assistant editor 25
Attributes tab 26
audio
  background state 305
  playing, in background 303
  recording, for pre-defined amount of time 187
audio files
  playing 182, 184
audio session
  categories 304
audio session categories
  CategoryAmbient 304
  CategoryAudioProcessing 305
  CategoryPlayAndRecord 305
  CategoryPlayback 304
  CategoryRecord 304
  CategorySoloAmbient 304
AutoReverses property 278
Autosizing property 110
AVAudioPlayer class 174, 304
AVAudioRecorder class 174, 186

B

back button 90
background
  audio, playing in 303
  code, executing in 300, 301

background code
  considerations 302
BackgroundColor property 52, 55, 270
background state, for audio 305
BackgroundTimeRemaining property 302
BaseController class 100
BaseController.cs file 99
battery information
  retrieving, for device 219, 220
BatteryLevel property 220
battery monitoring
  disabling 221
BatteryState property 220
BecomeFirstResponder method 222
BeginAnimations method 269, 270
BeginBackgroundTask method 301
BeginImageContext method 291
BeginInvokeOnMainThread() method 71
BinaryFormatter class 125
BookApp
  creating 338
bool parameter 90, 134
Bounce property 74
Bounds property 270
breakpoints, FinishedLaunching method 42
built-in compass
  used, for determining heading 242, 243
button
  adding, to user interface 27
buttonChangeColor object 50
buttonChangeColor_TouchUpInside event 51
Button control 31
ButtonDone_Clicked method 143, 145
ButtonEdit_Clicked method 143, 145
ButtonInput 27, 29, 35
ButtonInputAction 35
ButtonInputActionViewController class 35
ButtonInputViewController class 31
ButtonInputViewController.xib file 27
buttonTap 31
buttonTap outlet 32

C

C# 12
CABasicAnimation class 278, 279
calendar
  managing 208, 209
CalendarEventsApp
  creating 208
CallEventHandler 194
camera
  media, capturing with 177, 178
CameraOverlayView property 178
CanBecomeFirstResponder property 222
CanMoveRow method 146
CanSendMail property 202
CanSendText 198
CanSendTweet static property 345
cell styles, table
  default 140
  subtitle 140
  value1 140
  value2 140
Center property 270
CGAffineTransform class 272
  about 273
  methods 273
CGAffineTransform class, methods
  CGAffineTransformInvert 273
  MakeIdentity 273
  MakeRotation 273
  MakeScale 273
  MakeTranslation 273
  Multiply 273
CGAffineTransformInvert method 273
CGContext class 281
Changed() method 64
ClearsSelectionOnViewWillAppear 96
CLHeading class 244
Clicked event 31
CLLocationManager class 238-243
CLLocationManager.HeadingAvailable static
    property 244
CLLocationManager.LocationServicesEnabled
    property 242
CLLocationManager object 246
CLLocationUpdatedEventArgs parameter 241
CLRegion class 246
CMGyroData object 235
CMMotionManager class 234
code
  executing, in background 300, 301
CombinedControllerApp 104

353

CommandText property 117, 120
CommitAnimations method 269, 270
CommitEditingStyle method 143
compass availability 244
Compass class 238
Console.WriteLine() method 41, 64
contacts
  displaying 205, 207
content
  navigating through, UIPageControl class used 74-77
  scaling 153
content, larger than screen
  displaying 72-74
ContentMode property 60
ContentOffset property 73
ContentSize property 73
ContentStretch property 270
control states, UIControlState
  application 51
  disabled 51
  highlighted 51
  normal 51
  reserved 51
  selected 51
CopyDatabase() method 123
core animation 267
core graphics 267
CoreLocation framework 238, 239
CoreMotion Framework 234
CoreTelephony framework 193
C# programming language 12
CreateButton() method 50
CreateLabel() method 55
CreateSQLiteApp project 119
CreateSQLiteAppViewController class 116, 118
CreateSQLiteDatabase method 117
curves
  drawing 279, 280
custom buttons
  creating 52
CustomControllerApp 99
custom drawing
  implementing 279, 280
CustomerData class 124, 125

CustomerData object 128
custom gesture recognizer
  creating 228, 229
custom gesture recognizers
  benefits 230
custom gestures
  creating 228, 229
custom overlays
  creating 264
CustomRowsApp
  creating 139
custom view
  creating 80-83
CustomViewApp
  creating 81
custom view controller
  creating 99
  working 100

D

data
  displaying 132
  displaying, in table 135-137
  inserting, to database 118
  searching through 149, 150
  storing, .NET serialization used 123, 124
  storing, XML used 126, 127
  updating, to database 118
DateTime.ToLongDateString method 316
DateTime.ToLongTimeString method 316
dbReader variable 121
debugging
  MonoTouch application 40
DecelerationEnded event 74
DecelerationStarted event 74
DefaultRepresentation property 190
degrees
  radians, converting to 235
DegreesToRadians method 272
Delegate object 199
Delegate property 64
DeleteRows method 144
DequeueReusableAnnotation method 261
DequeueReusableCell method 137
DerivedController() constructor 100
Descendants() method 128

deserialization 127
Deserialize method 125
Designer 25
destinationIndexPath parameter 146
DetailTextLabel property 138, 141
developer certificate
  about 322
  creating 320
development tools
  Intel-based Mac computer running Snow
      Leopard 7
  iOS SDK 8
  iOS Simulator 8
  Lion (10.7.*) operating system 7
  Mono 8
  MonoDevelop 8
  MonoTouch 8
  reference link 12
  Xcode 8
device
  battery information, retrieving 219, 220
  orientation changes, detecting 212, 213
device album
  images, importing from 174-176
  videos, importing from 174-177
device orientation
  about 214
  detecting 212, 213
device screen
  disabling, proximity sensor used 217, 218
Dictionary 137
DidDismiss event 159
DidEnterBackground event handler 22
DidEnterBackground method 297
DidEnterFullscreenNotification 181
DidExitFullscreenNotification 181
DidReceiveMemoryWarning method 17, 102
DidRotate method 216
disabled control state 51
DismissModalViewControllerAnimated(bool)
      method 97
DisplayContactApp
  creating 206
DisplayedPerson property 207
distribution certificate, ad-hoc distribution
      bundle 325

DocumentPreviewApp
  creating 157
documents
  displaying 157-159
double sided pages, page curl effect 342
DraggingEventArgs class 20
drawing
  clearing 289
drawing application
  about 286
  creating 287, 288
DrawingView class 284
Draw method 281
DrawString method 285, 286
DurationAvailableNotification 181
Duration property 278

E

EditingEnded() method 64
EditingStarted() method 64
editingStyle parameter 144
EditingTableDataApp 142, 145
editor area, Interface Builder 25
EKEventSearchCallback 209
EKEventStore class 192, 209
EmailMessageApp
  creating 200
e-mail messaging
  used, in phone application 200-203
e-mails
  sending 194-196
Empty project 23
EndBackgroundTask method 302
Entitlements.plist file 327
EnumerateEvents method 209
enumeration flags, UIButtonType
  ContactAdd 52
  custom 52
  DetailDisclosure 52
  InfoDark 52
  InfoLight 52
  RoundedRect 52
Environment.GetFolderPath(SpecialFolder)
      method 114
Error property 166
Excel (.xls) 154

EXchangeable Image File format. *See* Exif data
Exif data
   reading 190
external applications
   opening 196

F

Failed event 240
FileCreationApp
   about 114
   creating 114
   documents folder 115
FileCreationAppViewController class 114
files
   creating, on iOS device filesystem 114
FileStream class 115
filesystem, iOS devices
   files, creating 114
FillPath method 283
FinishedLaunching event handler 22
FinishedLaunching method
   about 20, 21, 42, 89, 251
   breakpoints 42
FinishedLaunching() method 54, 87, 91
Finished method 199
FinishedPickingMedia handler 177
FirstController class 106
FirstOrDefault() 129
FirstViewApp
   creating 44
FirstViewAppViewcontroller.cs 53
FirstViewAppViewController.xib file 44
float parameter 57
formatted text
   displaying 155, 156
   specific links, allowing 156
forSearchString parameter 150
FrameEndUserInfoKey 349
Frame property 46, 270, 273
framework
   layers, animating 276, 278
FromKeyPath method 278
FromName static method 58

G

geocoding 257
gesture recognizers
   advantage 227
gestures
   about 226
   creating 228, 229
   recognizing 225-227
   responding to 225-227
GetCell method 137, 151
GetImageFromCurrentContext method 292
GetNextViewController 341
GetPeople() method 204
GetPhones() method 205
GetPreviewItem method 158
GetPreviousViewController 341
get-task-allow key 327, 328
GetTitle method 134
GetViewForAnnotation method 260
GetViewForOverlay method 264
Global Positioning System. *See* GPS hardware
Google maps 253
GPS accuracy 241
GPS hardware
   about 237
   responding, to region-specific position changes 245, 246
   used, for determining location information 238-241
graphics context, UIImageView 282
Grouped style 148
GTK# designer 11
GyroAvailable property 235
gyroscope
   about 234
   availability, determining 235
   using 233-235

H

heading
   determining, built-in compass used 242, 243
highlighted control state 51
HorizontalAccuracy property 241
html_content folder 153

I

IEnumerable interface 171
image context
   creating 290, 291
imageDisplay 58
Image property 314
images
   animation, performing 274, 275
   displaying, UIImageView class used 58, 60
   editing 179
   importing, from device album 174-176
   slideshow, creating 274, 275
   using, for different screen sizes 61
ImageViewerApp
   creating 58
ImageViewerAppViewController class 59
ImageView property 141
individual assets
   retrieving 190
Info.plist 22
Info property 176
information
   providing, based on location coordinates 255-258
InsertRows method 146
Inspector pane 26
installation
   pre-requisites 8
Integrated Development Environments (IDEs) 7
Intel-based Mac computer running Snow Leopard 7
Interface builder
   about 24
   working 25
Interface Builder 44
   about 11
   areas 25
   editor area 25
   navigator area 25
   utility area 25
Interface Builder document 95
int GetComponentCount () 133
int GetRowsInComponent () 133
iOS 5 features
   about 337

   page curl effect, reproducing 338, 339
   split keyboard, working with 346, 347
   Twitter integration 344, 345
   views, styling 342, 343
iOS Developer website
   URL 320
iOS devices 237
iOS SDK 8, 267
iOS Simulator 8, 11
iOS versions
   and UIKit animations 270
iPadControllerApp
   creating 105
iPad-specific controller usage 109
iPad-specific view controllers 86
iPad view controllers
   about 105
   creating 105, 107
   working 107
iPhone application options
   about 39
   Application name 39
   Deployment target 39
   iPhone Bundle Signing 39
   iPhone IPA 39
   Version 39
iPhone build options 38
iPhone project
   AppDelegate.cs 18-20
   creating, with MonoDevelop 13-15
   Info.plist 22
   iPhone application options 39
   iPhone build options 38
   Main.cs file 21, 22
   MyFirstiPhoneProjectViewController.cs 16, 17
   MyFirstiPhoneProjectViewController.designer.cs 17, 18
   MyFirstiPhoneProjectViewController.xib 16
iPhone Single View Application project
   creating 122
IsAnimating property 275
IsFirstResponder property 47
IsSourceTypeAvailable method 178
issues
   split keyboard 349
items
   combining, for UIBackgroundModes key 306

ItemTitle property 158
ItemUrl property 158
iTunes
  ad-hoc app bundles, syncing with 328
iTunes Connect
  about 333, 335

J

JavaScript Object Notation data. *See* JSON data
JSON data
  about 170
  reading 169, 171
  serialization 171
  working 170
JsonDataApp 169
JSON data format 161
JsonValue class 171

K

KeyboardApp
  creating 65
KeyboardAppViewController class 66
KeyboardFrameChanged callback 349
keyboards
  types, in iOS 67
keyboard usage
  important aspects 65, 66
Keynote '09 (.key) 155
Keynote (.key.zip) 154

L

label
  adding, to user interface 27
labelInfo field 55
labelStatus 31
labelStatus variable 41
landscape orientation
  supporting 346
Language INtegrated Query (LINQ) 127
launch image 330
layers
  about 279
  animating, for framework 276, 278

lines
  drawing 279, 280
Linker 38
Linker options
  about 39
  Dont Link 39
  Link all assemblies 39
  Link SDK assemblies only 39
Linker usage 39
LINQ to XML
  used, for managing data 127-129
Lion (10.7.*) operating system 7
lists
  providing 132-134
LoadError event 153
LoadFinished event 153
LoadHtmlString method 156
LoadRequest method 153
LoadStarted event 153
LoadStateDidChangeNotification 181
local content
  displaying 153
  navigating, through content 154
LocalContentApp
creating 153-155
localizable resources
  about 312, 315
  displaying 312, 314
  loading 312, 314
LocalizableResourcesApp
  creating 312
Localizable.strings file 310
localization
  about 309
  real-world application scenarios 312
LocalizedString method 311
location information
  determining, GPS hardware used 238, 240, 241
LocationInView method 83
LocationManager_UpdatedLocation method 250
location services
  about 238
  availability, determining 241

region monitoring service 238
significant-change location service 238
standard location service 238
usage, indicating 242
using, while application in background 249-251
location services availability 241
location services usage indicator 242

M

Mac
  Mono, downloading 10
  Mono, installing 10
magnetic heading
  versus, true heading 244
MagneticHeading property 243, 244
magnetometer 242, 244
MailController_Finished method 202
mailto: url scheme 196
MainController class 104, 132, 163, 164, 238, 243, 245, 252
Main.cs file 21
MainViewController class 86, 109
MakeIdentity method 273
MakeRotation method 273
MakeScale method 273
MakeTranslation method 273
map
  annotating, for information display 258-261
map annotations
  adding 258-261
MapKit framework 253, 255
maps
  displaying, on screen 252-254
  overlays, used for drawing 262-264
Master-detail application 23
MaximumZoomScale property 73
media
  capturing, with camera 177, 178
MessageComposeDelegate property 200
MessageComposeResult parameter 199
MeteringEnabled property 186
Method property 171
methods, MyFirstiPhoneProjectViewController.cs
  DidReceiveMemoryWarning 17

ShouldAutorotateToInterfaceOrientation 17
ViewDidLoad 17
ViewDidUnload 17
methods, NavigationItem property
  SetHidesBackButton 90
  SetLeftBarButtonItem 90
  SetRightBarButtonItem 90
MFComposeResultEventArgs.Result property 202
MFMailComposeResult
  values 202
MFMailComposeViewController class 192, 202
MFMessageComposeViewController 191, 202
MFMessageComposeViewController class 198, 199
microphone
  used, for recording sounds 185, 186
MinimumFontSize property 57
MinimumZoomScale property 73
MKAnnotation class 238, 261
MKAnnotationView class 261
MKCircleView class 264
MKMapView 238
MKOverlay class 238
MKPlacemark class 257
MKPointAnnotation class 260
MKReverseGeocoder class 257, 258
MKReverseGeocoderDelegate class 257
modal controller
  accessing 98
  restrictions 98
ModalControllerApp 96
ModalController class 97
ModalTransitionStyle property 98
Modal view controller 96
Model property 134
Mono
  about 8
  features 11
  URL 12
MonoDevelop
  about 8, 212
  features 11
  project, compiling with 37, 38

updates 13
URL 12
used, for creating iPhone project 13-15
MonoDevelop 2.8+
downloading 10
installing 10
MonoDevelop WCF support 169
Mono, for Mac
downloading 10
installing 10
Mono Framework 161
MonoTouch
about 8
downloading 10
features 12
installing 10
URL 8, 12
WCF services, consuming with 167, 168
web services, using with 164-166
MonoTouch.AddressBook namespace 204
MonoTouch.AddressBookUI namespace 206
MonoTouch application
debugging 40, 41
performance, when debugging 42
MonoTouch assemblies
reference link 23
MonoTouch.CoreAnimation namespace 278
MonoTouch.CoreGraphics namespace 272
MonoTouch.CoreLocation namespace 238
MonoTouch.CoreMotion namespace 234
MonoTouch.CoreTelephony namespace 193
MonoTouch.EventKit namespace 209
MonoTouch.Foundation namespace 20, 36
MonoTouch installation guide
URL 12
MonoTouch.MapKit namespace 253
MonoTouch.MessageUI namespace 198
MonoTouch.ObjCRuntime namespace 268, 269
MonoTouch project
about 38
SOAP web service, using 161-164
MonoTouch.UIKit namespace 20
MonoTouch.UIKit.NSObject sender 36
MotionBegan method 222
MotionCancelled method 222

MotionEnded method 222
motion events
about 222
handling 221, 222
MoveRow method 146
MPMediaPickerController 173, 183
MPMoviePlayerController
about 173, 181
notifications 181
MPMoviePlayerController, notifications
DidEnterFullscreenNotification 181
DurationAvailableNotification 181
LoadStateDidChangeNotification 181
NaturalSizeAvailableNotification 182
NowPlayingMovieDidChangeNotification 182
MPMusicPlayerController 174, 184
MTTestWebService web service 164
MTWebService 161
Multimedia Messaging Service (MMS) 200
multiple album items
managing, directly 187-189
MultipleLanguageApp
creating 310
MultipleTouchEnabled property 225
multiple view controllers
displaying, in tabbed interface 91, 92
navigating, UINavigationController class used 88, 89
Multiply method 273
MultiplyNumbersAsync method 165
MultiplyNumbersCompleted event 165
MultiplyNumbersCompletedEventArgs class 166
MultiplyNumbersCompletedEventArgs.Result property 166
MultiplyNumbers_CompletedHandler method 166
Multipurpose Internet Mail Extensions (MIME) 203
multitasking
about 295, 297
device support, verifying for 297
music
playing 182, 184
MyAppDistribution 325
MyFirstiPhoneProject 24

MyFirstiPhoneProjectViewController class 18
MyFirstiPhoneProjectViewController.cs
  about 16, 17
  methods 17
MyFirstiPhoneProjectViewController.designer.cs 17, 18
MyFirstiPhoneProjectViewController.xib 16

N

NaturalSizeAvailableNotification 182
navigation bar
  about 90
  bar buttons, managing 90
NavigationControllerApp
  creating 88
NavigationItem property 90
navigator area, Interface Builder 25
NetworkActivityIndicatorVisible property 166
network connectivity checks
  performing 305, 306
NewHeading property 243
NewLocation property 241
NIB file 25
normal control state 51
note
  tab bar interfaces 94
notification observers
  adding, in application 299
  removing 300
notifications
  receiving, for application states 298, 299
NowPlayingItem property 184
NowPlayingMovieDidChangeNotification 182
NSAction parameter 302
NSBundle.PathForResource method 311
NSDictionary object 349
NSLocale.PreferredLanguages static property 311
NSNotificationCenter 299
NSNotificationCenter.DefaultCenter static property 67
NSNotification class 349
NSObject 18, 68, 349
NSOperationQueue class 234
NSSet parameter 82
NSString class 285

NSUrl class 154
NSUrl object 181
NSUrlRequest object 153
NSUrl variable 193
NSValue class 279
NumberOfSections method 147
Numbers '09 (.numbers) 155
Numbers (.numbers.zip) 154

O

OldLocation property 241
OnActivated method 296
OnButtonTap 35
OnResignActivation method 297
OpenGL application 23
OpenUrl method 193, 194
ORDER BY statement 121
Organizer 10
Orientation property 214
OS X Lion
  Xcode and iOS SDK, installing 10
OS X Snow Leopard
  Xcode and iOS SDK, installing 9
OutletAttribute 32
outlet mechanism 32
Outlets
  about 8
  adding, through code 33, 34
  used, for accessing UI 29-32
overlays
  used, for drawing on map 262-264

P

Page class 339
page curl effect
  reproducing 338, 339
  working 340, 341
PageNavApp 75
PageNavAppViewController class 75
Pages '09 (.pages) 155
Pages (.pages.zip) 154
Parse static method 171
PathForResource method 312, 314
PDF (.pdf) 154
PeakPower method 187

phone application
  address book, managing 203, 205
  calendar, managing 208, 209
  contacts, displaying 205, 207
  e-mail messaging, using 200-203
  e-mails, sending 194-196
  invoking 192, 193
  text messages, sending 194-196
  text messaging, using 197-199
PhoneCallApp
  creating 192
phone calls
  starting 192, 193
Photos application 226
PickerViewApp 132, 133
placemark parameter 257
Plain style 148
Play() method 184
PopToRootViewController(bool) method 90
Portable Document Format (PDF) 132
Powerpoint (.ppt) 154
pre-defined amount of time
  audio, recording for 187
PredicateForEvents method 209
pre-requisites
  installing 8
PresentModalViewController() method 97
PreserveAttribute 39, 125
PreviewItemCount method 158
profiles
  creating 319
progress
  displaying 68-70
ProgressApp
  creating 68
ProgressBar 69
project
  compiling, with MonoDevelop 37, 38
properties, UITabBarController class
  SelectedIndex 94
  SelectedViewController 94
  ViewControllers 94
properties, UITableViewCell class
  Accessory 141
  AccessoryView 141
  ImageView 141
provisioning profile
  about 322, 323
  creating 321
  expiration 324
provisioning profile, ad-hoc distribution bundle 325
proximity sensor
  used, for disabling device screen 217, 218

Q

QLPreviewController class 132, 157, 158
QLPreviewControllerDataSource class 158
  GetPreviewItem method 158
  PreviewItemCount method 158
QueryData method 122
querying
  SQLite database 119-121
query performance, SQLite database 121

R

radians
  about 235
  converting, to degrees 235
ReadLine method 115
reateSQLiteApp 115
ReceiveMemoryWarning event handler 22
Recipients property 200
Record() method 186
RectangleF 46
reference link
  development tools 12
  MonoTouch assemblies 23
Reflection 39
regional formatting
  about 315
  used, for displaying formatted numbers and dates 315, 316
RegionalFormattingApp
  creating 315
RegionEntered event 245
RegionLeft event 245
region monitoring
  availability, determining 247
  using 245, 246
region monitoring availability 247
RegionMonitoringAvailable property 247
region monitoring service 238

region-specific position changes
  GPS hardware, responding to 245, 246
Register attribute 82
RegisterAttribute 18
RemoveAppStateObservers method 300
RemovedOnCompletion property 278
RemoveFromSuperview() method 47
reserved control state 51
ResignFirstResponder() method 47, 64
restrictions
  modal controller 98
reverse geocoding 257
Rich Text Format Directory (.rtfd.zip) 155
Rich Text Format (.rtf) 155
RootViewController class 88
RotationRate property 235
row removal animations 144
rows
  customizing 138-141
  deleting 142, 143
  inserting 145, 146
  re-ordering 146
RowSelected property 138
RowsInSection method 137, 151

S

SaveToPhotosAlbum method 178
screen
  maps, displaying on 252-254
ScrollApp
  creating 72
ScrollAppViewController class 72
Scrolled event 74
Search Bar 149
SearchButtonClicked event 151
SearchDisplayController property 149, 150
search functionality
  providing to other controllers 152
SearchTableApp project 149, 150
SecondController class 106
SectionIndexTitles method 148
selected control state 51
SelectedIndex property 94
SelectedViewController property 94
SelectFont method 285
SendTextApp 194

SerializableAttribute 125
Serialization 39
SerializationApp 123
Serialize(XmlWriter, object) method 127
SetActive method 151
SetAnimationCurve method 269
SetAnimationDelegate method 269
SetAnimationDuration method 269
SetAssetsFilter method 189
SetBackgroundImage() method 52
SetCenterCoordinate method 254
SetCompletionHandler method 346
SetContentOffset() method 78
SetEditing method 143
SetHidesBackButton method 90
SetImage() method 52
SetInitialText method 346
SetKeepAliveTimeout method 306
SetLeftBarButtonItem method 90
SetLineJoin method 289
SetMessageBody message 203
SetNeedsDisplayInRect method 281
SetNeedsDisplay() method 281, 292
SetPhones method 205
SetQueue method 184
SetRightBarButtonItem method 90, 143
SetShadow method 283
SetShadowWithColor method 283
SettingsController class 104
SetViewControllers method 93, 341, 342
SGetDrawingImage method 291
ShadowOffset property 56
shake gestures
  intercepting 221, 222
  responding to 221, 222
shapes
  drawing, on view 282, 283
  filling, with transparent colors 284
SharedAccelerometer property 231
Short Message Service (SMS) 200
ShouldAutorotateToInterfaceOrientation()
    method 17, 108, 216, 342, 346
ShouldReloadForSearchString method 150
ShowsCameraControls property 178
ShowsUserLocation property 254
ShowTextAtPoint method 285

significant-change location service
  about 238
  availability, determining 249
significant-change location service availability 249
SignificantLocationChangeMonitoringAvailable property 249
significant location change monitoring feature
  using 247, 248
Silverlight Service Model Proxy Generation Tool (slsvcutil.exe) 168
simple web browser
  creating 152, 153
Simulated Metrics 26
simulator
  user interface orientation 216
Single view application 23
slideshow
  creating, of images 274, 275
slsvcutil tool 167
SOAP 161
SOAP web service
  using, in MonoTouch project 161-164
Soft Debugger 41
Software Development Kits (SDKs) 7
sound files
  playing 184
sounds
  playing 182, 184
  recording, with microphone 185, 186
sourceIndexPath parameter 146
SourceType property 176
split keyboard
  issues 349
  working with 346
SplitKeyboardApp
  creating 347
  working 348
SQLite
  about 113
  performance 119
  URL 113
SqliteCommand.ExecuteReader() method 120
SqliteCommand object 118
SqliteConnection.CreateFile(string) static method 117
SqliteConnection object 117
SQLite database
  creating 115, 116, 117
  data, inserting 118
  data, updating 118
  existing file, using 121, 122
  querying 119, 120
  SQL table, creating 117
SqliteDataReader class 120
SqliteDataReader instance 121
SqliteDataReader object 120
SqliteDataReader.Read() method 121
SqliteException 123
SqliteIntegrationApp 122
SqliteIntegrationAppViewController class 122
SQL table
  creating 117
standard location service 238
standard overlay objects 265
StartAnimating method 275
StartMonitoring method 246
StartMonitoringSignificantLocationChanges method 248, 251
StartProgress() method 71
StartUpdatingHeading method 243
StartUpdatingLocation method 241, 246
Status Bar 26
Stock Keeping Unit (SKU) number 335
StopAnimating method 275
Stop() method 184
StopUpdatingHeading method 244
StopUpdatingLocation method 241
Storyboarding application design 23
StreamReader class 115, 171
StreamWriter class 114
StringBuilder object 126
string GetTitle () 133
StringSize method 286
style buttons
  working 343
StyleButtonsApp
  creating 342
styled text
  drawing, with outline 284, 285
Superview parameter 47

System.Globalization namespace 317
System.Object 18

T

tab bar interfaces
    note 94
Tabbed application 23
TabControllerApp 91, 101
table
    editing 142
    indexing 147
    rows, customizing 138-141
    rows, deleting 142-144
    rows, inserting 145, 146
    rows, re-ordering 146
table controller
    creating 94, 95
TableController class 135, 139
TableIndexApp 147
TableSource class 137, 139, 147
TableViewApp 135
TakePicture method 178
text
    displaying, labels used 53-56
    drawing 284, 285
TextAlignment property 55
text blocks
    displaying, UITextView used 62-64
TextColor property 56
TextLabel property 138, 141
TextMatrix property 285
TextMessageApp
    creating 197
text messages
    sending 194-196
text messaging
    used, in phone application 197-199
TextViewApp
    creating 62
TextViewAppViewController object 64
TimingFunction property 278
TitleForHeader method 148
toolbar
    displaying 78-80
ToolbarApp
    creating 78

ToolBarAppViewController class 79
To property 278, 279
ToucheEnded method 225
TouchesBegan method 224, 229
TouchesCancelled method 224
TouchesEnded method 224, 229
TouchesMoved method 82, 224, 289
touch events
    handling 223, 224
touch gestures
    recognizing 225-227
    responding to 225-227
TouchUpInside event 31, 36, 51, 64, 170
TouchUpInside event handler 71, 122
ToUrl method 186
Transform property 270, 272
transparent colors
    shapes, filling with 284
true heading
    versus, magnetic heading 244
TrueHeading property 244
TweetApp
    creating 344
Twitter integration
    implementing 344, 345
    working 345, 346
TWRequest class 346
TWTweetComposeViewController 337, 345, 346
TWTweetComposeViewControllerResult 346

U

UI. *See* user interface
UIAcceleration class 232
UIAccelerometer class 231
UIAppearance class 337, 343
UIApplicationDelegate class
    about 20, 22, 296, 299
    methods 296, 297
UIApplicationDelegate class, methods
    about 296
    DidEnterBackground 297
    OnActivated 296
    OnResignActivation 297
    WillEnterForeground 297
UIApplication object 21, 22

UIApplication.SharedApplication static property 21, 166, 193
UIApplicationState property 297
UIBackgroundModes key
  about 251
  items, combining for 306
UIBarButtonItem[] array 108
UIBarButtonItem class 79, 80, 90
UIBarButtonItem object 90
UIBarButtonItem parameter 145
UIButton class 48, 343
UIButton component 44
UIButton.ContentMode property 52
UIButton.FromType(UIButtonType) 50
UIButton.SetTitle(string, UIControlState) method 51
UIButtonType
  enumeration flags 52
UIButtonType.RoundedRect button 50
UIColor class 52
UICompletionHandler 341
UIControlState
  control states 51
UIControlState parameters 52
UIDatePicker class 135
UIDevice.BatteryLevelDidChangeNotification key 220
UIDeviceOrientation type 214
UIGestureRecognizer class 229
UIGestureRecognizerState
  about 227
  values 227
UIImage.AsJPEG() method 203
UIImage class
  about 61
  file formats 61
UIImage.FromFile method 314
UIImagePickerController 173, 176
UIImageView class
  about 60
  drawing on 292
  graphics context 282
  used, for displaying images 58, 60
UIImageView component 44
UIKeyboard class 67
UIKeyboard.FrameEndNotification(NSNotification) method 67

UIKit animations
  about 268
  and iOS versions 270
  UIView properties 270
UILabel class
  used, for displaying text 53-56
  rotating, by applying transformation 270-272
UILabel component 44
UILabel fonts 57
UILabel object 55
UILabel(RectangleF) constructor 55
UINavigationBar 90
UINavigationController 206
  about 86
  displaying, within UITabBarController 103
UINavigationController class 200
  about 142
  used, for navigating multiple view controllers 88
  working 90
UINavigationControllerDelegate 200
UI orientation
  about 214
  adjusting 215, 216
UIPageControl class
  uses 78
  using, for navigating through content 74-77
UIPageControl component 44
UIPageControl.ValueChanged event 77
UIPageViewController class 337, 338, 340
UIPickerView class
  about 131, 132
  customizing 135
  using 132
UIPickerViewModel class 132, 133
UIPopoverController 107
UIPrerenderedIcon key 332
UIProgressView class 69
UIProgressView component 44
UIRequiredDeviceCapabilities key 251
UIResponder class 47, 222
UIScrollView class
  DecelerationEnded event 74
  DecelerationStarted event 74
  events 74
  Scrolled event 74
UIScrollView component 44

UIScrollView control 72, 73
UIScrollView.DecelerationEnded event 77
UIScrollViewGetZoomView 73
UIScrollView.PagingEnabled property 77
UIScrollView.SetContentOffset(PointF, bool) method 77
UISearchBar 150
UISearchBar class 132
UISearchDisplayController class 150
  about 132
UISplitViewController class 106, 108
UISpliViewControllerDelegate class 108
UITabBarController class
  about 86, 91
  working 93
  properties 94
UITabBarItem 93
UITabBarSelectionEventArgs object 93
UITableView
  about 94
  working 95
UITableViewCell class
  about 141
  properties 141
UITableViewCell object 135, 137
UITableViewCellStyle 140
UITableView class
  about 131
  used, for displaying data in table 135-137
UITableViewController
  about 86
  adding 94
  creating 94
UITableViewController-specific property
  ClearsSelectionOnViewWillAppear 96
UITableView.ReloadData method 146
UITableViewRowAnimation enumeration 144
UITableViewSource class 136
UITextField component 44, 347
UITextField object 65
UITextView component
  about 44
  used, for displaying editable text 62-64
UITextViewDelegate class 63, 64
UIToolbar class 78, 158
UIToolbar component 44
UIToolbar items

setting 80
UITouch object 82, 83
UIView class
  about 46, 269, 270
  overriding 80, 81
UIView component
  about 44
  adding, Interface Builder used 44
  customizing, Interface Builder used 44
  View Content Layout 48
  working 45, 47
UIViewContentMode
  values 48, 60
UIViewContentMode.ScaleToFill 48
UIViewController
  about 85
  used, for loading view 86, 87
  working 87
UIViewController methods
  about 88
  ViewDidAppear() 88
  ViewDidUnload() 88
  ViewWillAppear() 88
  ViewWillDisappear() 88
UIViewController.TabBarItem property 93
UIWebView class 153
  about 132
  LoadError event 153
  LoadFinished event 153
  LoadStarted event 153
  used, for displaying formatted text 155, 156
UIWebView supported files 154
UIWindow object 21, 22, 46
Unique Device Identifier (UDID) 320
UniversalApp 109
UpdatedHeading event 243
UpdatedLocation event 240-246
UpdateInterval property 232
UpdateLocation event 241
UserInfo dictionary 349
UserInfo property 349
user input
  receiving, buttons used 48-52
UserInteractionEnabled property 224
user interface
  accessing, Outlets used 29-32
  button, adding 27

creating 26
creating, for different devices 109, 110
label, adding 27
titles, setting on buttons 29
working 28, 32
user interface designer 24, 25
user interface orientation. *See* **UI orientation**
user touches
intercepting 223, 224
responding to 223, 224
Utility application 23
utility area, Interface Builder 25

V

values, FMailComposeResult
cancelled 202
failed 202
saved 202
sent 202
video files
playing 180, 181
video player interface
displaying 180, 181
videos
importing, from device album 174-177
view
loading, UIViewController used 86, 87
ViewController1 class 88
ViewController2 class 88
ViewControllerApp
creating 86
view controllers
about 86
combining 103, 105
displaying modally 96, 97
iPad-specific view controllers 86
subclassing, from XIBs 100
UINavigationController 86
UITabBarController 86
UITableViewController 86
UIViewController 86
using 101, 102
working 102
ViewControllerSelected event 93
ViewControllers property 94
view controller usage

guidelines 101
ViewDidAppear() method 88, 222
ViewDidLoad() method 17, 31, 49, 64, 97, 102, 116, 122, 174, 243, 245, 247, 342
ViewDidUnload() method 17, 88, 102, 214
ViewForZoomingInScrollView property 73
views
adding, Interface Builder used 44
adding programmatically 47
animating 268-270
shapes, drawing on 282, 283
styling 342, 343
transforming 270-272
ViewWillAppear() method 88
ViewWillDisappear() method 88
Voice over Internet Protocol (VoIP) 306
void Selected () 134

W

WcfServiceApp 167
WCF services
about 167
consuming, with MonoTouch 167, 168
creating 169
WCF web services 161
WebBrowserApp 152
WebServiceApp 161
WebServiceApp2 164
web services
consuming 161-164
invoking 164-166
using, with MonoTouch 164-166
WHERE statement 121
width parameter 56
WillDismiss event 159
WillEnterForeground method 297, 302
WillHideViewController() method 108
WillTerminate method 297
window.MakeKeyAndVisible() 21, 89
WinForm 96
wireless streaming 182
Word (.doc) 155
WriteLine(string) method 114
WWDR intermediate certificate
downloading 320
installing 320

X

Xcode
about 8
features 10
Interface Builder 11
iOS Simulator 11
Organizer 10
Xcode and iOS SDK
downloading 9
installing, on OS X Lion 10
installing, on OS X Snow Leopard 9
XElement object 128
XIB file 25

XML
used, for data storing 126, 127
XML data
managing, LINQ to XML used 127, 128
XMLDataApp 126, 127
XMLDataAppViewController class 126, 128
XMLDataAppViewController.cs file 128
XmlSerializer class 126
XmlWriter class 127
xsp4 162
xsp lightweight web server 161
shutting down 164

Z

ZoomingEventArgs class 20

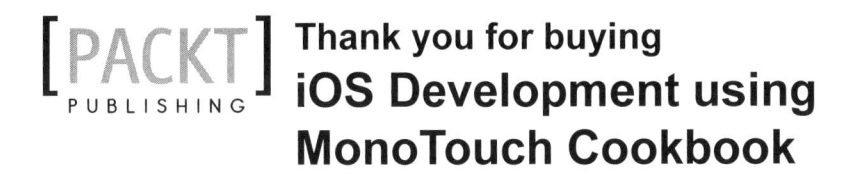

Thank you for buying iOS Development using MonoTouch Cookbook

About Packt Publishing

Packt, pronounced 'packed', published its first book "*Mastering phpMyAdmin for Effective MySQL Management*" in April 2004 and subsequently continued to specialize in publishing highly focused books on specific technologies and solutions.

Our books and publications share the experiences of your fellow IT professionals in adapting and customizing today's systems, applications, and frameworks. Our solution based books give you the knowledge and power to customize the software and technologies you're using to get the job done. Packt books are more specific and less general than the IT books you have seen in the past. Our unique business model allows us to bring you more focused information, giving you more of what you need to know, and less of what you don't.

Packt is a modern, yet unique publishing company, which focuses on producing quality, cutting-edge books for communities of developers, administrators, and newbies alike. For more information, please visit our website: `www.packtpub.com`.

Writing for Packt

We welcome all inquiries from people who are interested in authoring. Book proposals should be sent to `author@packtpub.com`. If your book idea is still at an early stage and you would like to discuss it first before writing a formal book proposal, contact us; one of our commissioning editors will get in touch with you.

We're not just looking for published authors; if you have strong technical skills but no writing experience, our experienced editors can help you develop a writing career, or simply get some additional reward for your expertise.

[PACKT] PUBLISHING

iPhone JavaScript Cookbook

ISBN: 978-1-84969-108-6   Paperback: 328 pages

Clear and practical recipes for building web applications using JavaScript and AJAX without having to learn Objective-C or Cocoa

1. Build web applications for iPhone with a native look feel using only JavaScript, CSS, and XHTML
2. Develop applications faster using frameworks
3. Integrate videos, sound, and images into your iPhone applications
4. Work with data using SQL and AJAX

Core Data iOS Essentials

ISBN: 978-1-84969-094-2   Paperback: 340 pages

A fast-paced, example-driven guide guide to data-drive iPhone, iPad, and iPod Touch applications

1. Covers the essential skills you need for working with Core Data in your applications.
2. Particularly focused on developing fast, light weight data-driven iOS applications.
3. Builds a complete example application. Every technique is shown in context.
4. Completely practical with clear, step-by-step instructions.

Please check **www.PacktPub.com** for information on our titles

Xcode 4 iOS Development Beginner's Guide

ISBN: 978-1-84969-130-7　　　Paperback: 432 pages

Use the powerful Xcode 4 suite of tools to build applications for the iPhone and iPad from scratch

1. Learn how to use Xcode 4 to build simple, yet powerful applications with ease
2. Each chapter builds on what you have learned already
3. Learn to add audio and video playback to your applications
4. Plentiful step-by-step examples, images, and diagrams to get you up to speed in no time with helpful hints along the way

iPhone Applications Tune-Up

ISBN: 978-1-84969-034-8　　　Paperback: 256 pages

High performance tuning guide for real-world iOS projects

1. Tune up every aspect of your iOS application for greater levels of stability and performance
2. Improve the users' experience by boosting the performance of your app
3. Learn to use Xcode's powerful native features to increase productivity
4. Profile and measure every operation of your application for performance

Please check www.PacktPub.com for information on our titles

1440579R00204

Printed in Germany
by Amazon Distribution
GmbH, Leipzig